Encyclopedia of Cage and Aviary Birds

Encyclopedia of
Cage and Aviary Birds

CYRIL H. ROGERS

VAL CLEAR, ADVISORY EDITOR

Harry V. Lacey, Photography

Macmillan Publishing Co., Inc.
NEW YORK

Macmillan Publishing Co., Inc.,
866 Third Avenue, New York, N.Y.10022

Library of Congress Catalog Card Number: 75 845

First Printing 1975

This book was designed and produced by
Rainbird Reference Books Ltd,
Marble Arch House, 44 Edgware Road, London W2

Designer: Yvonne Dedman
Line diagrams drawn by Thompson Santer
Genetic diagrams by Harold King

The text was set by Jolly & Barber Ltd, Rugby
The book was printed and bound by
Cox & Wyman Ltd, Fakenham, Norfolk

Printed in England

Foreword

WALTER J. PAGE
Editor of *Cage and Aviary Birds,* 1955–75

Birdkeeping is an expanding and worldwide hobby which many people find unequalled as a means of relaxation. Those attracted to it may want to keep a single bird as a pet, or to build up a colourful collection, while others may delight in keeping those species whose singing and mimicking abilities are remarkable for their range and quality. To a growing number of people the aim is to breed birds that conform to accepted standards of perfection and to enter such birds in competitive shows.

There are, too, those who devote the knowledge gained from their recreation to further a study of bird behaviour, of adherence to genetic patterns, of colour production and other fascinating aspects of birdlife. Recently the practical experience of birdkeepers has contributed to efforts being made to conserve species which, through changing environmental and other factors, are in danger of extinction.

Whatever the reason for wanting to keep birds, those who decide to make a start must be able to turn to a reliable guide. Numerous books have been written on bird culture but many are of an advanced nature or are too specialized for the beginner who needs a readily understandable introduction.

To write an encyclopedia covering the large number of species suitable for cage and aviary calls for a wide knowledge of the hobby, the aims of those who participate in it and, most important, the day-to-day requirements of the birds. I can think of none better than the author, with whom I have been friendly for many years and whose undiminished energy as a breeder, exhibitor, judge, writer, lecturer and club official over so long a period never ceases to amaze me.

Cyril Rogers commands a wide knowledge of British and exotic birds, knows the intricacies of the Canary fancy and is an acknowledged expert in the Budgerigar and Zebra Finch fields. His familiarity with the rare colours in Budgerigars is unsurpassed and I doubt whether anyone else equals him as an authority on colour mutations of other species, such as the Zebra Finch and the Bengalese.

I have no hesitation in saying that Cyril Rogers has presented the subject in a way that will earn praise from the experienced aviculturist and thanks from the newcomer, who will benefit from having the book handy for constant reference.

Preface

For the reader's convenience, this book is divided into seven parts, each describing species and subspecies, or varieties within a species (as is the case, for example, with Budgerigars), which are either related or require similar management. Sections on housing, feeding and breeding accompany each part, although more specific information on these aspects of aviculture may be found included in the individual entries. Symptoms of the commoner avian diseases and complaints are dealt with separately; the section on genetics explains Mendel's Laws of inheritance in simple terms. Lists of specialist societies, journals, and a bibliography of more specialized reading matter are given for those readers who wish to pursue the subject further.

The species and types in each part are described in alphabetical order of the common names generally used in Great Britain and the U.S.A.; synonyms are given where necessary. The index, however, should assist the reader as it lists the bird under its common and scientific names. The latter are those that are in general use today, but the reader should appreciate that, over the years, the scientific names may have been changed and thus the same bird may be described under a different name in other books.

Although a wide range of birds suitable for cage and aviary life are described it is not practicable in a book of this length to mention every single member of a genus, nor is it deemed necessary, when so many require similar management. The selection of species is based on their popularity, the freedom with which they reproduce and the relative ease with which they can be kept by the general aviculturist. Species requiring specialist management, such as humming birds, sunbirds, sugar birds, trogons (e.g. Quetzels) and fruit pigeons have not been included. Such birds are delicate and if managed wrongly, a high rate of mortality can result. It is better that such species are kept by zoological gardens or similar establishments, where the resources are so much greater and the necessary expert and full-time care can be given.

It is hoped that this book will be of use not only to newcomers but also to the more experienced aviculturist as a general reference book of cage and aviary birds.

CYRIL H. ROGERS

Contents

Color Plates

continued on page 41

8

1

2

3

4

5

6

7

8

9

10

11

12

13

14a

14b

15

16

17

18

19

20

21

22

23

24

25

26

27

28

29

30

31

32

33

34

35

36

37

38

39

40

41

42

43

44

45

46

47

48

49

50

51

52

53

54

55

56

57

58

59

60

61

62

63

64

65

66

67

68

69

70

71

72

73

74

75

76

77

78

79

80

81

82

83

84

85

86

87

88

89

90

91

92

93

94

95

96

97

98

99

100

101

102

103

104

105

106

107

108

109

110

111

112

113

114

115

116

117

118

119

120

121

122

123

124

125

126

127

128

129

130

131

132

133

134

135

136

137

138

139

140

141a

141b

142

143

144

145

146

147

148a

148b

149

150

Introduction

Man's first interest in birds was undoubtedly because of their value as food and this eventually led to the domestication of several species. The Red Jungle-fowl (the parent of the present domestic races) for example, was first domesticated in Burma for it is known that the Chinese received poultry from the west about 1400 B.C. Parallel with this, and as civilizations developed, birds were, because of their mysterious power of flight, endowed with magical properties and became associated with many gods. There are many beautiful examples of representations of bird gods in the museums of the world.

The dove has long been a symbol of Peace and its domestication, in Mesopotamia, dates from 4500 B.C. (so there must have been nest boxes at that time). Its naturally friendly habits made it an easy species to domesticate and suitable for keeping in places of worship. From Saxon times onwards, fine dove or pigeon cotes were incorporated in farm buildings and more recently this bird has been used to enhance the grounds of stately homes. Many types of pigeon have been developed from the wild species but their culture is a separate subject beyond the scope of this book.

It is difficult to establish exactly when and where Man first kept birds in cages purely as a pastime. We do know that some of the ancient Asian civilizations kept birds as pets instead of for food or religious reasons. Alexander the Great is credited with bringing back to Greece the Indian Ring-necked Parakeet. The same species was kept more recently by Indian princes in wonderfully constructed aviaries and special servants were employed for their care and maintenance. They also sent out bird trappers to collect abnormally coloured individuals (mutations). These, having been discovered, were taken from the nest just before they were ready to fly and hand-reared. Such rare specimens still have a considerable value in the world bird markets.

Many countries have a range of native song birds that can be acclimatized to cage life; Europe, for example, has the Goldfinch, Bullfinch and Linnet; the Middle East has its bulbuls, India has the Shama, and America has its cardinals. The Canary, however, in spite of this competition from birds of richer colour or greater song volume, is still the most widely kept pet singing bird.

The early cages for housing singing birds were often made of wicker and wooden bars, and frequently far too small for the comfort of their inmates. In the nineteenth century various metal wires were used in cage construction, the designs becoming more elaborate – some museums have good examples of these. More attention was paid to the outward appearance of indoor and outdoor aviaries than to the consideration of the inmates they were built to house.

It was in the 1920s and 1930s that aviculture began to develop and expand – a process that, apart from the war years, has continued until it has reached the world-wide scale of today.

Aviculture, particularly of many exotics has expanded greatly during the last two decades; there are two reasons for this. The first is that air transport has enabled birds to be sent quickly and safely (although, sadly, there have been instances of appalling losses due to quite inadequate in-flight housing), so they arrive in fine condition and adapt to captivity more easily. Their breeding potential is thereby increased and thus many more species are becoming domesticated. The second reason is that technical advances in materials and equipment have made it easier to feed and house newly imported specimens than was possible formerly.

Of all the thousands of species of birds in the

world, only a comparatively small number are suitable for cages and aviaries, and of these some breed more freely than others in captivity. I believe that many more would do so if they were correctly fed, well housed, in true pairs of course, and if their owners have the necessary patience. Each species has its own peculiarities and the more the owner can learn about the habits and habitats of the species in the wild the better. Many good books have been published that contain a wealth of information, not only on birds in captivity but also on the birds of various countries and areas. There are many societies, national and local, general and specialist, which publish journals and whose members are only too pleased to pass on their experiences, and magazines on the subject are published in most countries. The basic point is that environment, the

Edwardian bell-shaped cage *(Budgerigar Information Bureau)*

nesting materials, the nesting receptacle, the food (before and after nesting has started) must all be correct – that is to say, everything must be as nearly as possible like the natural conditions. It has been noticed, for example, that some species tend to nest far more readily when their enclosure is also inhabited by a totally different family of birds. One species seems to give support and encouragement to the other.

Once, foods, cages, aviaries, and other equipment were difficult to obtain and much ingenuity was shown by the enthusiast. The latter is still true, of course, but food of the right kind and quality is, because of present-day agricultural machinery and manufacturing techniques, within the reach of all aviculturists. There is a large choice of cages, aviaries and their associated equipment, all of the highest quality.

Exhibiting cage birds is an important facet of aviculture. It fosters a keen, yet friendly, competitive spirit among bird breeders and encourages them to continually improve the standard of their stock. Bird shows, whether small local ones or large open exhibitions, serve as a shop window for the cage bird fancy and are of great interest to beginner and expert alike. They enable the former to judge the quality of his stock against those being shown before deciding whether to enter a future show and the latter will meet his friendly rivals to discuss those many points of common interest.

All the domesticated species have standards of exhibition perfection, formulated over the years by the specialist societies concerned. The ideal standards, set out in the publications of the societies, are detailed descriptions of the shape, size and colour of the type bird. They enable breeders to match their breeding stock so that the young produced will show a steady improvement towards the ideal.

The specifications of the various show cages for the individual types must also conform to the standards laid down by the societies. The necessary details and dimensions, generally accompanied by illustrations, are given in the societies' publications. Show cages are made to standard proportions and designs in order that the birds may be exhibited to their best advantage when facing the judges and to

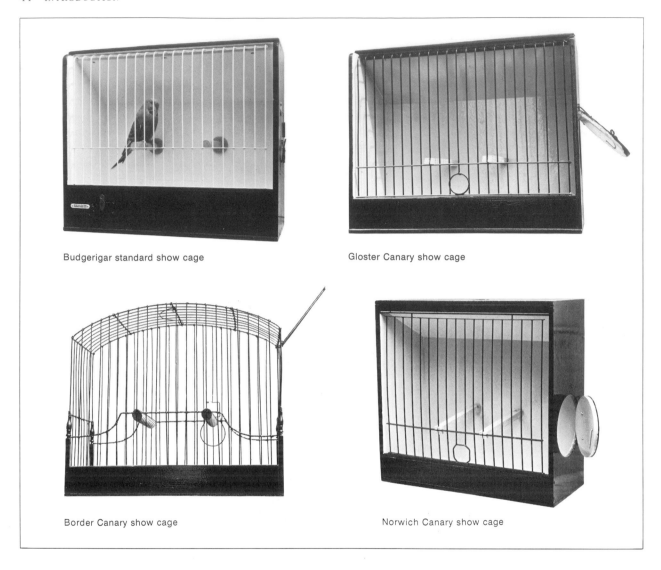

Budgerigar standard show cage

Gloster Canary show cage

Border Canary show cage

Norwich Canary show cage

give the birds the maximum of freedom and comfort.

There is, of course, a considerable amount of preparation before exhibiting birds. The necessary rules and regulations can be obtained from the exhibition secretaries, further information can be obtained from some of the books listed on p.193, and it is recommended that intending exhibitors join one of the societies given on pp.194 and 195. The majority of species travel extremely well by road or rail, and travelling boxes that take varying numbers of the standard show cages can be obtained.

Cage and aviary birds should only be bought from reputable dealers – the advertisement columns in the national magazines, and the societies are a great help in this respect. When obtaining new stock it is advisable, in most cases, to purchase birds bred in the current year, and Budgerigars, Bengalese and Zebra Finches should wear a closed year-dated ring. Young birds will settle down in their new quarters more easily and live longer.

The fact that birds are good travellers makes it easy for the purchaser to buy stock from a distant place. The travel arrangements are made between the seller and buyer, the birds generally being put on a train or plane and collected by the new owner. The birds are usually packed in small boxes, made according to the size of the species concerned, that allow sufficient room for movement but not for flight. A good layer of the bird's usual seed covers the floor of the box, which has enough small holes arranged around the top to give plenty of air and light. The boxes can be made of wood, stiff card, or a mixture of both; those for the powerful-beaked parrot-like birds should be made of stout wire and strong wood. Should the journey take more than a day, the softbills require their special food and water containers. Show cages and their travelling boxes can be used to great advantage in sending stock by rail, and this method is advisable for the more fragile and costly species. When sending by air the carriers require that special travelling boxes are used, details of which the airline will supply.

Generally speaking, cage and aviary birds may be freely imported into Great Britain and the quarantine regulations do not apply. Among the exceptions are birds of prey and poultry, neither of which types are dealt with in this book. It is advisable, however, to obtain a health certificate for the imported birds from the exporter as this may be required by H.M. Customs. In any event, the intending importer should always check with the Ministry of Agriculture, Fisheries and Food for the current position of the laws, as they are liable to change from time to time. At the time of writing, for example, it is proposed that the importation of psittacine species (parrots and all their allies) should be banned because of the incidence of psittacosis. This law has yet to be formulated and passed through Parliament. Wild birds are covered by the Protection of Birds Acts 1954–74 and the British reader is referred to p.153, where more details are given.

Aviculturists in the United States have been hit by two serious restrictions imposed by the Federal government. In an attempt to protect the poultry industry from the threat of Exotic Newcastle Disease, the Department of Agriculture established stringent quarantine regulations in 1973. The following year the Department of the Interior published sweeping prohibitions against the importation of most forms of wildlife. Based upon the Lacey Act, passed seventy-four years earlier, the Secretary of the Interior judged all forms of foreign wildlife injurious, but concluded that some were less injurious than others and therefore created a 'low risk' category, members of which could be imported without permit. All species not on the 'low risk' list are prohibited for commercial importation. Provision is made for zoos and educational institutions to obtain special permits. The list of commercially acceptable species can be secured by writing to Sport, Fisheries and Wildlife Service, Department of the Interior, Washington, D.C. Birds admitted to the United States under these regulations still have to pass the rigid quarantine procedures established by the Department of Agriculture. There are no federal restrictions on the movement of specimens bred by aviculturists in the United States, although

Yorkshire Canary show cage

some states have their own laws that may create problems. Airline freight departments usually have up-to-date information on interstate shipments.

All countries have laws governing the export of indigenous wildlife, and rightly so, particularly of the rare species. One of the main purposes of this book is to encourage the bird enthusiast to breed his own birds. By this means an acclimatized breeding strain can be built up, made available to all and thus make unnecessary the export of birds from foreign countries, which will help to prevent the extinction of many delightful species.

Regulations that may concern the aviculturist in Great Britain are the bylaws governing the erection of new structures and the alteration of existing buildings. Depending on the size and location of the birdroom or aviary it may be necessary to have the plans approved by the local council. It would be a wise precaution to have this done before starting work. Some American states have similar regulations – again, if in any doubt, the local authorities should be consulted.

The scientific names of birds are sometimes thought to be not only difficult but also unnecessary – neither is true. The birds dealt with in this book are described under their common names as it was felt more appropriate to do so. This, in itself, produces a problem, for one bird may also be known by a different name within a country, and perhaps by yet another name in other parts of the English-speaking world. Whenever it was felt necessary synonyms have been given. Naturally, the common name in another language will not be the same. Man

has always been a great cataloguer and classifier, and the scientific names, which are Latinized in form and always printed in italic type, are an attempt to give each species a unique and, hopefully, constant name understood by everybody wherever they may be. Each refers to one and only one species and indicates relationships. This name generally consists of two elements: the first, always having a capital initial letter, gives the genus to which the bird belongs and the second, without a capital initial (although older ornithological books may differ in this respect), is truly unique to one kind of bird and is the species. For example, the Derbian Parakeet is *Psittacula derbyana* and the Ring-necked Parakeet of Africa and India is *Psittacula krameri*. They have many features in common and thus are placed in the same genus. There are higher categories of classification – subfamilies, families and orders – but they have not been used in this book. A lower category, the subspecies, is important and has been used. *Psittacula krameri*, for example, has two subspecies, *P. k. manillensis* and *P. k. krameri* (note that it is unnecessary to repeat the whole of the generic and specific words when it is quite clear what is meant). The subspecific name is the third element and is an indication, in this particular example, that the species occurs in two distinct forms. Subspecific differences may be of colour, markings or size and are mostly races separated by a geographical barrier – a high mountain chain or the sea. Their ranges may overlap, in which case, because they are the same species and therefore able to interbreed, hybrids between the two subspecies may occur.

Canaries

The wild species *(Serinus canaria)* inhabits the Canary Islands, Madeira and the Azores, but it seems likely that it was introduced to Europe as a cage bird in the early part of the sixteenth century. Canaries quickly became adapted to captivity and enterprising bird keepers soon found that the birds bred quite happily in cages and aviaries. The practice of breeding spread throughout Europe and as more and more birds were produced mutations started to appear and during the last four centuries many types and colours have been developed. Records are not clear, but it seems that at first variegated birds were produced, and from these, the clear Yellow (and Buff) birds were developed. Cinnamon, Grey (Blue) and White birds were reported during the latter half of the seventeenth century but at the time these did not find much favour, the main object being the birds' song. Quite an industry was developed in Germany for songsters which were called Roller Canaries. Rollers are now exten-

sively produced in that country as well as Great Britain and America, where special singing strains are in great demand and highly valued. Other type-breeds were evolved, mainly in Britain and Europe.

Probably the greatest single colour event in the history of Canary breeding was the introduction in the late 1930s of a new ground-colour derived from the use of fertile hybrids bred from the Red Hooded Siskin *(Spinus cucullatus)* paired with the Canary. These Red Factor birds altered the whole colour conception of Canaries; they were quickly seized upon by scientifically-minded breeders, who recognized the possibility of obtaining further colour shades. Their breeding efforts and the inclusion of further mutations resulted in forms both richly and delicately tinted. With our present knowledge of the genetic inheritance of colours it is even possible that further colour shades will be produced.

TYPE AND COLOUR VARIETIES

The variety of forms and colours bred from the wild greenish-coloured species of Canary is considerable. This is because it is possible to produce birds of all types in three different ground-colours – yellow, white and red (a ground-colour is one on which other colours can be superimposed). The ground-colour of the wild bird is yellow and this, like the other two colours, is divided into two feather textures, known as yellow (jonque) and buff (mealy). The feathers of the Yellows are shorter, firmer, and richer in colour than those of the Buff birds, the feathers of which are longer, softer, and appear less deep in shade. The feathers of the Buff birds have a paler edging, which is usually more noticeable on the back of neck and head. The different characteristics of the feathers of the clear White birds are more difficult to describe but when the birds are closely examined it will be seen that the 'yellow' Whites are tighter feathered than the 'buff'

Whites. The feather types of Red Factor birds are easy to distinguish and in this instance, it is usual to call the buff feathers frosted.

It is extremely important that Canary breeders are fully aware of these variations in feather texture. To preserve the general quality of the feathers a Yellow should always be paired with a Buff, and such pairings give 50 per cent of each kind. If two Yellows are mated together, called double-yellowing, the feathers become tight and the birds are too slim. The reverse happens when double-buffing takes place, when fluffy over-feathered specimens result. In the course of this book Canaries will be written of as Yellow and this term should be taken as including the Buff forms. The distinction is, of course, apparent in the birds themselves, except in the White-ground Canaries where the lack of pigment makes the difference difficult to see. In these forms, therefore, neither term is used. In a deeper discussion of their genetics both terms would have to be used.

Agate

This is the name given to a colour dilution character which appeared at the end of the seventeenth century, and then reappeared during the early 1900s. When this mutation reappeared in Holland, the birds were known as Ash Greys but later the name was changed to Agate. This mutation and its name are of European origin and it is also known in Great Britain as the Sex-linked Dilute. The agate dilute character and its effect on other colours will be discussed under the heading New Colours. There is no separate variety for this colour and it can be introduced into all type-breeds by careful and calculated pairings.

Belgian Fancy

The beak is neat and well formed, eyes large and dark, set in a rather flat, snake-like head on a long, slender, tapering neck curving downwards from the shoulders, which are broad, full and rounded, to the well-filled back with a curve. The line from the shoulders downwards, including the tail, is almost straight with just a slight inward curve. The top of the shoulders to the crown of the head is as near as possible horizontal, thus giving the head a thrusting-forward appearance. The chest should be well-developed and the waist long, neatly-formed with an inward curve to the thighs. The legs and thighs should be long, straight and well formed; the tail nicely piped; the wings tight and placed close to the body. Overall the Belgian Fancy should appear easy and graceful and for this reason it is known as a bird of position.

The exact length of this bird is difficult to estimate because of its strange shape; the body size, however, is approximately the same as that of the Yorkshire Canary. It is usually clear yellow or clear buff in colour, although marked, variegated and self specimens (all dark) can and do appear. In recent years White and Red Factor kinds have been produced. The Belgian Fancy is one of the breeds of which the colour is not enriched by the use of colour-food and, therefore, they may appear to be somewhat more pallid than the colour-fed Yorkshires and Norwich Plainheads.

The exact date when this old breed first appeared does not seem to be recorded but it is known that the birds are of Belgian origin and are one of the few Canary breeds that takes the name of the country of its origin. Unfortunately they are not commonly seen in Great Britain now although during the late 1800s they were quite well

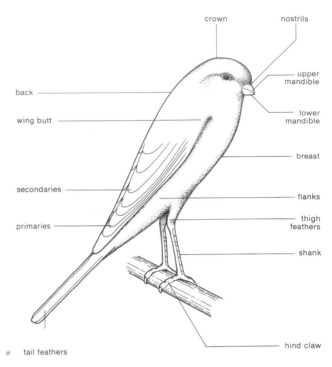

External anatomy of the Canary

favoured by British Canary breeders. It has been suggested that the Belgian Fancy is rather delicate and difficult to breed, but European and British breeders find it no more so than similar breeds. At one time, owing to the very limited number of Belgian Fancies in Britain, rather intensive inbreeding took place with a deleterious effect that has since been overcome by the greater availability of European stock.

The Old Varieties Canary Association was formed in Great Britain in 1971, its aim being to increase the numbers and to popularize rarer breeds. The efforts of the Association have led to a marked increase in the numbers of certain of these old breeds, including the Belgian Fancy. A few specimens have been seen at some shows, where they have created a stir among the younger Canary breeders seeing them for the first time. It is a pity when such a variety is allowed to lapse into obscurity but the Belgian Fancy should now be safe.

Blue Canary

The description of the various blue Canaries will be found under the headings of the type-breeds in which this colour is found. In fact, the birds called Blue Canaries certainly exist and have done so for quite a time; their colour is more of a greyish-blue tone and must not be confused with the brilliant blue of the Blue Budgerigars. Books published in the eighteenth and nineteenth centuries mentioned grey and grey-marked Canaries but as White Canaries were in existence in the seventeenth century, these so-called grey birds were undoubtedly our present-day Blues. Blues are the white-ground form of the Greens which have, of course, the yellow ground-colour. It is possible, therefore, to have a blue form of any variety of Canary where a green kind already exists. Blue Canaries include self and foul forms but not the ticked or variegated forms. White birds can be ticked or marked with blue, either lightly, evenly or heavily, just as ordinary Yellow and Buff birds can be marked with green. The purity of the tone of the blue colour depends to a great extent on the breeder's skill in selecting the breeding pairs and the quality of the green-coloured birds used in their initial production. Most present-day Blues have been evolved from the use of birds with a dominant white ground and as a result are likewise of a dominant breeding potential (see under White-ground Canaries for particulars of the mechanics of the dominant white-ground inheritance, which is the same for the Blues).

Border Fancy

The beak should be small and conical; eyes bold, dark and centrally situated in a small, well-rounded head, having a nice rise to the top of the skull, giving the birds an alert appearance. The neck and back should be well rounded, nicely filled and free from hollows or lumpiness. The chest should be well filled and rounded, tapering gently away towards the underparts, which should be clear cut and free from fluffiness. The stance of a good show-specimen should be at an angle of about 60 degrees when standing on a perch, and an overall length of not more than 5½ in (14 cm). The Border Fancy Canary of all colours should show a quick alert action at all times, either in stock or show cages.

These are the most popular of the type-breeds – a position they have reached during the past few decades. They are good free-breeders and reliable parents – so much so that they are often used as foster parents for those types that are not so reliable in the breeding quarters. They have a neat, active and alert appearance with a clear-cut shape that is appealing to the eye. They are available in a wide range of colours, including yellow (buff), white, green, cinnamon (Plate 2), dilute, blue, and fawn forms in clear, ticked, marked, lightly and heavily variegated (Plate 1), and self (Plate 1). Border Fancies are one of the breeds where natural colour is essential and no kind of artificial colouring agents must be used for enrichment. These qualities plus the fact that quality stock pairs can usually be bought at quite reasonable prices make them ideal for the beginning Canary breeder.

Some of the first Border Fancies were produced in the Northern Border counties of England – hence the name – and are now firmly established as a true breeding-type. It was thought that the ancestors of the Border Canaries may have been produced by blending Lizards, Rollers (singing Canaries), Norwich Canaries and possibly London Fancies, but whatever their origin, these birds are certainly most satisfactory.

Borders were once known as Cumberland Fancies, a name which strongly suggests that they were first evolved in the County of Cumberland. They came into being at a time when the popular type-breeds of Canaries were of the larger kind such as Norwich Plainheads, Yorkshires, Belgian Fancies, etc., and the need was felt for a smaller bird. As the popularity of these compact little birds grew and spread to other parts, the name Border Fancy Canaries was generally adopted by the Canary Fancy and today they are universally known under that name.

As the methods of breeding and colour inheritance are the same for all types of Canaries, this information will be found in the section on breeding, pp.69–73.

Cinnamons Plates 1, 2, 3

As with blue, there can be a cinnamon sort in all types of Canaries in clear, ticked, variegated and self forms. The colouring is a soft brown cinnamon shade with darker markings on wings, tail and flanks, all black colouring being absent from their plumage. The outstanding feature of this particular colour is that when the young birds are first hatched, they all have distinct 'pink' eyes, which stand out quite clearly from the black eye-colouring of the normal birds in the nest. As the birds become adult so the eye-colour changes to a rich, deep plum and when viewed at certain angles a distinct reddish gleam can clearly be seen. Another interesting point about Cinnamon Canaries (and all cinnamon-coloured birds for that matter) is that the genetic character that causes the cinnamon colour is sex-linked. This is discussed in the section on breeding.

The Cinnamon mutation was known to breeders during the early part of the Canary's domestication and the subsequent breeding of the separate type-breeds and, because their colour was somewhat more sombre than that of the Clear and Variegated Yellows and Buffs, they were once known as 'Dun' or 'Quaker' Canaries. Cinnamons were also regarded as a distinct breed and the majority of the first specimens bred were, in fact, similar in type, though not in colour, to the Norwich Plainhead. Exhibition birds were even given a separate standard of excellence and their own scale of points.

Cinnamons were crossed with other breeds in order to introduce the colour, and because its introduction was already known to have a beneficial effect on the feathers, giving them a softer and more silky appearance. Only recently, however, have breeders become aware of the sex-linked feature associated with this colour. Breeders do not always realize that perfectly clear Yellow or clear Buff birds can be Cinnamons because the colour is not visible in the plumage.

At the present time no separate breed of Canary is recognized that is simply called Cinnamon, but there are cinnamon forms of all other breeds – with the exception of the Lizards. The standard of excellence for each cinnamon form corresponds with that for each individual breed.

Copper Hybrids

As the second part of their name indicates these are not true Canaries but a cross between the domesticated Canary and the Red Hooded Siskin (*Spinus cucullatus*) from South America (see p.170). The results of the cross have played an important part in introducing to the Canaries a further colour character – the Red Factor that at one time was thought to be quite impossible.

Over the years different species had been crossed with Canaries, in many countries, and the results of these pairings were always thought to be sterile. South American breeders crossed the Red Hooded Siskin with their Canaries in the same way as breeders in Great Britain used the native Siskin (*Carduelis spinus*). Such crosses gave cock birds of an attractive black and copper colouring and a pleasing song, and hens of a more sombre plumage. When these Hybrids were kept in aviaries with hen Canaries, it was noticed that some of the fully mature cock Hybrids mated with hen Canaries. Breeders were surprised to find that from certain of these pairings second generation crossbreeds resulted. The hen Hybrids, however, although they would mate quite freely with cock Canaries only produced infertile eggs. The second generation cross-bred birds showed more of an orange-copper shade and their black was less intense. Because the first-cross Hybrids had proved fertile the breeders deliberately mated the second generation birds with Canaries but again it was only the cocks that proved fertile. The

European Copper Hybrids are said to have been bred first in Germany in about 1925 – after which they were quickly developed.

It soon became obvious to breeders that a new colour character had been introduced to the Canary via the Copper Hybrids. It was not long before deep orange-coloured Canaries were being produced by colour-feeding but this was a true natural colour. Very soon these Red Factor birds, as they became known, were developed and a host of Canaries with new shades came into being. (For further details see Red Factor Canaries.)

Crests Plate 4

Whenever a species of bird is bred for a number of generations under domestic conditions colour mutations are likely to occur, and these are invariably followed by feather mutations, such as a head crest or feathers on feet and legs. Early in the evolution of the type-breeds a crested mutation occurred, as a result of which there are now several crested breeds, each known by an individual name. The type that is commonly called the Crest, but was once referred to as the Crested Norwich, is unlike the Norwich Plainhead in that the birds are not colour-fed but are shown in their natural colouring.

The Crested Canary is shaped like its close relative the Norwich Plainhead except that the head carries a circular

Crested Norwich

crest. The crest should be full and even all over the head to just above the eyes from a central point. The crest feathers should be long, well formed, of the same length and the crest should not have any irregular breaks in its circle. The body feathers always seem to be a little longer and softer than those of the Plainheads. The birds bred from a cross of one crested parent are called Crestbreds and have somewhat longer and thicker feathers on their heads than do the normal Plainheads.

The genetic character that causes birds to develop a crest on their heads is a dominant one. There is, however, an unusual feature associated with the breeding of all types of crested Canaries which is that two crested birds should not be paired together. The reason being that if two crested birds are mated they will give, genetically, three kinds of young – the non-crested (Crestbred), the single-character Crest and the double-character Crest. Unfortunately the latter are not viable and usually die in the shell thereby reducing by 25 per cent (see Dominant Inheritance (A)2 on p.73) the possible number of chicks bred. Because of this lethal element, crested birds are paired to crestbreds and such matings give 50 per cent of each kind (see p.73). Fortunately this important fact was discovered in the development of Crested Canaries.

Dilutes

There are several mutations which cause the normal plumage colours to be shown in various degrees of dilution. It is possible to introduce these dilute characters into all type-breeds of Canaries although they are now generally confined to the New Colour group of birds under the names of agate, opal, melanin and Ino. Details of these interesting colour mutations will be found on pp.57–8.

Dutch Canaries

These are a very old breed of large Canaries which do not seem to exist today in their pure form. In books published in the eighteenth century they are simply called Dutch Canaries but they were probably a type of Frill and the ancestor of the present-day frilled varieties. Dutch Canaries played an important part in the evolution of such types as the Frills, Belgian Fancies, Scotch Fancies, Lancashire Coppies and Yorkshire Fancies. Not seen today, they are important because of their part in the creation of some of today's fine varieties.

Fawns

Fawn is found in all the type-breeds in clear, ticked, variegated and self. Fawn is the white-ground form of the Cinnamons (yellow ground) and is of a soft, fawn brown shade with the characteristic darker markings on flanks, wings and tail. Like their yellow-ground counterparts, the Cinnamons, they have the special feature of distinct 'pink' eyes when first hatched and this clearly distinguishes them from the others in the nest. When adult the eye colour of the Fawns changes to a pleasing deep plum shade which has a reddish tint when viewed at certain angles of light. The fawn character is sex-linked as the birds are the white-ground cinnamon forms, but the mode of inheritance is more interesting as there are two kinds of white-ground birds – the Dominant German Whites and the Recessive Whites; details are given under White-ground Canaries on p.62.

Although Fawns appear to be a comparatively recent addition to Canary colours, it is thought that they must have been bred on earlier occasions for both White and Cinnamon birds were known centuries ago and thus it would seem a little strange if a few Fawns had not been bred during those early years and as the Whites dropped out of favour so too the Fawns must have.

The modern fawn colouring does not seem to have been monopolized by any one special variety – some of the best examples being found in Rollers, Borders, Norwich, Yorkshires and Gloster Fancies.

Fawn, ranging from self to ticked, can be introduced by crossing within the different varieties of Canaries so as to transfer the colour to them but, like the Cinnamons, they are a colour form and not a type-breed. Clear White birds can, in fact, be Fawns but because the character does not show, such birds look just like the ordinary Whites. The colour of the eyes of these clear White Fawn birds have the characteristic reddish gleam when seen at certain angles in a good light. All varieties of Canaries with fawn in their plumage make a pleasing addition to a mixed collection, either in cages or in a garden aviary. The fawn character can be used to breed even further delicate shades of colour.

Fife Fancies

The beak should be fine and the eyes centrally placed in a neat, small, well-rounded head. The neck should be full and the chest well filled and nicely rounded without appearing to be heavy. The back should be neatly rounded with the wings lying close and the tips just touching, the tail well piped and filled and in line with the wings. The thighs should be inconspicuous and clear-feathered; the legs of medium length allowing the bird to stand firmly on its perch at an angle of about 60 degrees. The plumage is a natural rich intense colour of firm texture and fine quality. The overall length is not more than 4½ in (11·5 cm).

Fife Fancies are one of the newest of the type-breeds and were evolved, as their name shows, in Fifeshire, Scotland, during the 1940s. They were bred by a group of dedicated fanciers who thought the Border Canaries were at that particular time becoming too large and coarse to merit the name of 'wee gems'. Although it is not known exactly what varieties were used in their initial production it is certain that small Border Fancies were one and Gloster Fancies possibly another. The birds that were ultimately produced, now called Fife Fancies, are neat, smart, active little birds and full of colour. A number of different colour shades are possible but the Yellow and Buff birds seem to be the most popular among present-day breeders. When their distribution becomes wider and more fanciers take to breeding, no doubt other colour shades will be produced in this dainty bird.

Frills Plate 5

The beak should be neat and the eyes well placed in a small, nicely rounded head and neck; the latter should be long. The back and shoulders should be well made with the flanks heavy and well proportioned to the shoulders. The breast should be covered with symmetrical frilled feathers of a soft texture. Legs and thighs should be long and straight without frilled feathers. The overall length of the birds ranges from 6¾–7¾ in (17–20 cm), and there are several kinds of Frills in which the area of frilled feathers varies: Dutch Frills, Parisian Frills, and an Italian variety.

The differences between the Frill breeds are not very great and as they are mainly the concern of the exhibitor are not given here. Undoubtedly Frills are an ancient breed and our present-day varieties probably owe their existence to the old Dutch Canaries with the variations being achieved by selective pairings over a number of years. Frills were one of the first of the rarer breeds to be produced with the white ground-colour. I saw examples of Clear White, Lightly Marked White, and Heavily Variegated White Frills in the late 1920s, but it was not until some five or six years later that I bred my first Clear White Frills. At that period in the British Canary Fancy it was difficult to arouse interest in rare breeds although, at one time, Frills did make a certain amount of progress in popularity. With the difficulty of getting new stock this enthusiasm soon began to wane and Frills went back more or less into obscurity.

During recent years Frills have once again started to come to the fore in the U.S.A. and in Britain, where with the help and support of the Old Varieties Canary Club their future is assured. I always found them excellent breeders and first-rate parents – an asset to any breed of cage or aviary bird.

Frills are and have been bred more frequently in Europe than in Britain. Europe is their native home where some fine examples of these large birds are to be seen in breeders' birdrooms. Experiments introducing the Red Factor and dilute characters into Frills have had some success. The few Red Factor Frills I have seen appear to be most attractively coloured, as their frilled feathers give the orange-red tinting an unusual blend of shades. I have yet to see the Dilute Frills but I have seen a colour transparency of a Dilute Cinnamon which looked very pleasing. Those breeders who like large Canaries that are a little out of the ordinary and who like to experiment with colour breeding would find Frills ideal for this purpose. If some of the newer shades were produced in Frills they would quickly become more popular, leading to a considerable demand for stock.

Gloster Fancies Plates 3, 6, 7

There are two kinds of this breed: the *Corona*, which should have a neat crest, falling evenly all round the head, a small beak and the eyes clearly discernible, and the *Consort*. The latter, a crestbred bird, should have a small beak, a broad round head, with a good rise over the dome and boldly showing eyebrows. The neck should be full, the back and chest well rounded, with the wings close to the body, the tail well folded and legs of medium length. The plumage should be tight and of a good level colour and free from looseness at thighs and vent. Overall length approximately 4¾ in (12 cm).

Gloster Fancies are a non-colour-fed breed and are available in numerous colours, the main being buff, yellow, cinnamon, green and white. Birds with dark crests and evenly-marked wings are of particularly attractive appearance as are dark birds with light crests. An interesting fact is that Buffs are far more plentiful than Yellows and this is undoubtedly due to their original breeding. Gloster Fancies are a comparatively recent innovation – they were the result of the skilful blending of Crested Rollers with small Border Fancy Canaries in the 1920s. As their name suggests they were bred in Gloucestershire. A great deal of the credit for their creation must go to a Mrs A. Rogerson, who did so much in the early days to make the breed available to other fanciers and to get them recognized as a distinct type-breed.

There are now several specialist societies in Great Britain for the Gloster Fancy Canaries and enthusiasm

Corona Gloster Fancy

for them is world wide. This great interest is understandable for they are such active little birds and the crest makes them rather more exciting to produce. A further point in their favour is that they are among the varieties of which good-class stock can be still bought at reasonable prices. Their record as successful breeders is extremely good and they are generally so reliable that owners of rare varieties have no hesitation in employing them as foster parents.

It is of interest to note that although there is now a bias in the bird fancy towards larger domesticated birds, the two most recent productions in the Canary world are the smallest of all our type-breeds. This is an indication that many Canary lovers still prefer small, neat, active, tight-feathered birds to those having more bulk. If a breed is first developed to be small and compact every effort should be made to retain those qualities. In fact, whatever the shape and size of a breed, improvements within that breed should always be carefully considered and controlled so that a symmetrical balance is maintained.

Hybrids

Under Copper Hybrids there was a description of how a whole range of new colours has been introduced into Canary breeds by the use of these fertile hybrids. A question which undoubtedly springs to the minds of enquiring Canary breeders is whether it is possible to obtain other colours by using similar methods. Some experimental work has already been carried out in this field but so far

significant changes in colour appear not to have been achieved. This does not mean that new colours cannot be produced providing the right cross-pairings are made with finch-like birds with the necessary colour attributes.

The black Canary, like the black Budgerigar, has eluded breeders for many decades and yet both would seem reasonable possibilities. At one time some experimenters believed that the Red Hooded Siskin (*Spinus cucullatus*), with its jet-black hooded head and wings, could introduce black as well as red into the Canary. After some experiments, however, it was found that the black of the Red Hooded Siskin was not helping breeders to produce the black Canary. Crosses with the Hooded Siskin (*Spinus ictericus*), another South American bird showing a fair amount of black feathering, have produced hybrids, some of which have proved fertile. However, back-crossing the hybrids with Canaries has not brought the black Canary any nearer.

For many years now the Alario Finch (*Alario alario*), which has black on head, neck, flights and a wide streak on flanks, has been crossed with the Canary. The hybrids produced have a dull brownish colour and I am told that a few, perhaps surprisingly, have produced young when back-crossed to Canaries. The black is still elusive for the second generation birds which, although showing some brown, have a more general yellowish colour. The song of these Alario Finch Hybrids is of a pleasing and musical quality. A further species which would seem to be a possibility and from which a number of hybrids have been produced is the Grey Singing Finch (*Serinus leucopygius*). As far as I have been able to ascertain, the hybrids have not been used for back-crossing with Canaries so it is not certain if they are fertile, although they are expected to be; nor do we know what is the result of a second generation cross. Hybrids with other black-carrying finch-like birds have been bred in various aviaries from time to time, again without achieving the desired colour.

It is possible that the Recessive White Canary would be more useful for hybridizing experiments than the usual Yellow or Buff birds. Recessive Whites are not plentiful and the breeders who own them may not be interested in producing hybrids as it takes a number of years to obtain results. Anyone with a spare Recessive White hen might try crossing it with black-carrying finch-like birds, bearing in mind that black is the ultimate aim.

The chances of producing true blue Canaries, as opposed to the present grey or silver-blue types are slight, for the finch-like species having blue in their plumage are too remotely related to the Canary for successful hybridizing.

Inos

These are a dilute colour group of Canaries that have red eyes. The name given to the birds depends entirely on their ground-colour: Albinos (white ground), Lutinos (yellow ground) and Rubinos (Red Factor ground). Ino (pronounced *ai-no*) Canaries can be bred in all colours and type-breed, all have the common distinguishing factor of red eyes. The term Albino and Lutino must not be confused with those used to describe Budgerigars and other species of birds as the usage differs in several respects. The Ino Canary mutation is recessive and does not completely remove all the dark pigments from the feathers. The mutation is more like that of the Fallow Budgerigar which is also recessive in its manner of inheritance. Because the Ino character is recessive, both cocks and hens can be carriers of the character and, to reproduce the visual characteristics of Inos, both parents must be carriers. Thus there are three kinds of matings that can produce visual Ino young; Ino cock to Ino hen; Ino to Ino carrier; and Ino carrier to Ino carrier. The Ino character has the effect of modifying the pigment present in the plumage of the birds and the colour expressed varies according to the ground-colour and other characters that may be present. This interesting mutation therefore offers a number of possibilities to breeders.

The first reported breeding of the Ino mutation was in Belgium in 1964 from a pair of Cinnamon Red Factors and was therefore of the kind now known as Rubino. When it was realized that this first red-eyed bird was a mutation, breeding experiments started at once. Within a few seasons it was discovered that both yellow- and white-ground birds could also have the character, and such birds were named Lutino and Albino respectively. Other mutant characters were also included in the Ino-breeding scheme and these gave rise to a further range of delicate colours. For more details see New Colours (p.57).

Irish Fancy

This variety, as its name indicates, is being developed in Ireland and is a refined edition of the Roller Canary. The birds have the general appearance of the Roller but the head is more rounded, the back a little fuller and the body more streamlined with the wings and tail tight and compact. The aim of the breeders is to produce a neat small bird with a smart contour and a rich singing voice. I have judged these birds over a number of years and during my last visit to Ireland I was pleased to note a distinct advance in the general conformity of the type and style of the Irish Fancy. These birds, which can be produced in all colours,

Lancashire Coppy

will steadily gain favour with fanciers, thereby adding a further variety to our list of Canary type-breeds.

Lancashire Coppy

Syn: Manchester Coppy

Crested   The crest of this old breed should be flat, neat and fall evenly all round the head, which should be less rounded than that of the Yorkshire or Norwich Canary.

Plainhead (Crestbred)   The head should be similar to that of the Crested, with the feathers over the eyebrows standing out clearly giving the impression of a large top. The eyes of the Crested should be bold and not covered by the fall of the crest. The beak should be strong and short in both types. The neck should be thick and full and the back long and nicely rounded. The body should be substantial, with the chest well filled but not heavy looking. The wings should be long and held close to the sides and the tail well folded, straight and long. The bird should stand clear of the perch on long legs with little thigh showing; its overall appearance should be one of substance and length, with tight feathering all round. Overall length is approximately 7–7½ in (18–19 cm).

This variety originated in Lancashire, its centre of popularity being the city of Manchester. Exactly when the breed was first evolved does not seem to have been recorded but it is known that it was well established over a hundred years ago. Lancashires are the largest type-breed of Canary of British origin and have been used in the production of some other varieties. It is thought that they were evolved in the first instance from the Old Dutch (Dutch Frill) Canary by breeding out the frilled feathers and introducing the crest (or coppy as it used to be called in the fancy).

A rather unusual feature of this breed is that the birds are invariably clear, not showing the variegation of most other breeds. In the Crested birds, however, the crest is sometimes grizzled with the remaining parts all clear. The Lancashires are non-colour-fed; that is to say their colour is natural and not deepened by giving them colour-food. The only exception to Yellow and Buff Lancashires that I have seen is White. Self or variegated birds in cinnamon, green, fawn, blue, dilute and Red Factor are all possibilities that could be evolved by keen experimental breeders. The Lancashire Coppies come under the jurisdiction of the Old Varieties Canary Association which fosters the promotion of Lancashire Coppies and their Plainhead counterparts.

Lizards Plates 7, 8
The beak should be fine and dark in colour and the eyes clear and set centrally in a nicely rounded head. The neck and chest should be well proportioned, well rounded, and tapering smoothly to the vent, with the back filled and falling gently to the tail, which should be straight and tight. The wings should be close to the body and in line with the tail, the thighs just showing above the dark legs and feet, with an overall plumage of tight silky feathering.

The arrangement of colour in Lizard Canaries is extremely important; it is a unique pattern and is the only example of this particular arrangement of colour in Canaries. The Lizards are in two shades, corresponding to the yellow and buff of the other varieties, called gold and silver, which are quite appropriate terms. Both Gold and Silver Lizards have the same feather pattern, spangling on the back and rowing on the breast and flanks. The spangles are dark spade-shaped marks edged with light and the rowings are lines of dark marks of similar shape; the flight and tail feathers are dark.

The whole of the top of the head (cap) is either clear, broken or solid. The types are known as Clear-capped (Plates 7, 8), Broken-capped (Plate 8) and Non-capped Gold or Silver Lizards. The spangles and rowing are superimposed on a basic colour. The basic colour of the Gold Lizard is a deep rich bronze green with the edges of

the spangles and the cap a soft golden-yellow shade. In the Silver the colour is more greyish green and the yellow areas are paler than would be expected from a buff feathering. The ideal arrangement of colour is a perfectly clear symmetrical cap with the spangles and rowing clear cut and even throughout, and the flight and tail feathers completely dark.

Young Lizard Canaries do not have the characteristic feather markings until after the first moult. Unfortunately, with the second and subsequent yearly moults the richness and clearness of the colour recedes and the flight and tail feathers become progressively more grizzled. Because of these peculiarities Lizards are known as one-year birds, although both young and adult can be exhibited in different classes. Both adult and young birds can be colour-fed. The overall length is approximately 5 in (13 cm).

The breeding of White-ground (Blue) Lizards is mentioned in eighteenth- and nineteenth-century books on Canaries but no further information is given. Blue Lizards, however, are now a fact and they are attractive with their white caps, blackish spangling and rowing on a warm blue-grey body. In 1949 the first Blue Lizard was bred and shown (by the author's wife) at a National Exhibition. This bird won the A.O.C. (Any Other Colour) class and its appearance created much interest amongst colour-breeders at the show. Since then Blue Lizards have appeared at various British shows. With the exception of the Blue (White-ground) Lizards, it is not practical at the moment to try and produce other colour forms, but no doubt something may be achieved in the future.

The origin of the Lizard is not in the least clear; it is possible that it was brought to Great Britain by the Huguenots. Equally the opposite might have happened. Lizards could have been evolved in Great Britain and then taken to Europe (see London Fancies for further information on this point). Whatever the truth their colour was not produced by selective breeding by fanciers but as the result of a natural mutation of the original colour pattern in the wild species. It was similar to the mutation that changed the undulating pattern markings of the normal Budgerigar to that of the Opaline Budgerigar – a redistribution of the dark pigmentation areas of individual feathers. Drawings and prints of this delightful breed, dating back to 1840, show that the pattern of the Lizard Canaries has remained remarkably unchanged for many generations.

The skill of the breeder has to be extended to its fullest to produce and maintain the correct colour perfection in the Lizards and consequently crossing with other breeds is not undertaken. Special care has to be taken when matching the breeding pairs to avoid producing young that have the cap running down the back of the head or spilling over onto the face. The judicious use of Broken-capped and Non-capped Lizards as mates for Clear-capped birds can be advantageous but over-capped specimens should not be mated as this will only exaggerate this failing. Occasionally double-silvering is carried out when a larger size is required, and when the resulting young are back-crossed to Golds excellent results are obtained. Otherwise it is the practice to mate Gold to Silver, always bearing in mind the cap formation and markings.

After World War II the stocks of Lizards were so low that it was feared that the breed might cease to exist. Fortunately there were a few dedicated breeders who devised a plan to protect and increase the then existing stocks. Their efforts were successful, the Lizard Canary Association was formed, and the popularity of the Gold and Silver Lizards increased until today, when they are part of almost every cage bird exhibition in Great Britain.

London Fancy

The beak should be short and dark in colour and the eyes well set in a nicely rounded head. The proportions of neck, back and chest should be well balanced and rounded. The wings should be tight against the body in line with the tail, which should be nicely folded and straight; the thighs should just show above the dark legs and feet with the overall feathering tight, soft and of a silky texture. The overall length is approximately 4¾ in (12 cm).

Today no examples of the London Fancy are known to exist but the description is given as it may be possible to revive the breed again. Perfectly marked examples must have looked very handsome and it is a pity that such birds no longer exist. In colour, London Fancies were as unique as the Lizards to which they are said to be closely allied. They were Yellow and Buff or, as their breeders used to call them, Jonque and Mealy; ideally the feathers should be clear throughout with the exception of the flight and tail feathers, which should be black. The full beauty of London Fancies lasted for only one year while in their first adult feather. In their second and successive moults the body colour remained the same but the backs, flights and tails became progressively grizzled.

Few fanciers have actually seen living examples of the London Fancy as the breed was quite rare before it became extinct in about 1934. I bred and exhibited them for a number of years and, as far as I know, I was the last

LONDON FANCY CANARY.
(The Property of Mr. J. Waller. Third Prize at the Crystal Palace.)

London Fancy Canary – an illustration from *The Canary Book* by Robert L. Wallace, published in the last quarter of the 19th century

breeder to own true London Fancies. I was also the last secretary of the London Fancy Club which was wound up in the early thirties because of insufficient breeders and stock. While I was breeding London Fancies I produced from my stock the first and I think the only white-ground example. I could not continue with London Fancies because my entire stock was destroyed in a single night by a marauding stoat, and with this tragic event went the last hope of reviving London Fancies from pure original stock. It might be possible to reconstitute the breed by using the Lizards as foundation stock and carrying out a series of predetermined experimental pairings.

Like the Lizards the exact origin of the London Fancies is unrecorded although there are several theories on their evolution. One is that they were a further mutation from the Lizard, another that they were developed from the Lizard by selective breeding. A third suggestion is that the Lizards were produced from London Fancies by carefully introducing the dark markings which appeared in some examples of the latter. These theories are, of course, conjectural but it is possible that if a group of keen fanciers were to try breeding from Lizards some truth might eventually emerge. It would certainly be a great achievement if London Fancies were to become a live fact instead of fading pictures and mental images.

Malinois

These song Canaries are similar in size and build to the Roller Canaries to which they are said to be related. Their song is quite distinct from those of either the Roller or the Timbrado. They were bred in Belgium, where they are quite popular and there are breeders in other European countries, although they are practically unknown in Great Britain and America. The majority of Malinois are clear yellow (buff) or lightly variegated in colour – colour is of no real importance as they are bred for their strong, sweet singing voice. They have been recognized by the World Ornithological Confederation as a separate singing variety of the Canary.

Mule Plates 9, 85

This is the name given in Britain to hybrids resulting from crossing Canaries with various species of finch-like British birds (see pp. 154–6 and p.158). A large number of hybrids result from the wide range of crosses, many hundreds being bred each year. The height of perfection is considered to be a clear mule – a bird showing the shape of both parents but clear yellow (or buff) in overall colour. One of the most favoured crosses is Goldfinch × Canary (Plate 85) and from such matings come the largest number of clear and variegated birds. Many very beautiful dark mules are bred showing the lovely Goldfinch colour pattern in slightly altered tones. Another very popular cross is the Greenfinch × Canary (Plate 9) and if Cinnamon or White-ground Canaries are used, blue- and cinnamon-coloured mules can result. Bullfinches, Linnets, Twites, Redpolls and Siskins are often used as mates for Canaries, and the resultant mules are pleasing in colour and song. A rare cross, sometimes attempted by experienced breeders, is the Crossbill × Canary and a

very fine example of the mule was acclaimed 'Best Bird in Show' at the 1964 and 1965 National Exhibition of Cage and Aviary Birds in London.

Some rather unusual mules can be produced by using the various crested Canaries. The resultant crested mules are of no special value beyond their unusual appearance and, of course, the extra interest to the breeder in producing them. By using the smaller finch species, such as the Redpoll and the Siskin, as mates for the small breeds of Canary the results are attractive miniature mules. If the Canaries are Red Factors then the miniature mules are beautifully coloured and a favourite cross in Britain is that of the British subspecies of Goldfinch (*Carduelis c. britannica*) × a small Red Factor Canary, the offspring of which are highly coloured. An American favourite for similar crosses is the larger and more dramatic Siberian Goldfinch which, like the British subspecies should not be confused with the American Goldfinch (*Spinus tristis*) which is a Siskin.

Canaries can also be crossed with various exotic birds, some of which, including the Red Hooded Siskin (*S. cucullatus*) crosses, have been detailed under Hybrids. With this particular cross a number of fertile birds were produced, the discovery of which led to the development of the Red Factor Canary (see p.59). Until this discovery breeders had taken it for granted that any birds bred from Canaries and other birds were automatically sterile, however, as the Red Hooded Siskin cross proved this assumption to be incorrect, breeders are now wondering which other crosses will produce fertile young. It is likely that among the existing Greenfinch, Linnet, Twite and Siskin Mules some of the mature cock birds would prove to be fertile if given the opportunity to reproduce. Although it seems unlikely that such birds could add to the colours already achieved in Canaries it does suggest possibilities in the production of new coloured finches. By the skilful mating of mules back to their finch propagator new and interesting domesticated races of finches might be created. By the use of Lutino Greenfinches as partners for Canaries the possibility of obtaining sex-linked Lutino and Albino Canaries is greatly increased. With any such pairings there are always failures and disappointments but with perseverance something exciting should be achieved. Planned experiments are now being carried out, the objective being Albino Greenfinches and Albino and Lutino Canaries.

New Colours

'New Colours' include the whole range of colour mutations and their combinations that have appeared within recent years. This new Canary group does not contain such varieties as Cinnamons, Dominant Whites or Recessive Whites, although such breeds are used in combination with the new mutations.

The reappearance of the agate mutation (see p.48) was fortunately established reasonably quickly owing to the advance in our knowledge of colour breeding. Like the cinnamon character the agate is sex-linked which means that it is *only* cock birds that carry the character; if a hen bird has the agate character it shows in her plumage. No matter from what pairings the hens are bred they cannot be carriers (this applies to every sex-linked colour). The Agate mutant can be bred in the same way as the Cinnamon and, of course, the Cinnamon can be, and very often is, included in the pairings.

Opal is a recessive mutation which has a dilute colour effect on all birds that have the character in full strength in their genetic make-up. When the character is carried in half strength it does not show and the bird is known as a carrier. The opal character is produced in the same manner as the Ino mutation (see p.54) and both parents must have the character before any visual Opals are bred. With these diluting mutations it is the Self Greens and Cinnamons (yellow ground), Self Blues and Fawns (white ground) and these kinds in Red Factor ground that show the mutation to its best advantage. The reason for this is that the opal mutation turns black feather pigments into grey, and brown pigments are almost removed.

Another recessive mutation is melanin pastel (commonly called pastel) which affects the pencil markings only (Plate 10). The depth of the colour of the markings is reduced considerably in the darker colours and is absent in the palest colours. Again, all the different colours can be altered and of course the pastel mutation can be combined with other new mutations.

The opal, Ino and melanin pastel mutations affect the pigments carried by Canaries but there is one that influences only the ground colours and is known as lipochrome pastel. This mutation has no effect on the white ground beyond reducing the yellow wing tinting in the Dominant Whites. The yellow of the yellow ground is less deep but it is on the Red Factor ground that the mutation is seen at its best. It should be remembered that ground-colours and pigments are quite independent genetically; they both follow the rules of inheritance and a mutation can affect either one or both of them.

The production of New Colour Canaries is a specialized study and requires a certain amount of scientific knowledge: these birds are not suitable for the beginning Canary breeder.

Norwich Plainheads Plates 7, 11, 12

The beak is short and stout, eyes well set and not obscured, in a bold head that has a nice rise to the front making it well rounded all over the skull and cheeks. The neck should be thick and short, running smoothly from the back of the head down to well-proportioned shoulders with the breast rounded and full. The wings should be nicely placed touching at the tips and lying closely onto the rump, with the tail short, well filled and straight; legs and feet set well back. The plumage should be of a fine silky texture, smooth and clear cut throughout, and rich and level in tone. This is a colour-fed breed and the colour should be even in depth with the Buff form (Plate 12) showing plenty of mealing. The total length should be approximately 6–6¼ in (15–16 cm) with the birds having a solid, bold appearance.

The Norwich Canaries are, without doubt, one of the finest examples of selective breeding. The nineteenth-century drawings of Norwich Plainheads clearly show that the birds then existing were very different from today's magnificent specimens: they were much slimmer in build and appeared much longer. The tendency to produce birds of more substance probably started when it was found that colour-feeding could be carried out without any harmful effects. Before colour-feeding the Norwich Plainheads had been bred for their richness of colour and when this became less important breeders turned their attention to achieving shape with substance.

There are several ideas as to the origins of Norwich Canaries: some say that the prototypes were of European parentage and others that Lizards and London Fancies were crossed with nondescript birds and that Norwich Plainheads were produced by selective breeding over several generations. No actual dates for their appearances are ever quoted although it was probably during the early part of the eighteenth century. It is known, however, that East Anglia was the place of their evolution with the city of Norwich, from which they took their name, the centre of their early culture. The influence of these birds on local activities is to be found in the name given to Norwich City Football Club, affectionately called 'the Canaries' by its supporters.

Originally the perfect Norwich Canaries were considered to be the Clear Buff and Clear Yellow (Plate 11), Evenly-marked birds coming next. As their popularity increased Lightly and Heavily Variegated, Foul and Self Greens and Cinnamons became more freely bred and exhibited. Shortly after the dominant white ground-colour appeared it was introduced into the Norwich Plainheads and some beautiful bold Clear White, Variegated White and Self Blue and Fawn forms were produced and exhibited. Although these white-ground character birds are very attractive they do not seem to appeal to the majority of Norwich breeders, who still prefer the Yellow and Buff kinds. At one time it was thought that the Red Factor colouring might be introduced to the Norwich but this potential has not yet been realized. If this factor could be introduced it would do away with the necessity of colour-feeding. In the future we may see an escalation of the colour varieties in this fine bold Canary.

Opals

Again, this is not a breed of Canary but a colour mutation, which gives a special dilute pattern to the birds that have this character in their genetic make-up. This means that any type-breed can have this character and that it will alter the visual appearance of their existing colour. This mutation first appeared in Germany in 1949 in a Green (yellow-ground) bird. The opal character has the effect of changing the colour of the feather pigments: the black mainly appearing as pale grey and the brown as ghost-like pencillings. A Green bird with the opal character has a lime-green shade with light grey pencillings and a Cinnamon looks much like a clear Yellow but with very faint overlay of a pale pigment. The underflue (small soft feathers close to the body) of an Opal Cinnamon is a light beige colour, whereas in a normal Yellow the underflue is white. When the dominant white-ground character of a Blue Canary is combined with the opal character then both Yellow- and White-ground Opals are produced. These Opal Blues have a silvery tinted plumage that shows pale silver-grey markings and the Opal Fawns are whitish with a slight tinting of fawn. When the cinnamon character appears on a white ground it is then known as fawn. An interesting fact is that the opal character does not affect the colour of the beaks and legs, which are the same as their normal counterparts.

Because of the particularly delicate colouring of the group it is preferable to use only Self birds in their production as Variegated birds will only give an incomplete picture of the soft colouring produced by the opal character. The character that actually produces these Opals is recessive, and therefore to breed visual Opals both parents must have the character in their genetic make-up. The pairs can either be two Opals, one Opal and a normal, carrying Opal, or two normal-carrying Opals. The inheritance of recessive characters will be found in more detail on p.72.

Red Factors Plates 13, 14a, 14b

The introduction of the red ground-colour in Canaries opened up a whole new range of colour possibilities that could be introduced to the existing type-breeds. However, the majority of these Red Factor birds belong to a group commonly known as Red Factor Canaries – small birds with a strong Siskin influence showing in their type and deportment. Birds of various shades, ranging from the palest pastel pink to the deepest red orange, that have the Red Factor ground-colour are called Red Factors. The Buff examples are known as Frosted because the whitish mealing of their feathers makes the birds look as though they are covered with frost.

The first step taken by the breeders to introduce the red character carried by the Red Hooded Siskins (see p.170) to the Canaries is to pair Red Hooded Siskin cocks and Yellow (or Buff) Canary hens. Such matings result in birds that have neither the yellow ground of the Canary nor the red ground of the Siskin but show a copper ground due to both red and yellow pigments being present in the feathers. As already noted under Copper Hybrids (p.50) the cock birds are fertile, their sisters sterile. The next step in the breeding scheme is to mate the Coppers of the first cross to further Yellow Canary hens which results in young of Copper, Orange and Yellow, with the hens again being sterile. In the further matings of Copper and Orange with Yellow more Copper and Orange birds result, moreover both sexes are fertile. It is now possible to mate these birds together and by selective pairings the beautiful rich Red Orange and the deep Orange Canaries result.

If, in place of Clear Yellow birds, Self Cinnamons and Self Greens are used, these colours are produced on a Red Factor ground. The specimens resulting from such pairings are Self Orange and Self Red, Orange Green and Cinnamon – all very attractive birds of dark plumage. When Red Hooded Siskins are paired to Recessive White Canaries the resulting young are somewhat different from those of the Yellow Canary crosses. Such matings give young that show a sexual difference in their colour, the cocks being copper and the hens grey with a copper flush on breast and rump. This seems to be a modified form of sexual dimorphism (see Glossary), which is a characteristic of the Red Hooded Siskin.

This Red Factor has provided a large number of colour possibilities when incorporated with the new colour mutations that have been evolved within recent years, particularly by European breeders, but the breeding of these new and still rare coloured forms is a matter for the experimental specialist fanciers. However, information given above should help the inexperienced fancier to recognize the birds of the Red Factor group. Should the reader wish to study this subject more deeply, further information can be obtained from published literature. (See bibliography p.193.)

There are a number of specialist societies in Britain, Europe and America, which are doing sterling work in standardizing the shades of these red-ground varieties. Some of the tints of the Pastels, for example, are difficult to recognize because of the slight differences in their colouring – if these are not standardized one colour can be confused with another. Breeders keenly interested in the advancement of these handsomely coloured Canaries should join one of the societies and receive the benefit of their guidance and knowledge of the subject.

Roller Canary (Song Canary) Plate 15

These small Canaries are bred entirely for their song; although they adhere to a particular type this is of little importance to their breeders. Roller Canaries, as these birds are called, are about the same size as Border Fancies but are of a heavier build. Bird lovers were first attracted to the wild Canary because of its sweet singing voice and as domestication proceeded Canaries were divided into two groups – the singing birds and the type and colour kinds. The song of Roller Canaries has now been highly developed and it covers a wide range of musical notes. These birds have a wide following in most countries and singing contests are frequently staged so that the breeders can put their best birds against others. Undoubtedly these contests have greatly encouraged the breeders to improve and develop the song of their birds. The competing birds must be ringed with special closed and coded year-dated rings issued by the Roller Canary societies. These rings are put on the legs of young birds (see p.72) when they are a few days old and must not be removed and they serve to identify the birds for contest work. The unringed specimens can of course be used for breeding.

Different strains of Roller Canaries render various arrangements of notes and the training of birds to sing these 'tours', as they are called, begins when they are quite young. The training is carried out by 'schoolmaster' singers (i.e. prize-winning birds) of particular tours and it takes time and patience to bring the young trainees to a high standard. Nowadays records and tapes are also used. The breeding and establishment of a strain of contest Rollers is exacting and the breeder must keep extremely careful records of all the stock used. Breeding pairs must be matched with great accuracy, their records of performance and relationship being taken into consideration in order to achieve the greatest song potential in the resulting young. The colour of the birds has no bearing on their singing qualities – they can be bred in the whole range of both old and new colour shades. It is interesting to note, in fact, that most of the colour mutations have occurred in the stocks of Roller-type Canaries.

Even if they are not bred and trained to execute 'classical' song tours, Roller Canaries naturally inherit beautiful singing voices and thus they make good single household singing pets and delightful colonies in decorative garden aviaries. When breeding birds under aviary conditions it is usual to have a far greater number of hens than cocks in the same enclosure. This helps to minimize the fighting between the cock birds, thereby creating a more harmonious climate that is conducive to successful breeding. The ratio of cocks to hens will vary according to the particular circumstance, two or three hens per cock being the average. Hens also sing although not so lustily as their mates. An aviary can be further enhanced with an assortment of the many different colour shades not available in Roller Canaries. An aviary mixture might well consist of specimens in Yellow, White, Cinnamon, Green, Blue, Fawn, Red Factor, Dilute, etc. in Clear, Variegated and Self birds.

Since Roller Canaries are extremely good breeding-stock both in cages and aviaries, they are invariably prolific and make first-class parents. Breeders of some of the rarer kinds of Canary sometimes employ Rollers as foster parents. The production of birds for household pets has become an industry in some countries, particularly in Germany where, in the Harz mountains, thousands of birds are exported each year. At one time this area was the chief source of the world supply of pet singing Canaries and it still plays an important part in that trade. These mass-produced Canaries have excellent songs although they do not have the range or quality of the pedigree contest singing birds.

These contest songsters are divided into groups according to the type of tours and rolls they are trained to sing. Such tours have distinctive musical characters and their own special names such as Hollow Roll, Schockel, Bass, Gluck, the last being an important element in the repertoire of all contest singers. It is because of these variations that it is so essential for breeders to keep careful records of all their stock. (For further details see the section on Breeding, pp.69–73.)

Scotch Fancy Plate 16

The beak is small and neat; the eyes well placed in a small, clean-cut, flat, snaky head; the neck is long, fine and or Buffs and, like the Belgian Fancies, they look quite pallid beside the colour-fed Yorkshires and Norwich Canaries. It is possible that cinnamon, fawn, blue and white forms may soon be evolved in these birds of unusual shape. There is a distinct increase in the interest now being taken in the breeding of Scotch Fancies – much of which is due to the activities of the Old Varieties Canary Association.

The place of origin of the Scotch Fancy is indicated by their name and the centre of production was Glasgow. Originally this type was known as the Glasgow Don but as improvements were made in form and size they were more generally kept in Scotland and the name of Scotch Fancy was adopted. As Glasgow Dons they emerged some time before 1837 and were somewhat smaller birds than the present-day Scotch Fancy. It is said that Dutch 'Frilled' Canaries and Belgian Fancies were used to cross in with the Glasgow Dons to improve their substance and type. There is, of course, a distinct resemblance in the structural features of the Scotch and the Belgian Fancies and as the latter are the older breed it can be conjectured that they played an important part in the evolution of the Scotch Fancy. It is said that they are delicate and difficult birds to breed; this may be true of some closely inbred specimens but not of strong and healthy birds, which are good and gentle parents. In my opinion the Scotch Fancy is ideal for Canary lovers who want to take up an unusual variety that has considerable potential.

Spanish Timbrado

The beak should be conical, the eyes black and head small and rounded. The neck and back should be rounded with the neck slender and of medium length. The wings should be carried close to body and slightly crossed; tail forked and slightly spread. The body should be roundish and free from hollows or lumpiness. Legs small, delicate, with knees flexed. The plumage should be tight, thick, but markedly ruffled feathers are a fault. Colour: all colours except Red Factor shades, which disqualify the birds from competition. The birds should stand clear on the perch with an overall length of 5 in (13 cm), about the same size as the well-known Border Canary.

The Spanish Timbrado is a small bird that is produced for its song – its colouring is of little importance. It would appear, however, that the dark coloured specimens are likely to be better singers than the light coloured ones. The Timbrado was classified as a separate variety by the World Ornithological Confederation in 1962 and great credit must be given to the Spanish breeders for their achievement. They are not widely known outside Spain

THE GLASGOW DON, OR SCOTCH FANCY CANARY

Scotch Fancy Canary – an illustration from *The Canary Book* by Robert L. Wallace, published in the last quarter of the 19th century

curving; the back is long and narrow but well filled and tapering from prominent shoulders to tail; the chest is well filled with the waist long and fine. The thighs are of medium length with the legs long, and the tail long, compact and circled inwards. The overall shape, from the top of the head to the end of the tail, should be as a section of a circle. Its length is approximately 7 in (18 cm).

Scotch Fancies ('Birds o'Circle' as they are sometimes known) are another non-colour-fed variety; the most popular colour forms are clear or green-marked Yellows although during the past few years they have found enthusiastic support with some breeders in both North and South America. It is thought that the breed may have been evolved by selective crossings of a Spanish singing strain with wild Canaries and possibly a blend of Roller Canaries. This would seem to be borne out by the presentation of their song which has a more bell-like sound and gives the breed their name Timbrado, from the Spanish *timbre* (bell). Their song has been divided into three groups known as Bells, Clucks and Embellishments. The song of the Timbrado is very distinct from that of the Roller Canary breeds.

White-ground Canaries
This colour, or rather lack of colour, is available in two different breeding kinds – the Dominant Whites of German origin and the Recessive Whites that originally came from New Zealand. The Dominant Whites can be recognized by the leading edges of their flight feathers which have a distinct yellow tinting, absent in the Recessive kind.

White-coloured Canaries were known in Germany as long ago as 1667 and they appeared in France in 1709, though it is not known whether the latter birds were the same strain as the German ones or the result of a further mutation. The same applies to the White Canaries first recorded in Great Britain in 1737. None of these early references recorded whether these White birds were Dominant or Recessive as the Canary breeders did not then know about the rudimentary facts of inheritance.

The first White Canary to be produced since these early birds appeared in New Zealand; it came from a pair of normal-looking Buff Canaries and in the same year a further White bird was bred from Yellows by a fancier in London, England. Normal coloured birds from this British White strain were exported to Holland where, in due course, further Whites and carriers were produced. In 1912 a collection of the New Zealand Whites were sent to Great Britain and were becoming well established in several strains, when World War I prevented further breeding; the war also affected Dutch strains. Fortunately, a few Recessive Whites were still being bred in New Zealand in the post-war period and in 1926 four birds reached England in a shipment of mixed specimens and were obtained by the great pioneer Canary colour-breeder, A. K. Gill. It was through his untiring efforts that the Recessive White Canaries once again became an established breed and it is generally thought that all the Recessive Whites now known are descended from this strain. When or how the first Dominant White Canaries were produced is not known beyond the fact that it was in

Germany that they were first noted and reported. It is most improbable that they could have been descendants of the early German mutation since the character is of a dominant nature and could not have been carried in 'split' form; had it been visible it would have been reported earlier. It must be assumed, therefore, that these Dominant Whites arose from a fresh mutation which could, of course, be genetically the same as the previous one.

During the 1920s and 1930s the implications of the Mendelian principles of heredity in the breeding of Budgerigars and Canaries began to be understood. Much of the extensive pioneer work with both of these species was carried out by Dr Hans Duncker of Germany, whom I had the pleasure of meeting with his co-investigator, Gen. Konsul C. H. Cremer, and discussing with them the various aspects of bird breeding as revealed by the Mendelian laws.

The genetic behaviour of the Dominant Whites differs from that of other Canaries (except the crested kinds) in that when two Dominant Whites are paired a quarter of their resulting young are not viable. For this reason Dominant Whites are always paired to Yellows or Buffs to give half Dominant White and half Yellow or Buff young. The expectation of Dominant White paired to Dominant White is 25% Yellow (or Buff), 50% Dominant White with a single white character and 25% non-viable Dominant White with double white character.

At an early stage in the initial development of the Dominant White Canary strains some breeders attempted to cross them with Recessive Whites in the hope that this would eliminate the yellow tinting on the flights of the Dominant kind. Such matings were discontinued when it was discovered they were of no value in helping reduce or completely remove this unwanted yellow tinting. In fact the only way in which this yellow tinting can be somewhat reduced, although not eradicated, is through a series of careful selective pairings.

The dominant white character is simpler to introduce into various type-breeds than the recessive character and breeders were not slow to take advantage of this. As soon as Dominant Whites became sufficiently plentiful in their original Roller type, breeders started to use them in the production of the Border Fancy, Yorkshire Fancy and Norwich Plainhead in white ground-colour. The Gloster Fancy soon followed, as did Frills and a few examples of some of the other type-breeds.

When white ground is added to green the blue colour takes the place of the green of birds with the yellow-ground character and the results range from birds with a blue tick right through to a Self Blue. In the Self Blue range are the Blue Lizards, which are discussed on p.55. If in place of green the cinnamon character is used in crosses with the white-ground, then the rather attractive fawn shade is produced. Because fawn is derived from cinnamon it is sex-linked no matter what type-breed is concerned. Although Blue and Fawn birds were bred in Europe it was not until 1926 that they were produced in Great Britain, but the Recessive kind had been bred in New Zealand as early as 1914.

Border Fancies, being close to the White Rollers in size and shape, were the first type-breed to be bred in white-ground forms. It is, perhaps, surprising that the long slender Yorkshire Fancies were the next to be bred with the white-ground character, moreover they were of good quality. The first White Yorkshire I bred was a wing-marked Fawn hen and came from a Variegated Cinnamon Yellow cock and a second generation White Roller Yorkshire hen. This same Variegated Cinnamon Yellow cock also sired my first Self Fawn Yorkshire, a bird of a most pleasing soft fawn shade that was much admired by all who saw her. It was some time before White-ground Norwich Fancies began to appear – this is a much more substantial variety and took longer to develop in size.

I have had no breeding experience with Recessive Whites but I saw A. K. Gill's birds on numerous occasions and also had the opportunity of discussing with him the way the Recessive Whites reproduced. He told me that his original Recessive Whites were rather delicate but this weakness was soon overcome by out-crossing them to a vigorous unrelated stock. As expected, the colour of the blue and fawn markings of these Recessive White birds is visually identical with that of the Dominant kind.

Both varieties of these birds with the white-ground character have been used in Red Factor breeding and have resulted in further colour shades being produced. White Canaries have widened the whole range of possible colour types and even though they are not popular with Canary exhibitors they will always be attractive to the enthusiastic colour-breeder.

Wild Canary (Serinus canaria)

The beak is short and of medium stoutness; the eyes bold and centrally situated in a neat round head; the neck is short and rounded flowing into the body without a break; the breast and back are well rounded, the wings short and carried in line with a neat straight tail; the legs are of medium length. The general colour is a greenish yellow with more green on the rump and dark blackish streaks on flanks and mantle and some greyish markings on neck and wings; flight and tail feathers are blackish with some light edgings. The hens are easily identified as they do not show quite so much yellowish green as the cocks and there is more grey in their plumage. Overall length is approximately 5 in (13 cm).

Canaries, as outlined on p.47, are indigenous to Africa and some of its off-shore islands. It is difficult to discover exactly when they were first introduced to Great Britain but they are known to have existed there in the sixteenth century. These birds were wild-caught specimens or birds that were bred in captivity and on the road to domestication. Canaries reached America as pets with the families of some of the early settlers and today their popularity is considerable. A few wild Canaries are still exported to various countries as aviary specimens or for special scientific experiments. They have been paired with the domesticated Canary and other finch-like birds, and young have been successfully raised from these crosses. No benefits to the existing breeds can be achieved by these wild Canary crosses but they are of considerable scientific interest.

It has been suggested that the likelihood of fertile Mules being produced would be greater if the wild species were used instead of the domesticated types. This might well interest some advanced experimental breeders.

Yorkshire Canary Plates 17, 18

The beak should be neat and fine, eyes centrally placed in a round, full head with plenty of back skull; the shoulders should be wide, rounded and carried well up to the head. The breast should be deep and full and coming up to the beak, the body should be nicely rounded and tapered all through and the bird should stand erect on long legs with a bold fearless look. The plumage should be short, neat and tight with the wings long and compact, lying centrally down the back with the tail well set and closely folded. Their overall length is approximately 6¾ in (17 cm).

Yorkshire Canaries are often called 'the Gentlemen of the Fancy' because of their stylish appearance. The origin of the type-breed is obscure but it is known that earlier examples were much smaller and slimmer than the present-day birds. There is an old saying that a good exhibition Yorkshire should be able to be passed through a wedding ring! It would seem that Belgian Fancies, both pure and crossbred, Manchester Plainheads and Dutch Canaries, all contributed to the evolution of the Yorkshire Fancies. At the turn of the century, breeders felt that the variety was in need of more substance and extra length and to achieve this aim more Dutch 'blood' was introduced. Nineteenth-century drawings of Yorkshires show that the birds were much slimmer, lacked shoulders, and did not have such an erect position on the perch. Owing to the mixture of other varieties these old Yorkshires were probably difficult to breed consistently true to type. However, skill and perseverance have produced improved strains of first-class true-breeding birds. Like all varieties of 'type' Canaries, the popularity of Yorkshires varies – at the time of writing their numbers are increasing.

Yorkshires are available in a variety of colours: the Clear and Even-marked Yellows and Buffs are the most popular followed by the Greens and Cinnamons. There used to be special strains of Green Yorkshires, known as Manchester Greens, that had distinct bright green colouring. It is probable that these particular birds were the result of cross-breeding Yorkshire strains with Green Lancashire Plainheads. Although bright green, the birds were not colour-fed (as is customary with Yorkshires), since colour-feeding alters the shade of the green as it does the cinnamon.

The inclusion of the cinnamon character in Yellow (Buff) strains has a highly desirable effect on the feather quality. Many Cinnamons in Clears, Marked, Variegated and Selfs, have particularly good tight silky feathering which is so much desired in this variety. Some of the Clear Cinnamon specimens have soft feathering that takes the colour-feeding very well, giving an extremely rich deep shade. The majority of breeders have some Cinnamons in their studs for the purpose of maintaining and improving feather texture.

Nearly all White Yorkshires (see White-ground Canaries) are of the Dominant kind, and thus breeders can produce both Yellow and White-ground kinds from the same breeding pairs. It is surprising that these birds are not more widely bred; if breeders were to add to their stocks a few Whites, they would find their breeding rather more attractive. Self Blues are pleasing birds but, personally, I find Self Fawns the most attractive of the ordinary colours. (It is a good thing that breeders have individual tastes, otherwise only one kind of bird would be bred.)

Self Blue and Variegated Blue birds can be simply produced by mating Self Green or Variegated Green birds with Whites. As the white ground is dominant, marked White birds can be produced from the first cross. By carefully pairing the heaviest marked Whites with further Self Greens, Self Blues and heavily Variegated Blues can result. In all such pairings the general overall quality should be considered in addition to a good pure colour. The Greens used to breed Blues should be a clear, bright shade of green otherwise the resultant blue shade will be dull and greyish.

THE YORKSHIRE FANCY CANARY.
(First Prize Crystal Palace, 1875.)

Yorkshire Fancy Canary – an illustration from *The Canary Book* by Robert L. Wallace, published in the last quarter of the 19th century

The breeding of Self Fawns and Variegated Fawns is not so simple because sex-linkage is involved. If, for instance, a White cock is paired with a Self Cinnamon hen the young will be Variegated Green and Variegated Blue with all the young cocks being carriers of the sex-linked cinnamon character. When these Variegated Blue carrier cocks are paired with Self Cinnamon hens, the fawn colours will be in both cocks and hens. With the fawn and blue colours it is the 'yellow'-feathered birds that show the clearest and brightest shades of colour (this applies to all the different varieties of Canary).

A few British and European breeders have experimented with introducing the Red Factor ground-colour into the Yorkshires. Apparently this is much more difficult than it is with the white ground because of the type of the Red Factor birds that have to be used. Those usually available are small and have quite a different stance to that of the Yorkshires. It takes a number of generations to bring back the Yorkshire quality and style in the birds possessing the Red Factor ground-colour. For those breeders who are interested in producing studs of Yorkshires having a lovely rich colour without the use of colour-food this is a challenging and rewarding project.

HOUSING

It should be obvious, that Canaries need to be housed according to the purpose for which they are kept. The single singing pet bird is best housed in one of the fancy all-wire or plastic and wire ornamental cages. Such cages should be easy to clean and should not be covered with ornate metalwork that could trap a leg or wing. Cages should be sturdy, well made and roomy, even though this may mean a little extra initial outlay. If the metal work is plated it will look smarter and last longer. As well as the seed and water pots that are supplied with the cage it is necessary to have a small flat dish to put on the cage floor for holding grit.

Most cages have a removable sand tray on the floor as well as a loose bottom, which is useful when the cage is given its periodic cleaning. It is advisable to give a new cage a thorough wash with warm water and a mild soapy liquid to remove any possible source of contamination before the bird is introduced: small pieces of metal, galvanizing, paint or plastic can be dangerous if the bird eats them. The sand tray can be covered with special bird sand or with sanded sheets designed specially for this purpose. Sanded sheets are useful and quick to change but the old-fashioned bird sand is preferable – it contains grit and minerals and absorbs moisture far better than the sanded sheets. Holders for pieces of cuttlefish bone and for greenfoods are also available from suppliers. The scattering of seed and husks can cause some inconvenience but this can be largely overcome by fitting over the outside of the cage bottom a fabric or plastic cover which catches the bulk of the scattered debris and keeps the area around the cage neat and tidy.

The Canary cannot bathe satisfactorily in the small water vessel usually provided with the cage. A shallow dish or saucer can be put into the cage so the bird can bathe in comfort, but special baths for hanging on the open cage doors give more room and are much more practical as they prevent the cage from getting too wet from splashing. The water used for baths should be boiled tap or rain water, provided the latter is from a clean source.

The siting of the pet Canary's cage is most important as this can have a direct bearing on the bird's continued good health. The room in which the bird is to be housed should be maintained at a reasonable temperature. Continual fluctuations in the temperature will cause a series of partial moults and besides making the Canary's feathers look rough this does not help the bird's natural comfort. A direct draught from window or door can soon become the cause of a chill which can develop into a more serious condition if not dealt with immediately. Canaries, like many other birds, will live happily in cool temperatures – it is the sudden changes that upset them.

The cage should be hung or stood in a position free from direct draughts and the full rays of the sun. Although sunshine is extremely good for birds they cannot stand being kept for long periods in the direct rays without being able to hop into the shade whenever they wish. The cage can be stood on a table, hung on a wall, or from a stand, whichever is the most suitable and convenient for the owner. The special cage-stands are the safest and best way of having a bird and cage in a room. They are easy to move from room to room and prevent domestic animals from getting too close to the bird, thereby causing unnecessary fright.

A fancy cage is ideal for housing a single pet Canary but birds kept for controlled breeding need a different type of cage. For such purposes single or double wooden or metal breeding-cages should be used. The size of such cages will vary according to the amount of space available and the type of Canaries kept. Single breeding-cages are usually about 24 in (60 cm) long by 14 in (35 cm) high and 10 in (25 cm) deep; double breeding-cages are about 36 in (92 cm) long by 14 in (35 cm) high and some 12 in (30 cm) deep. The double breeding-cage is divided into two parts by a movable wooden and/or wire slide so that the cock bird or the young can be separated from the hen while the second clutch of eggs is being laid. It is particularly important that the perches in *all* breeding-cages, either single or double, are really *firmly* fixed. Loose perches prevent the birds from mating successfully and a number of clear eggs usually result.

The food and water vessels for breeding-cages are generally fixed on the outside for easy cleaning and

Canary breeding-cages – note the sliding panels that separate the birds and which can be removed when mating is desired. The birds here are of the Border Fancy variety and the relevant standard show cages can be seen on top of the breeding-cages.

replenishing; the birds are able to reach them through round holes made in the bottoms of the wire fronts. Grit pots are generally placed inside the cages in shallow dishes, cuttlefish bone and greenfood can be held in place with clips similar to those suggested for use in the ornamental cages. Soft food is generally given in finger trays that are held in place by the sliding door of the cage itself. The wooden breeding-cages can be decorated inside and out with emulsion paint or one of the non-lead containing paints, which are harmless to the birds.

The arrangement and siting of the breeding-cages in the birdroom varies according to the individual breeder's requirements and the available space. Some prefer to have the cages built in tiers with the rows divided by slides. In this case some rows of cages can be made into long flights for keeping stock birds during the non-breeding season and, of course, for the young birds when taken from their parents. The slides can be kept in the remaining rows to provide individual cages for the preparation of exhibition stock. To obtain the maximum amount of light in the bird house all the decoration should be white. Some suitable decorative cages and breeding-cages are shown on this page.

Canaries of most kinds, especially the smaller breeds

Decorative cages with stands *(Genyk Products Ltd)*

such as Rollers, Borders, Red Factors or Gloster Fancies, make excellent outdoor or indoor aviary birds. Several factors, however, deter fanciers from keeping them in aviaries, the most important being that it is not possible to control the breeding of free-flying birds – essential for the production of the type- and colour-breeds and the contest Roller Canaries, all of whose pedigrees must be known and recorded. Another factor is that few people realize that healthy Canaries are tough little birds and can stand cold conditions provided they have good food and dry, draught-proof quarters.

Aviaries in which to keep and breed Canaries can be of many shapes and designs but must have certain common factors. The aviary should have a well-lit, dry, draught-proof section for sleeping, feeding and breeding; to this is attached an all-wire, mesh-covered flight of about twice the area of the covered portion. A part of the flight roof may also be covered so that the birds can be out in the open air during wet weather without getting unduly wet.

The floor of the flight can be covered by stone slabs, sand, fine gravel, or it can be planted with grass and small trees or shrubs. With careful planning it is possible to make a flight really attractive; it can include a shallow pool, ¾ in (2 cm) deep, for bathing, or even a planted rockery. The landscaping of a planted aviary gives the owner plenty of scope for artistic design.

The perching in the enclosed portion of an aviary is best made of dowelling of different thicknesses so as to give the birds a change of grip – important in preventing foot stiffness. The perches should be fixed firmly at varying heights, clear of the food, water and grit vessels. In the outside flight the perches can be made of branches, preferably from fruit, nut, hawthorn, wild plum, pine or beech trees. Such natural perches are always welcomed by the birds; they can be arranged so that the perching birds are seen to advantage from any angle.

In addition to these purpose-built flighted outside aviaries many other types of buildings can be successfully converted. If only a few birds are kept, a small portion of a verandah or sunroom can be wired-in to make a useful and handy flight. Old garden or tool sheds, summer houses, indeed any unused structure can be converted into a house suitable for different-sized flocks. A few brightly coloured, sweetly singing birds will brighten up an otherwise dull garden.

FEEDING

If the owner has only one pet Canary the simplest and most economical way of providing the bird with its staple

A garden shed being converted into an aviary – the front and right-hand end will be wired-in and any glass will either be covered with wire mesh or replaced with clear plastic.

A double-flighted aviary and birdroom suitable for Canaries, Budgerigars and all small foreign birds

seed mixture is to buy one of the branded packeted kinds. These seeds are of the best quality and are specially blended to suit the needs of such birds. There are several different brands on the market and it is best to try them all to discover which the bird prefers. Although the seed will keep in its original packet it will retain its freshness much longer if stored in an airtight tin or jar.

For those who keep a number of Canaries the staple seeds can be bought either ready-mixed or as separate kinds to be mixed by the bird keeper, to suit his stock. A standard blend can be made up of one part large canary seed, two parts small canary seed, one and a half parts sweet red rape seed and a handful of hemp seed. In very cold weather the amount of hemp can be increased and some pinhead groats or niger seed may be added. During the moulting period a small quantity of linseed is a useful addition to the standard mixture. Niger, hemp and linseed are oil-containing seeds which should be given in restricted quantities because of their fattening nature. Some weeks before the breeding season small quantities of maw, niger, teazel and gold of pleasure seeds can be given, either in the standard seed mixture or separately in finger dishes. The pet Canary will also benefit from periodic feeding of some of these tonic seeds, which can be bought ready mixed.

Seed bought in bulk should be of the best quality and should be obtained from reputable seed merchants. The seed should be bright, sweet and hard, and free from extraneous materials such as dust, husks, or vermin droppings. Seed is best stored in metal, plastic or wooden containers that have tightly fitting lids; to prevent an accumulation of stale seed, it is essential that the containers are emptied completely before adding a new supply. It is surprising how quickly stale or musty seed will upset the stomachs of Canaries which can be disastrous at all periods and especially at breeding times.

As well as the seeds mentioned above, mixed wild flower seeds are readily eaten by most Canaries; they provide a periodic variation of diet that contains valuable nutritious elements not found in the standard seed mixtures. If purchased, it is essential that the wild flower seeds are carefully checked for freshness before giving to the stock. Should the British owner wish to prepare his own mixture the following wild flower seeds can be collected from the countryside, taking care to avoid any that may have been contaminated by chemicals or animals: chickweed, rye and meadow grasses, dandelion, charlock, teazel, campion, persicara, plantain and hardheads. The seed heads should be collected fully ripe, thoroughly dried and stored in airtight containers. In an extensive aviary collection of Canaries the use of wild flower seeds will help to compensate for the rather high cost of plain canary seed and at the same time will provide a more balanced diet.

The regular use of soft food throughout the year is beneficial to the stock and helps to keep it in a fine condition of health and feather. Extra soft food should be given at moulting times and it must be given, of course, while the birds are breeding. Individual breeders have their own idea of what constitutes a good soft food; at one time it was thought that the only satisfactory soft food was a mixture of hard-boiled hens' eggs and crumbled biscuit. Although a few breeders still use this old-fashioned mixture and find it quite satisfactory, the majority find the scientifically blended and packed soft foods easier to use, and there is less risk of it going stale. These packeted soft foods contain biscuit, cod liver oil, dried egg and other ingredients needed by the birds in a carefully balanced mixture. They are simple to prepare and each packet contains instructions for its use.

As a change from the standard soft food, breeders sometimes give their birds bread and milk with a scattering of maw or gold of pleasure seed on top. Both white and wholemeal bread can be used but wholemeal is preferable as it is of greater nutritional value. This preparation is usually given to the birds as a midday feed but this is for the individual breeder to decide. Because milk quickly goes sour it is essential that any uneaten bread and milk is removed from the cage or aviary when the next feed is given – this applies to all soft foods.

The third essential part of the diet is fresh greenfoods. Pet Canaries will live reasonably well without any greenfood but they undoubtedly prosper from a regular supply and greenfood is an essential for breeding Canaries. A large variety of fresh greenfoods, some fruits and root vegetables, are eaten by Canaries. The consensus of opinion of breeders in many countries over a long period of years shows that chickweed (*Cerastium* species) is the most popular of all the fresh greenfoods. It is eagerly devoured by the birds at all times of the year and it is as acceptable in its full lush green form as when it is covered with tiny pods of ripe golden seeds. There are numerous instances of breeding pairs that have reared full nests of vigorous chicks on their usual hard seed mixture with unlimited supplies of chickweed. Next in popularity is fresh spinach – the birds like whole leaves and their juicy stalks. Spinach contains iron and is good for keeping the richness in the colour of the bird's feathers. Both spinach and chickweed are easy to grow, even in the smallest town garden. The heads of seeding grasses, especially the meadow (*Poa annua)* and the rye *(Lolium perenne)* grasses, provide another valuable greenfood, both in their green half-ripe state and when the seeds are fully ripe and dry. Further good greens are the young freshly grown leaves of dandelions *(Taraxacum officinale)*, and leaves and seed heads of sow (milk) thistles *(Sonchus arvensis)*, the seeding heads of shepherd's purse *(Capsella bursa-pastoris)*, lettuce leaves and seeding heads, chicory, endives, watercress, quickly-grown groundsel, cabbage hearts, Brussels sprouts, slices of carrot, sweet apple or pear. When fresh greenfood is in short supply, sprouted wheat, barley, oats or canary seeds can be given – they too will be eaten by the majority of Canaries. The birds need not, therefore, be short of greenfood at any period of the year and at most times it can be easily varied.

Canaries, like most birds, must have a constant supply of good mixed grits so that their food can be ground into a consistency for easy assimilation. The birds swallow the small sharp-edged pieces of grit and fill their gizzards where these stones grind the food by constant movement. By their continual movement the edges of the stones are gradually worn smooth – they then lose their potential and are expelled. This process is going on throughout the life of the stock so grit must always be available for replacement. Grits can be of several kinds such as flint, limestone or oyster shells, and are given either separately or mixed: all should be crushed and graded to suit Canaries. Grit can be bought in small bags or in bulk when larger quantities are needed.

Pieces of cuttlefish bone should be hung or clipped in all cages and aviaries. Cuttlefish bone is a source of almost pure lime, which helps to keep the beaks of the birds at a correct length and is needed throughout the year. Specially made iodine and mineral blocks are also beneficial as a source of elements that are needed for the well-being of the stock.

Fresh clean water must always be in cage and aviary, and a special check should be made on the water vessels during warm weather and when young birds are in the nests. Water pots should be kept perfectly clean: they must be emptied daily and thoroughly washed once a week to prevent accumulation of germs.

BREEDING

The many types of Canaries all need the same management at breeding times. Once the necessary accommodation and conditions have been established, the breeding stock of the variety decided upon should be obtained. Experienced local fanciers, who already keep the desired variety, may be able to offer advice and suggestions for obtaining the initial stock. With certain rare varieties it may mean going further afield to get the necessary birds. The Fancy paper *Cage and Aviary Birds* is an excellent source for discovering those breeders who have surplus stock for sale. This weekly publication also contains valuable articles on all aspects of the cage bird fancy and its general progress in Britain and abroad. The equivalent publication in the United States is *American Cage-bird Magazine*. Joining a local cage bird society is another good way of getting to know other enthusiasts in the area and gaining knowledge of their culture through discussions at meetings and shows.

The best time to buy breeding stock is in the autumn when most breeders have surplus birds for sale. At this time of the year the intending buyer will have a larger selection from which to choose and the birds will have time to settle in their new quarters long before they are needed for breeding.

It is usual to start breeding operations at the beginning of spring although the actual date will depend on the part of the country where the breeder lives and, most important, the birds' condition. Both members of the matched breeding pairs must be in full breeding condition before any attempt is made to mate them. If the pair, or one of the partners, is not in the desired condition then the mating will be unproductive. It is not necessary, as is sometimes thought, to mate all breeding pairs on a given date. The pairs should be put together as and when they are thought to be fully ready and not before.

It may be difficult for the new owner to decide when the birds are ready for breeding but there are certain clues. When cock birds are in full condition they will be seen and heard singing very lustily. Fit hens call to the singing cock birds and carry in their beaks anything that could be used as nesting material.

On close examination, the vent area of the hens appears slightly swollen, with the vent itself being flat; in the cock birds the area will be flatter, with the vent protruding. This examination of the hens should not be done too close to pairing time as catching the birds will undoubtedly disturb them.

When the birds are thought to be ready the general practice is to put them into a breeding-cage with the wire dividing slide between them; the slide is left in place for a day or two so the birds can become acquainted. If courtship is successful and mating is taking place the nesting receptacles and nesting material can be put in the cage.

The nests can be either round pottery or plastic 'pans' with linings of felt or other soft material or they can be

Round pottery 'pan' nest with a cowhair lining, provided by the owner, into which the bird has built her nest.

A Corona Gloster Canary hen sitting on a clutch of eggs in a pottery nest pan.

square wooden boxes with perforated zinc bottoms. The pottery or plastic nests can be bought complete with hangers at bird stores but the wooden kinds are generally made by the fanciers.

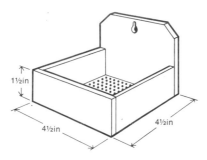

Wooden nest with perforated zinc bottom

I have used both kinds with equal success; in very warm weather the zinc bottom is cooler for the sitting birds as it allows air to circulate. Some breeders hang the nests on the back of cages and others at the side depending on the size of the breeding-cages. In my opinion the side position is preferable and a square of card fixed on the wire front gives the birds some privacy. I provide the birds with clean moss to make the main nest and then some cow hair to line the nest. Pieces of wool, cotton, string or any similar materials should on no account be given, as the birds easily become entangled and suffer serious damage.

After the pairs have been together for a week or so eggs will be laid on consecutive days during the early part of the morning. The clutches are mostly four to five in number. As each egg is laid it should be taken out of the nest and stored in a special felt-lined box divided into small numbered sections each to hold a complete clutch. If the cages are numbered the eggs can be put into the corresponding section in the egg box. To prevent the hens from becoming too upset, pot eggs are given to them to sit on in place of their own. On the evening of the fourth day the pot eggs are removed and the proper clutches are replaced or 'set'; the hens then begin their period of incubation of thirteen or fourteen days.

The breeder should record in his breeding register the date the clutches are 'set', how many of the eggs hatch and whether any unhatched eggs are dead-in-shell, clear or addled. Accurate records will serve as a guide to the breeding behaviour of individual birds and the pedigrees of the young will be readily available for future reference.

To ensure that the incubating clutches of eggs are not getting over-dry the sitting hens can be given the opportunity to bath at midday on several days before the hatching date. Many hens will not avail themselves of this, in

In this instance the breeder removed and replaced the first three eggs before the fourth egg was laid and . . .

. . . the latecomer was therefore at a fatal disadvantage in competing for food with its more advanced companions.

which case the eggs should be moistened with warm water when the hens leave their clutches for their morning feed.

The day before the eggs are due to hatch the parent birds should be given some soft food so they are ready to feed their young when they hatch out. Apart from giving food, water and greens, the nests of newly hatched chicks should not be interfered with for the first few days. Some hens, particularly first-year birds, will desert their nests or let the young die if they are unduly disturbed while the chicks are still very small.

Healthy young Canaries grow quickly so the amount of food given must be progressively increased to keep up with the demand of the fast developing youngsters. Food has already been discussed. The young will be ready to leave their nests when sixteen to twenty days old but will still depend on their parents for food for a further period of about ten days.

By the time the first clutch is ready to leave the nests, the hens are usually preparing to lay their second clutch of eggs; the hen should be given a new nest and a period of rest away from the cock and young. The cock bird can be allowed in with her for a little time each morning and evening so the birds can mate and she can lay fertile clutches. Once the young are feeding on their own they can be moved to nursery cages for final development and then into flight cages for moulting.

Just before the young birds are removed from their parents, if they are not closed-ringed, they should be ringed with either split metal or celluloid rings so they can be positively identified. The ring details should be en-

The mother with her three surviving chicks

METHOD OF RINGING A CHICK

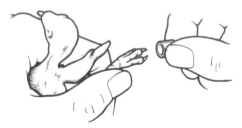

1. With the first finger and thumb of the hand in which the bird is held, gather the three long toes together, holding them in position by the ball of the foot.

2. Pick up the ring and slide it over these toes, then pass it over the ball of the foot, gradually sliding it up the leg.

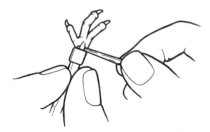

3. To release the short back toe, which is now held against the leg by the ring, insert a pointed stick, such as a matchstick, between the toe and leg and gently ease the toe through the ring.

4. The ring is now correctly positioned around the chick's leg.

tered in the breeding register so that the true ancestry of each bird is known, for it is virtually impossible to remember the parentage of each bird. Identification will assist the breeder to prevent indiscriminate inbreeding which would weaken the stock.

It is general practice to mate a Yellow with a Buff bird, irrespective of breed or colour. There are different methods by which colours are passed from one generation to another. A number of these colours are recessive to others and the inheritance of the recessive ones all follow a definite set of rules. Yellow including Buff is dominant to all recessive forms and the table which follows gives the results of such matings. The variegation carried by any birds is quite independent of other colour characters although the colours of the variegation can be affected by the other colours. As there is no sex linkage it does not matter which member of a pair is Yellow.

RULES OF RECESSIVE INHERITANCE

1. Recessive × Normal Yellow gives 100% Normal Yellow/Recessive (see fig. 1, p.104)

2. Recessive × Normal Yellow/Recessive gives 50% Recessive and 50% Normal Yellow/Recessive (see fig. 2, p.104)

3. Normal Yellow/Recessive × Normal Yellow gives 50% Normal Yellow/Recessive and 50% Normal Yellow (see fig. 3, p.104)

4. Normal Yellow/Recessive × Normal Yellow/Recessive gives 25% Recessive, 50% Normal Yellow/Recessive and 25% Normal Yellow (see fig. 4, p.104)

5. Recessive × Recessive gives 100% Recessive (see fig. 5, p.104)

This set of rules can be applied to all the different varieties and although percentages may not work out with single nests or pairs, if taken collectively they will be found quite accurate.

The reproduction of the sex-linked colour characters of which the cinnamon is the most popular often mystifies new breeders; however, once these rules are known the whole picture becomes clear. With this kind of inheritance the sex of the bird having the colour has a direct bearing on the colour of the young produced. It should be noted that it is possible for a bird to have more than one sex-linked character in its genetic make-up.

RULES OF SEX-LINKED INHERITANCE

1. Normal Yellow cock × sex-linked hen gives 50% Normal Yellow/sex-linked cocks and 50% Normal Yellow hens (see fig. 1, p.105)

2. Sex-linked cock × Normal Yellow hen gives 50% Normal Yellow/sex-linked cocks and 50% sex-linked hens (see fig. 2, p.105)

3. Normal Yellow/sex-linked cock × Normal Yellow hen gives 25% Normal Yellow/sex-linked cocks, 25% Normal Yellow cocks, 25% sex-linked hens and 25% Normal Yellow hens (see fig. 3, p.105)

4. Normal Yellow/sex-linked cock × sex-linked hen gives 25% sex-linked cocks, 25% Normal Yellow/sex-linked cocks, 25% sex-linked hens and 25% Normal Yellow hens (see fig. 4, p.105)

5. Sex-linked cock × sex-linked hen gives 100% sex-linked cocks and hens (see fig. 5, p.105)

There is a little variation in the dominant inheritance due to the fact that German Whites and Crests are also subject to a lethal character. Two set of rules make this clear.

RULES OF DOMINANT INHERITANCE (A)

1. German White single character × Normal Yellow gives 50% German White single character and 50% Normal Yellow

2. German White single character × German White single character gives 25% Normal Yellow, 50% German White single character and 25% German White double character which are not viable

DOMINANT INHERITANCE (B)

1. Dominant single character × Normal Yellow gives 50% Dominant single character and 50% Normal Yellow (see fig. 1, p.103)

2. Dominant single character × Dominant single character gives 25% Dominant double character, 50% Dominant single character and 25% Normal Yellow (see fig. 2, p.103)

3. Dominant double character × Normal Yellow gives 100% Dominant single character (see fig. 3, p.103)

4. Dominant double character × Dominant single character gives 50% Dominant double character and 50% Dominant single character (see fig. 4, p.103)

5. Dominant double character × Dominant double character gives 100% Dominant double character (see fig. 5, p.103)

If the inheritance rules given above are taken in conjunction with the other information given under the different breeds the owner can forecast the possible expectations obtainable from his matched breeding pairs.

The methods discussed are for breeding Canaries in cages but the procedure for aviary breeding is similar in most respects. The two main differences are that in aviary breeding control cannot be exercised over the pairing of the birds and several hens are given to each cock.

Budgerigars

It is, perhaps, difficult to believe that the collections of Budgerigars seen today in all their mixed colours were evolved from the wild species. It was in 1840 that the first live birds were brought to Britain from their native Australia by the naturalist, John Gould.

The very first breeding of Budgerigars in captivity is credited to Gould's brother-in-law, Charles Coxon, but it has not been established whether this was in Australia or Britain. This first success was followed by others and it was not long before the keeping and breeding of Budgerigars spread to other European countries. Kept in both large and small aviaries, the birds soon became acclimatized and bred quite freely.

When large numbers of a species are bred in captivity, it is inevitable that mutations occur. This, of course, is also true in the wild, but the mutations are generally swamped by the dominant wild type, whereas in captivity any mutations are noticed by the breeder. The first colour break among green-coloured is most likely to be yellow, and it was during the period 1870–5 that Yellow mutants were observed in several European aviaries among flocks of Light Greens; later other mutations were seen. There are three races (or subspecies) of Budgerigars in the wild: the principal type, which is found in most of the Australian states, scientifically called *Melopsittacus undulatus undulatus*; a race that is paler in colour on the neck and back, and darker on the head (*M. u. intermedius*), which inhabits the northern areas; and *M. u. pallidiceps*, which is generally paler, especially on the head, and comes from the western region. The three subspecies have overlapping territories and during migration all three have been noted flying together and must interbreed. Certainly they did so in captivity when collections from the different areas were brought together in the aviaries. It is this admixture of the three races plus the natural variation in the pattern of their markings that have contributed to the evolution of the numerous and varied domesticated strains seen today.

More importantly, when Mendel's laws of inheritance became common knowledge in the 1920s, selective breeding on a more scientific basis was possible, further mutations were discovered and there was an explosion of interest in Budgerigar breeding. In 1925 at the Crystal Palace Exhibition, London, a meeting of those interested in Budgerigar breeding was arranged and about twenty fanciers formed the Budgerigar Club. Five years later it became The Budgerigar Society, under the patronage of His Majesty King George V. The Society formulated colour and show standards, designed standard show cages, allocated ring code numbers, issued year books and bulletins to keep its members informed on the latest developments and organized all aspects of keeping, exhibiting and breeding Budgerigars. As the interest grew and spread, national societies were soon formed in many other countries, area and specialist societies came into being, all taking their lead from the parent Budgerigar Society.

Although the breeding of the many colour varieties is today a fine art and the newcomer to this field may wonder how the various forms have been arrived at, the basic facts are easily understood and applied. In the wild the Budgerigar, as previously noted, is a variable species having slightly different colours (shades or intensity of shades) and marking patterns on the plumage. Selected pairings by the breeder result in new combinations of colour and patterns that are more interesting than the straight colours. Unlike the Canary, the general shape of Budgerigars of all colours is the same. They do vary a little in substance and other qualities that are very noticeable in first-class breeding stock. Information on breeding is given on pp.100–5 and the reader should also turn to the section on Genetics (p.184).

An early plate of a Budgerigar *Nanodes undulatus* from Vol. X of the *Naturalist's Library* edited by Sir William Jardine, 19th century

Other details appear under the various colour mutations, where information is supplied on the first breedings and progress of the forms.

TALKING BIRDS

The ability of Budgerigars to imitate the human voice and other sounds has endeared them to millions of people all round the world. Their power of mimicry was first discovered, most probably in Germany, during the last part of the nineteenth century, but it is only over the last few decades that this talent has really been developed. Budgerigars of all colours can be trained to mimic and it is usually the young cock birds that make the best pupils, although some young hens will learn to talk and become very tame and friendly with their owners.

Budgerigars, like all living things, are very individual in their ability to learn and their aptitude to repeat the human voice varies. Some birds will start to talk soon after they have been taken into a household, others may take weeks or even months before they make a start; and a few never succeed. Even though the birds may not talk the majority become exceedingly tame and can be trained to do many little tricks. Much depends on the instructor; women and young people, because of their clearer higher voices, are usually the best tutors. The young bird chosen for training should be taken from the care of his parents as soon as he can feed on his own, put into a cage and taken into the home (see pp.96–7).

When the bird has become tame and used to its surroundings and its owner, a daily period of freedom can be allowed. A specially-made platform that can be fixed to the open cage door will encourage the bird to go in and out of the cage quite naturally. Before a bird is allowed out into a room it is essential that all doors and windows are securely closed and any open fires completely covered by a wire guard. Any pot plants or flowers should be taken out of the room while the bird is free (certain greenfoods are very good for a bird but most household greenery is harmful if eaten).

One person in the household should be designated to act as the bird's instructor because a number of different voices only confuse the trainee. The usual method of teaching the young Budgerigar to talk is to repeat its name in a clear voice each time the cage is approached and especially when the bird is being fed or just before it goes to roost. Once the first hurdle has been overcome and the bird can say its name, short sentences can be tried and continued until the bird has achieved a good vocabulary. During training the bird may pick up other

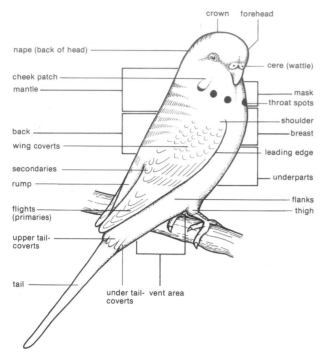

crown forehead

nape (back of head)

cere (wattle)

cheek patch
mantle

mask
throat spots

shoulder

back
wing coverts

breast

leading edge

secondaries

rump

underparts

flights
(primaries)

flanks
thigh

upper tail-
coverts

tail

under tail- vent area
coverts

External anatomy of the Budgerigar

words from hearing the family talking. An important point in the training is that the owner must have plenty of patience and at no time frighten the bird by sudden unexpected movements. If the pet bird is given good seed, grit, water and greenfood, but not sweet household food, it will keep in good health for the longest possible time.

COLOUR VARIETIES
These are listed in alphabetical order and not according to the year in which they first appeared. The colour descriptions are based on the standards of The Budgerigar Society.

Albino Plates 19, 35
Syn: Red-eyed Clear Whites
The almost pure white red-eyed forms have been developed in two ways and at one time were also obtainable in two separate breeding forms. Albino mutations have occurred in several countries and they have also been bred from Lutinos. Albinos were first reported in 1932, both in Great Britain and Germany, but it was only the German race that finally became established.

Although the British Albino produced a number of chicks when mated with a Blue cock no further Albinos are known to have come from that strain. The German kind was found to be sex-linked and it was not long before Albino cocks and hens were raised from the original Albino hen.

During the period of the development of the German sex-linked Albino a non-sex-linked type of Albino and Lutino were also raised in Germany but details of its origin are not available. Both forms were imported by British breeders and a certain amount of confusion arose when the two sorts were unknowingly mated (a Lutino cock of the non-linked kind paired with a sex-linked Lutino hen – both birds having red eyes – would only give normal coloured black-eyed young). The confusion was disentangled when it was realized that the two kinds of these red-eyed birds had different genetic make-ups.

It is most probable that the British Albino mutant was of the non-linked kind. If so, further Albinos could not have occurred unless the young of the original hen had been back-crossed to her or *inter se*. The non-linked Albino and Lutino strains of German ancestry disappeared from breeding establishments in Great Britain and examples have not been reported as breeding in any other countries for about thirty years.

By combining three other separate colour characters it is possible to produce what has been called the synthetic Albino (or Lutino). If the Cinnamon form of the Fallow White is bred it appears as an almost clear white red-eyed bird difficult to distinguish from a true Albino. I have carried out this cross-breeding experiment a number of times and find it a fascinating set of matings with interesting results.

The purest-coloured Albinos are those from one of the Grey series. The grey character reduces the depth of the suffusion that may be shown by the Albinos and being of a grey tint it is not so noticeable. In fact, some Albino Greys look almost pure white and are very desirable as exhibition birds.

The aim when producing Albinos is to breed birds that are as pure white as possible. There is one exception, the Albino Violet, where a heavy suffusion is required. This suffusion shows a very beautiful rosy pink shade and the heavier the suffusion the richer this shade. The Albino Violet is the closest to being a pink Budgerigar that has yet been bred.

There is no such thing as a pure Albino; it must be an Albino form of one of the Blue series. For instance, an Albino Skyblue, Albino White Cobalt, Albino Clearwing, Albino Grey, etc. There is an interesting Albino form which is produced by the inclusion of the Yellow-faced or Golden-faced characters giving birds with both yellow and white on their plumage and in some cases a complete yellow overlay which causes the birds to appear in attractive lemon shades.

Blue Series
The description given in the next paragraph, relevant to Skyblue (p.92), applies also to birds with the following body colours, when these are substituted in the description: Cobalt, Mauve, Slate and Violet (qq.v.). The tail feathers will be correspondingly darker. The Grey (Blue) series of these colours are the same but the body colours are different shades of grey and the cheek patches are light grey to silver and the tail feathers jet black.

Mask: white, ornamented by six evenly spaced large round black throat spots, the outer two being partially covered by the violet patches. General body colour: back, rump, breast, flanks and underparts, sky blue. Markings: on cheeks, back of head, neck and wings, black and well defined on a white ground. Tail: long feathers deep blue.

Cinnamons Plates 30, 34
Syn: at one time, Cinnamonwings
Cinnamon is a character in the genetic make-up of a bird, the presence of which dilutes the existing colour by inhibiting the production of the black pigment that is normally present. The brown (Cinnamon) pigmented markings thus become visible in the birds' feathers. The Cinnamon Budgerigars are not, in themselves, separate colour varieties, but there are Cinnamon forms of all the colour-types in the Green, Blue and Yellow-faced series. There can be, for example, Cinnamon Light Greens, Cinnamon Cobalts, and Cinnamon Yellow-faced Greywings. In common with Canaries and certain other birds, young Cinnamon Budgerigars, when newly hatched, show the characteristic pink eye and are therefore immediately recognizable as Cinnamons. The brightness of the pink in the eyes diminishes as the birds mature but, nevertheless, a slight reddish gleam can still be seen in the eyes of adult birds when viewed at an angle in a good light.

The first bird with cinnamon markings exhibited in Great Britain was a White Skyblue hen bred in Middlesex by Messrs Hughes in 1931. The bird was bred from a pair of Green/Blues without any known White (or Yellow) ancestry. It was a great loss to fanciers that this hen did not produce any issue as she appeared to be a mutant for both White and Cinnamon. In the same year as this Cinnamon White Skyblue further, but unrecognized, Cinnamon birds were noticed in a brood of related Dark Greens. The birds were all hens and all were green. These Dark Greens had been bred by Mr A. R. Simms of Hertfordshire, England, from an Olive Green cock paired with what was thought to be a Greywing Green hen which was, in fact, a Cinnamon Green hen. The young from the Dark Greens were various green and blue shades together with some 'Greywing Green' hens like their grandmother. In due course these 'Greywing Greens' were mated to White Skyblue cocks and, to the surprise of their owners, only produced normally coloured chicks. Greywing Green mated with White Skyblue is quite a good cross for producing Greywings and the owners were surprised and disappointed when only normally coloured birds resulted. I was shown these 'Greywing' hens and some of their young, and I suggested that the so-called Greywings were, in fact, a sex-linked variety – like Cinnamon Canaries.

With colleagues I obtained some of these hens and young cocks and it was not long before we were able to ascertain that these birds were sex-linked Cinnamon mutants. This new sex-linked mutation was at first called Cinnamonwing because the wing colour was a prominent distinguishing feature of the birds. As the stocks increased and more varieties were being bred, it became apparent that the name was not always appropriate because the Cinnamon forms of the Yellows and Whites did not have cinnamon wings. It was decided to call these new birds simply Cinnamons as this prefix was suitable for all the varieties having the character. The Cinnamon Blue series did not start life as a separate mutation, but was evolved direct from the Cinnamon Greens.

After the Cinnamons had become established in Great Britain in a range of colours further Cinnamon mutants were reported in Europe, Australia, South Africa and America. All were identical in colouring and breeding behaviour and in all cases when crossed with the British form gave only Cinnamon young. No Budgerigar with a cinnamon body colour has so far been bred (this particular colour shade is only seen in the undulations on head, neck, back, wings and tail). Such a bird would certainly be a step in the direction of a brown and ultimately a red.

Cinnamon Blues The ensuing description applies to the following body colours when these are substituted in the description: Skyblue, Cobalt, Mauve, Slate and Violet. The Grey (Blue) series of these colours are the same but the body colours are different shades of grey and the cheek patches are light grey to silver. The colour of the long tail feathers will also vary.

Mask: white, ornamented by six evenly spaced large round cinnamon-brown throat spots, the outer two being partially covered by the pale violet cheek patches. General body colour: back, rump, breast, flanks and underparts, pale blue. Markings: on cheeks, back of head, neck and wings cinnamon brown and well defined on a white ground. Tail: long feathers smoky blue.

Cinnamon Greens The subsequent description applies to the following body colours which will differ accordingly in the description, with a slight deepening of the yellow ground colour in the darker birds: Light, Dark, Olive, Slate and Violet Green. The Grey Green series has body colours that are different shades of grey green and the cheek patches are light grey to silver.

Mask: yellow, ornamented by six evenly spaced large round cinnamon-brown throat spots, the outer two being partially covered by the pale violet cheek patches. General body colour: back, rump, breast, flanks and underparts, pale green. Markings: on cheeks, back of head, neck and wings, cinnamon brown and well defined on a yellow ground. Tail: long feathers smoky blue.

Clearbodies

This variety appeared in America during the 1950s and, as its name indicates, is just the opposite in its colouring to the Clearwings. Although I have seen feathers and colour transparencies of these rather striking birds I have yet to see living examples. The first specimens to appear were in the Green series and had dense black undulations which set off their yellowish body colour. As more specimens were bred by selective matings, so the contrast between body colour and wings improved. Reports suggest that the clearbody factor is recessive to the normal colours although it is dominant to some of the other shades, in which case, it is inherited in the same way as the factor that produces the Clearwings. It is not really unexpected that such a mutation should occur since Clearwings had already emerged. It would be of interest to see the results of mating these clear-bodied birds with Clearwings – would the young be ordinary Normals or something quite different?

Clearflights Plate 36

These are the same as the Normal varieties except that their flights, tail and head spot are clear and their body colour is solid all through. See Whiteflights and Yellow-flights.

Clearwings see Whitewings and Yellow-wings

Cobalts *(for description see Blue Series, p.77)*
Syn: Dark Blues, Powder Blues

With the possible exception of the violet shades, the majority of Budgerigar lovers consider the cobalt forms to be the most beautiful of all the colour shades. This rich colour would not have been possible if a Dark Green mutation had not occurred in France (the Dark Green birds may have been imported in a consignment rather than been bred in France) at the large commercial Budgerigar breeding establishment of Blanchard at Toulouse, France, in 1915, the Cobalts appearing for the first time in 1920. A Dark Green bird is basically a Light Green with a dark character added and, similarly, a Cobalt is a Skyblue with a dark character in its genetic make-up. This dark character, which deepens the tone of an existing colour, is of major importance in Budgerigar breeding and is discussed further on pp.104–5.

There are numerous matings that can give various percentages of these Cobalts and, as might be expected, some produce more than others. Cobalts are often bred from Skyblue mated with Dark Green/Blue and they can be produced even when both parents are of the green shades of colour. When Cobalts were still quite rare, breeders were often puzzled by the extremely small number resulting from crossing Dark Green/Blue with Skyblue, whereas crosses between similar looking birds produced large numbers. Various theories were advanced but none were found to fit the facts until Dr Hans Duncker of Germany discovered the variability of the linkage of the dark with the blue character.

In certain instances the dark character forms a strong link with the blue and many Cobalts result, while in others the link is with the green when Skyblues predominate. After many sets of test pairings were carefully analysed, it was ascertained that two kinds of Dark Green/Blues were possible; they were designated Type I and Type II. When a Dark Green/Blue Type I is paired with a Skyblue the theoretical expectation is not, as might be expected, 25% Skyblue, 25% Cobalt, 25% Light Green/Blue and 25% Dark Green/Blue, but 43% Skyblue, 7% Cobalt, 43% Dark Green/Blue and 7% Light Green/Blue. The percentage of birds having the dark character in their make-up is the same but the individual colour differs. When Dark Green/Blue Type II is paired with Skyblue the results are reversed: 7% Skyblue, 43% Cobalt, 7% Dark Green/Blue and 43% Light Green/Blue. This rearrangement of the dark character will be found to operate in all the different varieties where Dark Green/Blue (or White) kinds are possible. There is, of course, no visual difference between the Type I and Type II Dark

Green/Blue kinds. The difference is in the genetic make-up and this can only be discovered from their pedigrees or the breeding results.

There can be a Cobalt form in all the different Blue series, including the Yellow-faced Blues and Golden-faced Blues. Breeders who are inexperienced with the colour inheritance of Budgerigars often wonder, when two Cobalts are paired, why only 50 per cent of the young are Cobalts like their parents, the remaining 50 per cent being Skyblues and Mauves. Rule 2 under Dark Inheritance (p.105) explains this. The various topics discussed above are also applicable whenever cobalt colours are mentioned elsewhere.

Crested

Whenever birds have been bred in captivity for any length of time colour mutations occur and these are invariably followed by feather variations of which the crest is the most frequent. This was so of Budgerigars, and in 1935 birds with a small crest of feathers appeared as a mutation in the aviaries of Mr A. Mathews of New South Wales, Australia. Some years later a further crested mutation appeared in Canada and then in France, and it was found that both these mutations were compatible.

Crested birds are usually paired with mates that have had a crested parent – on the same lines as practised in the breeding of Crested Canaries and other crest-bearing birds. In Budgerigars the crest appears in three forms – the Tufted, which is the commonest, the Half-circular, and the Full-circular, which is the rarest and thus the most sought after. The type of crest and the numbers that occur depend upon the nature of the genes. Each type has its own attraction but, in the author's opinion, a well-

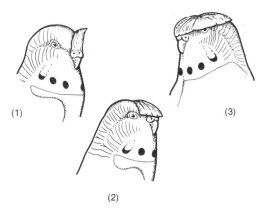

The three standard Budgerigar crests – (1) Tufted, (2) Half-circular and (3) Full-circular

formed Full-circular crest carried by a nicely proportioned bird looks particularly fine.

It is better to gain experience in keeping and breeding non-crested Budgerigars before attempting to breed the crested forms whose breeding is rather more complicated. The stock used for gaining experience can be incorporated with the crested forms – when they are obtained – as it is possible to breed the crested type in all colours and varieties; the colour of the birds has no bearing whatsoever on the formation of the crests.

Dark-eyed Clears

When these birds were first bred they were called, incorrectly, Black-eyed Lutinos and Albinos because of their pure, clear colour and dark eyes. Although they had appeared in aviaries of mixed colours, mainly in Europe, their origin was not clear. By a process of elimination it was discovered that these clear birds were the direct result of the combination of the Danish recessive pied and the dominant clear-flighted characters. Why the blending of these two different Pied kinds should produce some perfectly clear offspring in the second generation has not yet been established.

These Dark-eyed Clears (so called because they do not have the normal black pupil surrounded by a light area like ordinary Budgerigars do, but have the same deep plum colour of the Danish Recessive Pieds) are available as Whites, Yellows, Yellow-faced and Golden-faced: they are the only Budgerigars that are absolutely *pure* in colour and free from suffusion on any part of their plumage. Even the best specimens of Albinos and Lutinos can show some bluish or greenish suffusion on flanks or rump, when viewed at certain angles, but this is not so with the Dark-eyed Clears. It is possible that in due course pure yellow and pure white birds with the normal black eyes will be bred.

When two Dark-eyed Clears of a certain genetic make-up are paired, a percentage of their young will be lightly marked Danish Recessive Pieds. Other pairings of two Dark-eyed Clears will give only Dark-eyed Clear young depending on the pedigree of the parents.

The parents required in order to produce Dark-eyed Clears are a Danish Recessive Pied and a Clearflight (not Clearwing); the sex of these birds has no bearing on the results since one is recessive and the other dominant. Most of the clear-flighted birds now available have only a single character; they, therefore, when paired with Danish Recessive Pieds will give both Clearflight and Normal young all 'split' (see Glossary) for Danish Recessive Pied. Backcrossing these Clearflight/Danish Recessive Pieds with Danish Recessive Pieds, produces 25% Clearflight/Danish Recessive Pieds, 25% Normal/Danish Recessive Pieds, 25% Danish Recessive Pieds and 25% Dark-eyed Clears. In two generations, therefore, Dark-eyed Clears can be produced. When these (single character) Dark-eyed Clears are paired the results are 25% Danish Recessive Pieds, 50% Dark-eyed Clears, like their parents, and 25% Dark-eyed Clears with a double character.

Most Dark-eyed Clears are of the single character type because breeders seeking to improve their stocks do not mate them together, but to the best quality Danish Recessive Pieds. Dark-eyed Clears paired to pure Normals will give 50% Normal/Danish Recessive Pieds and 50% Clearflight/Danish Recessive Pieds. I am told that some well-marked Clear-flighted birds have been bred from such matings, but I have yet to try this.

It is rather surprising that these pure coloured Budgerigars have not become very popular – probably because of the difficulty of breeding the desired size. An enthusiastic breeder of Dark-eyed Clears, W. A. T. Morecombe, informs me that improving size is an extremely slow process because of the difficulty in obtaining Clear-flighted or Danish Recessive Pieds with the required extra substance. Nevertheless with careful selection and, above all, patience, Dark-eyed Clears can be gradually developed and their quality improved.

Dark Greens (for description see Green Series, p.83)
Plate 30
Syn: Laurel Greens, Satin Greens
As already mentioned under Cobalts, the Dark Greens were first noticed and bred in 1915 at Blanchard's Aviaries, Toulouse, France. This breeder undoubtedly used some wild Budgerigars to maintain his stock and it is therefore possible that the first Dark Greens actually came from Australia. There is a skin of a wild Dark Green Budgerigar in the Natural History Museum, London. Other Dark Greens may have occurred in their natural habitat but were not recognized as such.

The establishment of the Dark Green had a similar effect on the Budgerigar fancy as had the Skyblue mentioned above, for without the Dark birds, only a third of the range of Budgerigar colours was possible. Early French Dark Greens had a brighter and somewhat more ribbed satin-like appearance than most of those seen today. One of their earlier names, Satin Greens, supports this fact and it is thought constant out-crossing and selective breeding have made the colour even in tone. Dark Greens serve the useful purpose of introducing the dark

character into other colours and helping to maintain the brightness of those shades.

Dark Yellows (for description see Yellow Series, p.95)
These are the yellow counterparts of the Dark Greens but, unlike the Greens, they are not seen very frequently at exhibitions or in general breeders' aviaries. It was once thought that clear coloured Light Yellows could produce pure coloured Dark Yellows of a rich shade. They are useful for the production of Yellow Olive forms. Previously, the exhibition Light Yellows became exceedingly scarce and have remained so for the last twenty-five years. Now that there are two specialist societies in Great Britain catering for the Yellows, further developments of this colour are likely.

Dominant Pieds Plates 20, 21, 22
Syn: Australian Pieds, Banded Pieds
These are the same as the Normal varieties except that the flights, tail and head spot are clear and the body colour is broken with clear patches. One form has a clear band across the chest from wing butt to wing butt and is called a Banded Pied. It is essential that all these birds have a complete set of throat spots and unbroken flashes. Eyes · the same as Normal varieties.

Although Dominant Pieds had been reported as breeding freely in Australian aviaries as far back as 1935, it was not until about 1956 that the first examples reached Great Britain and were developed by Mr A. M. Cooper in Wales. The first mutation occurred in Sydney, Australia, and was one of the Green series Banded type; the initial pairing quickly proved beyond all doubt that this pied character was dominant. As a result, these Pieds soon became quite plentiful and breeders, not realizing the possible risks, crossed them with most of the other established colours. These indiscriminate matings eventually resulted in all kinds of interesting Dominant Pieds, but many of them lacked colour contrast.

The worst crossing error happened when Dominant Pieds were mated with Danish Recessive Pieds but the seriousness of this fault was not immediately apparent. In later pairings, for some inexplicable reason, certain Dominant Pieds appeared which had the Danish Recessive Pied pattern markings. These markings showed particularly in the facial area and caused cheek flashes to be broken and throat spots to be missing. Unfortunately, this particular pattern failure is difficult to eradicate once it has been introduced to a strain.

The Banded Pied is considered by many to be the most perfect of the Dominant Pieds, although the broken patterned kind is extremely popular as an exhibition and aviary bird. Because of the variability of the character producing the pattern of the Dominant Pieds, it is not possible to mate pairs with the certainty of producing the Banded kind. Fully or partially banded birds mated with pure Normals are more likely to increase the probability of Banded birds. Sometimes indifferently marked Pieds give rise to beautifully banded offspring – this is just one of the quirks of breeding. Chance, therefore, plays a part in the production of Banded Pieds.

Broken patterned Dominant Pieds in the Normal series showing approximately 50 per cent each of light and dark areas are rather attractive birds and can be bred quite freely. In the production of Dominant Pieds it has been found that Dominant Pieds crossed with first-class Normals are the most suitable pairings. If Dominant Pieds are mated together the majority of the Pied young will be lightly marked and will not look as attractive as the normally patterned ones. Except for experimental purposes it is not advisable to breed Dominant Pieds in the pallid or dilute varieties as the lines of demarcation between the colours are not distinct enough. Forms such as Albinos, Lutinos, Lacewings and Danish Recessive Pieds should be avoided because of the adverse effect they can have on the colouring of the resulting Dominant Pieds.

At one time it was thought it might be possible to breed Black-eyed Clears from the Dominant Pieds by a series of matings similar to those used in the production of the Dark-eyed Clears. A great many experimental crosses and back-pairings have been carried out but, alas, without the result desired. Birds with very few dark markings (rather like lightly marked Canaries) are produced quite frequently but no really clear birds appear. A few interesting lightly marked examples with different coloured eyes (one, a solid plum coloured, like the Danish Pieds, and the other, a dark, with a light iris ring, like the Dominant Pieds) have been bred. From an experimental cross of one of these odd-eyed Dominant Pieds with a Recessive Pied I produced (among normally-eyed birds) three further odd-eyed examples. They are thought to have no value except as curiosities.

The dominant pied character can be carried in either a single or double quantity, but the birds are visually similar. Few double character birds are actually bred for the reason given in the above paragraph. Most Dominant Pieds are single character birds and will give both Normal and Dominant Pied young when crossed with Normals. Any Normal birds bred from such matings are of no more value in breeding Dominant Pieds than Normals bred from Normal pairs. The dominant pied character

follows the usual rules of Dominant inheritance (see p.103).

Dutch Pieds

This variety originated from a single green coloured cock which I obtained from a mixed collection of colours imported from Holland. I was attracted to this bird because it was the only one having an even distribution of colouring (50 per cent dark and 50 per cent light) out of about two hundred Clearflights, Danish Recessive Pieds and Normals. He was paired with a number of different coloured hens and having dominant genes, these matings gave Normals and birds pied just like the cock. The young were cocks and hens and of green and blue shades. Several of the second generation won prizes in the Any Other Colour classes at the National Exhibition of Cage and Aviary Birds, London. One particularly outstanding specimen was a Cobalt hen, with well and evenly broken colour, bred from the original bird's son paired with a fine Normal Green/Blue hen.

A notable feature of Dutch Pieds, as I named them, was that when paired with Normals they produced as many hens as cocks, all with good pied markings. Dutch Pieds were said to be badly coloured specimens of the Clear-flighted with a bib over-spilling down the chest and some breaks in the colour on the wings. Although such Clear-flighted birds may look similar to the Dutch Pieds they are not the same mutation. It is difficult to breed Clear-flighted hens with well-marked colours but this is quite the reverse in Dutch Pieds.

Being short of space for other experimental pairings, I had to dispose of my strain of Dutch Pieds. I know that some breeders did quite well with them for a time, but when the Australian Dominant Pieds appeared on the scene they unfortunately displaced the Dutch Pieds in popularity. I have made exhaustive enquiries but have been unable to trace any breeder who now has specimens of this original strain of Dutch Pieds and I have reached the conclusion that the race must be extinct. It is just possible that a few specimens may be in an aviary and not recognized for what they are or, of course, a mutation of the same kind may suddenly turn up.

Fallows Plates 25, 26

The English name of this group of red-eyed Budgerigars is a translation of the German word used to describe the mutation when it first appeared in Germany. Unlike most of the other names used for the many Budgerigar mutations it is not a description of colour but an indication that the feather pigments are more or less uncultivated, that is, not fully developed. The name is now applied to a whole series of Budgerigars.

The first recorded examples of these red-eyed Budgerigars were raised by Mrs A. R. Hood of California, U.S.A., in 1931. However, this mutation was not established and it was some years before a further Fallow mutation appeared in America. At about the same time as Mrs Hood's birds were bred, a similarly coloured mutation occurred in the aviaries of Herr J. Schumann of Magdeburg, Germany, and further examples were soon being produced in both the Green and Blue series by Herr Kurt Kokemüller of Hannover. Herr Schumann's birds were the progeny of a normal looking Olive Green cock and a normal looking Cobalt hen, thought to be from the same nest. This pair gave Fallow young in three successive nests which suggests that one of the parents had the mutant gene in a single quantity. By chance, both the Olive Green and the Cobalt had inherited the new mutation in a single quantity. Such birds would, of course, be able to give Fallows in each nest.

These German Fallows, particularly the Dark Green and Olive Green kind, quickly became favourites with many British and European breeders, the first being bred in 1934. At the time, Dr H. Steiner of Switzerland, a world authority, said that Fallows were the most significant event in Budgerigar breeding since the Blue mutation appeared. Although the Fallow Blue series was not quite so appealing to the eye, the birds were often bred and in due course the Cinnamon Fallow Whites (synthetic Albinos) were bred through a series of planned matings.

In 1936 it was reported that Fallows had been bred by Mr F. Dervan of Luton, England, from green birds which he had been breeding in his aviaries for two generations. During a visit I recognized at once that they were similar in colour to the already established German Fallows, with the exception of the colour of their eyes. The German Fallows had the red iris surrounded by a light ring, whereas the new kind had solid, clear bright-red eyes without iris rings. In the following season both Fallow kinds were mated together to discover whether the two mutations were distinct or the same having only a slight difference of eye colour. All the chicks produced were normally coloured black-eyed birds as would be expected from the crossing of two different mutations. The results proved the existence of two distinct Fallow types.

Before the English Fallow mutation had occurred, a Fallow type had appeared in Australia, and was bred in all forms of the Blue and Green series. Information received suggests that this mutation belongs to the German type;

unfortunately it has not been possible to carry out the test pairings to prove this. Further Fallow mutations have occurred in Europe (these could have been of German origin), South Africa, America and two more in Great Britain, one of which seems to be a third Fallow breeding type.

Recessive characters can be handed down unseen for many generations so that once mutants carrying such characters have been crossed with other varieties it is difficult to prove the recessive nature of the character. The sudden appearance of a 'new' colour in a mixed aviary, where uncontrolled breeding takes place from stock of unknown parentage, occurs periodically. Some are undoubtedly new mutations, while others are the reappearance of a mutation, the character of which has been hidden in the stock. In such uncontrolled breeding conditions the chances of hidden recessive characters reappearing are very much accelerated.

During the past few seasons I have been trying to increase the numbers of German Fallows available and to breed them in some previously unknown forms. I have been fortunate on both counts and have bred a number of well-known kinds, including Opalines, as well as some new forms, including Fallow Danish Recessive Pieds in Greens and Blues, Fallow Yellow-wings, Fallow White-wings, Fallow Yellows and Fallow Violets in Normals, Danish Recessive Pieds and Danish Recessive Pied Whitewings. I hope to succeed with other colours, such as Fallow Dominant Pieds and Fallow Slates, both of which would be first breedings in Great Britain.

The colourings of the Fallows vary between individual birds, even those of the same colour: some strains have quite a steely brown wing colouring, whereas others have more of a cinnamon-brown shade. The body colours are mainly yellow and white and on the flanks and rump the individual green or blue colouring is shown.

Fallow Blues The subsequent description applies to all the following body colours which differ accordingly in the description: Skyblue, Cobalt, Mauve, Grey, Slate and Violet.

Mask: white, ornamented by six evenly-spaced large round brownish-grey throat spots, the outer two being partially covered by the dull violet cheek patches. Eyes: red with light iris ring (German) or solid bright red without light iris ring (English). Body colour: back, rump, flanks and underparts, pale whitish blue, upper breast almost clear white but varying. Markings: on cheeks, back of head, neck and wings, brownish grey clearly defined on a white ground. Tail: long feathers bluish grey.

Fallow Greens The ensuing description applies to the following body colours which differ accordingly in the description, with a slight deepening of the yellow ground-colour in the darker birds: Light, Dark, Olive, Grey, Slate and Violet Green.

Mask: yellow, ornamented by six evenly spaced large round brownish-grey throat spots, the outer two being partially covered by dull violet cheek patches. Eyes: red with light iris ring (German) or solid bright red without light iris ring (English). Body colour: back, rump, flanks and underparts, pale yellowish green, upper breast almost clear yellow but varying. Markings: on cheeks, back of head, neck and wings, brownish grey clearly defined on a yellow ground. Tail: long feathers bluish grey.

Golden-faced Blues *(for description see Yellow-faced, p.95)*
Plate 23

It is not certain when this rich form of the Yellow-faced series came into existence. Some of the first Yellow-faced mutations were originally called Golden-faced but the name Yellow-faced is now used universally. In the late 1940s I saw some Golden-faced birds that had been bred in Britain and also some imported originally from Europe. The Golden-faced birds were probably first crossed with the paler Yellow-faced kinds, as their owners did not recognize the difference between the types. The same applies to the different Yellow-faced kinds where these were mixed indiscriminately. When varieties are very similar in colouring, recognition is always a problem until their genetic make-up has been established.

During 1960–1 investigations into the genetics of the Yellow-faced varieties were carried out in Great Britain and America and it was established that at least two Golden-faced forms existed. A further study was carried out by Mr K. Gray of Tiptree, England, who found that his Golden-faced birds, which carried a single quantity of the particular character showed a heavy bright yellow overlay, and when the double factor birds were bred this overlay more or less disappeared, leaving the rich golden colour in the characteristic areas. There is much still to be learned about this yellow colouring in the Blue series and further studies may reveal other interesting points.

Goldwings

This was a name used in France to describe a strain of Yellows, now known as Yellows of deep suffusion. Goldwings were bred from birds selected for their rich yellow wing colour, faint markings and a deep green body suffusion. I owned some of these birds and, although they were attractive, they were only Yellows and when crossed with good coloured Light Yellows gave young of varying degrees of suffusion. It seems that Goldwings were bred originally from a particularly brightly coloured Green strain by pairing them with Yellows and back-crossing the Green/Yellows to Yellows. The Yellows resulting from the second generation crosses were selected for brightness of body colour, and richness and clearness of wings. Today, a number of deeply suffused Yellows might well be described as Goldwings. It is thus misleading to describe a colour phase of any variety by a fancy name.

Green Series

The description given in the next paragraph, relevant to Light (Normal) Green (p.86), applies also to birds with the following body colours when these are substituted in the description, with a slight deepening of the yellow ground-colour in the darker birds: Dark Green, Olive Green *(qq.v.)*, Slate *(q.v.)* Green and Violet *(q.v.)* Green. The long tail feathers will be correspondingly darker. The Grey Green series of these colours are the same with the exception that the body colours are different depths of grey green, the cheek patches are light grey to silver and the tail feathers jet black.

Mask: yellow, ornamented by six evenly spaced large round black throat spots, the outer two being partially covered by the violet cheek patches. General body colour: back, rump, breast, flanks and underparts, bright green. Markings: on cheeks, back of head, neck and wings, black and well defined on a yellow ground. Tail: long feathers deep blue.

Greys *(for description see Blue Series, p.77)*

The colours of these birds are controlled by a character which alters the colours carrying the character. The addition of the grey character to the Blue series causes the birds to be varying shades of battleship grey, and the Green series to be shades of grey green (a mustard-green tone). It seems that the first recorded example of a Grey Budgerigar was a mature hen bird found in a dealer's shop by Mr H. T. Watson of Bedford, England, in 1933. She was paired with a White Cobalt cock and produced two cobalt-coloured chicks, after which she unfortunately died. I had her skin for many years and was able to compare it with later Grey forms when they appeared. Her body colour was between that of the present-day Dominant Greys and the Slates; her tail, flights and undulations were jet black. No further examples have been recorded of this particular mutation.

In the following year, 1934, Mrs S. Harrison of Victoria, Australia, obtained a Grey Budgerigar cock from a dealer. This was paired with several Normal hens and in each nest Grey chicks were produced. During 1933, Mr W. E. Brooks of Surrey, England, bought a pair of Cobalt Budgerigars from a dealer and the next breeding season they produced ten chicks, three of which were Greys, not Mauves as would be expected from such a pairing. The breeding results from these two widely separate grey mutations indicated that the grey character of the Australian bird was dominant while that of the English was recessive. Further breeding experiments with both types proved these facts.

I received examples of Mrs Harrison's strain and was therefore able to compare this mutation with that of Mr Brooks when I visited his aviaries. The Australian kind were a light clear battleship grey, even in shade throughout, with jet-black tails, flights and markings. The English birds were of a much deeper shade and more leaden in tone; their colour, too, was quite even and they had jet-black tails, flights and markings.

Within a short space of time Dominant Greys were being bred freely in most of the other varieties. It was found that although the grey character masked all other colours carried by the birds having this in their genetic make-up, the dark character still operated in its normal way. This meant that there could be three shades of grey in all varieties – Light (Light Green and Skyblue), Medium (Dark Green and Cobalt) and Dark (Olive Green and Mauve). The shade of grey is extremely difficult to establish visually, so for exhibition purposes they were simply called Greys or Grey Greens. Although birds of the Grey and Grey Green series are rather dull in colour, they are popular with many exhibitors now and many fine examples of Dominant Greys in Normal, Opaline and Dominant Pieds, are to be seen at exhibitions in most countries.

The three shades of Recessive Greys are much darker than the Dominants. I have seen only one example of a Recessive Grey Mauve – an extremely dark coloured bird which looked more like a Slate Mauve but without any suggestion of a bluish background. It is a pity that this Recessive Grey mutation could not have been retained for there could have been some interesting results from pairing it with a Dominant Grey and a Sex-linked Slate.

Grey Greens (*for description see Green Series, p.83*)
Plate 27
These are the Green forms of the Dominant Greys (Blues) discussed above and the same facts apply. At one time there were Recessive Grey Greens but unfortunately they too disappeared like their Recessive Grey counterparts. Grey Greens are sometimes mistaken for Olive Greens because of a certain colour similarity. They can easily be distinguished, however, as Grey Greens have the characteristic jet-black long tail feathers whereas those of the Olive Greens are deep blue. Being a Dominant it is quite easy to increase the numbers of Grey Greens by pairing them with Normal Greens. As the majority of Grey Greens are only single-character birds, when paired with Normal Greens, they produce 50 per cent Grey Greens and 50 per cent pure Normal Greens. Although these Normal Greens are bred from parents, one of which is Grey Green, they have no more power to reproduce Grey Greens than have Greens bred from two Green parents. There can be a Grey Green form of all the other Green series.

Greywings
Syn: Apple Greens, Jade Greens, Satinettes, Silverwings
The origin of the Greywing mutants is hard to date since they were first thought to be badly coloured Yellows. It is known, however, that several mutations of Greywing Greens occurred between 1918 and 1925 (one appeared in my own aviaries early in 1925). At that time these birds were known to some Budgerigar breeders as Apple Greens, Satinettes, or Jades, depending on the depth of their body suffusion. Another group of breeders did not recognize them as a separate variety, insisting that the birds were only heavily marked Yellows. After studying several years' breeding results from a number of influential breeders, and considerable discussion, the variety was finally accepted and a standard laid down by the Budgerigar Society. The decision was justified when a Blue form appeared in 1927–8 as a mutation in the aviaries of Mrs P. Weiss of Graz, Austria, from a brother and sister mating of a pair of Green/Whites. They were called Silverwings. A further mutation occurred in Germany and was named Greywing because of the clear grey colour of its markings.

It was in 1925 that I exhibited the first example of the Greywing Light Green (then Apple Green) variety and three years later Mr G. F. Hedges exhibited the Blue form calling it a 'Pearl Blue'. The first 'Pearls' were reported as being bred the previous year in Great Britain by Mr A. Lewis of Dorset. It did not take breeders long to discover that the so-called Silverwings and the Greywings were nothing more than the Blue form of the already well-known Apple Greens. The name Greywing was adopted for both the Green and Blue series.

For a time, Greywings in all their colours became popular both with breeders and exhibitors. Greywings, being recessive to the Normal birds and dominant to the Yellows and Whites, were simple to reproduce in their ordinary form. Breeders soon discovered that other characters could be incorporated and Cinnamon and Opaline forms of the Greywings were produced. In spite of the initial wave of enthusiasm for Greywings, they soon gave way to new colour forms and now Greywings of any colour are rarely seen at shows or in aviaries. However, a new specialist society, the National Yellow Budgerigar Society, has decided to undertake the re-establishment of the Greywings.

Greywing Blues The subsequent description is for the Skyblue form and applies to the following body colours when these are substituted in the description: Cobalt, Mauve, Slate, Grey and Violet. The long tail feathers will be correspondingly darker.

Mask: white, ornamented by six evenly spaced large round grey throat spots, the outer two being partially covered by the pale violet cheek patches. General body colour: back, rump, breast, flanks and underparts, about 50 per cent of the normal depth of blue. Markings: on cheeks, back of head, neck and wings, light grey on a white ground. Tail: long feathers smoky blue.

Greywing Greens The subsequent description is for the Light Green form and applies to the following body colours when these are substituted in the description: Dark Green, Olive Green, Slate Green, Grey Green and Violet Green. The tail feathers will be correspondingly darker.

Mask: yellow, ornamented by six evenly spaced large round grey throat spots, the outer two being partially covered by the pale violet cheek patches. General body colour: back, rump, breast, flanks and underparts, about 50 per cent of the normal depth of green. Markings: on cheeks, back of head, neck and wings, light grey clearly defined on a yellow ground. Tail: long feathers smoky blue.

Greywing Yellows For many years it was considered impossible to produce Greywing Yellows and then, in the late 1930s one such bird was reported in Australia. A few individual birds with similar colouring had been reported in Great Britain slightly earlier. The specimens and skins that I saw appeared no more than heavily marked Yellows. This colour was not reproduced in their offspring, so it was not a definite inheritable mutation but a single individual colour expression.

We have seen in the section on Clearbodies, p.78, that clear-bodied birds with full normal markings had appeared and were established in America. The Clearwing mutation had appeared earlier in Australia in the Yellow (White), Greywing and Clearwing groups, so a further extension of this series is not unexpected. As I have only seen colour transparencies and a skin of the Australian Greywing Yellows I am not conversant with their pedigrees and therefore of what the results would be if they were paired to other members of the group. They have marked wings and clear bodies – just the opposite of the Clearwings. By mating them together one would expect the result to be deeply coloured Greywings.

Half-siders
Syn: Bi-colours
These rather intriguing birds are, in their full and complete expression, a combination of two distinct colour forms, divided vertically down the centre. For example, a bird may be a complete Green on one side and a complete Blue on the other, or in fact any two of the vast range of Budgerigar colours. The reasons for this peculiar cell division are complex and, because such birds are rare, I do not intend to go into the matter here. Few Bi-colours have a perfect division of colours; in most, the two colours are in differing proportions, some birds having only a small patch of another colour. During all my years of breeding Budgerigars only three Half-siders have appeared among my stock and only one had a perfect division of colours. As each bird appeared I carried out an experimental breeding programme in order to produce further specimens, but without any success. Other breeders have had the same lack of success. Some Half-siders, particularly the well-marked birds, have been proved to be sterile. Although Half-siders cannot be reproduced, they do make good show exhibits and always create interest whenever they are seen.

Harlequins see also Recessive Pieds
This is a name that was and sometimes still is used in Europe and America to describe the Recessive Pied varieties. The name arose from the fact that the Pied birds showed two distinct colours in their plumage.

Lacewings
Lacewings are one of the five strong sex-linked groups of Budgerigars and are the only new mutation to be established in Great Britain since the Dutch Pieds and Clearflights appeared in Europe. The first specimens must have been produced in 1946–7 and I was told that the parents of these first Lacewing hens were a Green cock and a Lutino hen. All the offspring from this pairing were

disposed of by the breeder because he did not wish to have bad coloured Lutinos in his strain! In 1948 I was fortunate enough to obtain a nest brother of the original Lacewing hens. I paired him with several different coloured Normal hens and eventually true Lacewing hens appeared in the nests, among numerous normally coloured cocks and hens. From this nucleus I was able to establish the variety in their Green, Blue and Yellow-faced forms.

The Lacewings have the same red-coloured eyes as the Albinos, Lutinos and German Fallows (the iris is deep red, surrounded by a light iris ring). They can be bred in all varieties but their body colours are yellow in the Greens, white in the Blues, and various shades of lemon and lemon-and-white in the Yellow- and Golden-faced forms. The depth of their cinnamon markings differs, the normal kinds having the deepest, and the yellow and white kinds the palest. The markings of the Lacewing Greens and Blues are a cinnamon colour of a depth between that of an ordinary Greywing and a Yellow of deep suffusion. The markings of the other Lacewing forms are the same depth as the ordinary kinds to which they are the counterparts. In most cases the Lacewing forms of the Greys and Grey Greens show the best depth of markings. A particularly attractive form is the Opaline Lacewing in either the Green or Blue series.

Lacewings are said to be the result of crossing Albinos and Lutinos with Cinnamons; though their colouring supports this idea, it is certainly not the case. It was the chance breeding of Lacewing Yellows and Whites by the use of Yellows, Whites and their 'splits' in the early days of Lacewings that led to this theory. They are, however, quite a separate mutation and operate in the same way as do all sex-linked mutations. Breeders have tried to produce Lacewings by crossing Albinos or Lutinos with Cinnamons but all the red-eyed birds ultimately bred from such crosses have been ordinary-looking Albinos and Lutinos. It is only in the last decade that Lacewings have been recognized by the Budgerigar Society as a separate variety and a standard of perfection produced. It is hoped that this recognition will help to increase the number of Lacewings being bred and exhibited.

Light Greens (*for description see Green Series, p.83*)
Plate 28
Syn: Greens, Normal Greens
It is from the original Light Green Budgerigars that all the other colours and varieties have been evolved either by a mutation or by the combination of more than one mutation. The vast array of colours makes it difficult to believe that most of the wild Budgerigars are only light green. Many Budgerigar enthusiasts maintain that Light Greens are still the most handsome birds with their bright grass-green body colour and black undulations on a rich yellow ground.

On page 74 details are given of the Light Green Budgerigar's arrival in Europe and its subsequent progress to domestication. From that time Light Greens have been bred continually in cages, pens and aviaries in most countries of the world. Strains of Light Greens have been used to improve new mutations when they appeared, often to their own detriment. Today it is difficult to find studs of pure Light Greens because of the constant outcrossing, but a few breeders have now begun to develop stocks of pure Light Greens both for show and experimental purposes. It can take many generations of careful selective breeding to eradicate all recessive and sex-linked characters that can be hidden in a strain. I find that the presence of a few Light Greens, either pure or 'split' birds, in a stock can have a beneficial effect on a breeding programme.

Light Yellows (*for description see Yellow Series p.95*)
Plate 34
Syn: Buttercup Yellows, Yellows of light suffusion
The Yellows were recorded as the first colour break in the domesticated Light Green strains some thirty or so years after the latter reached Europe. The first Yellows were reported in Holland about 1870 and others were reported from several places in Belgium during the next few years. When a recessive mutation appears in several places it is difficult to establish whether they are, or are not, connected. The Dutch Yellows seem to have been the ordinary suffused kind, but the Belgian forms were of two kinds – the suffused and the clear Yellow. The latter were all hens and must surely have been Lutinos; unfortunately the strain was not perpetuated at that time. However, several suffused Yellow kinds were established although for some years they were rare and expensive. The first Yellows of the Belgian stock to be bred in Great Britain were produced in 1884 by Mr J. Abrahams of London, and Yellows were exhibited some two years later. It was not until the 1920s that Light Yellow Budgerigars became more common in the aviaries of general Budgerigar breeders. They were also seen more often at cage bird shows being mostly shown, like all Budgerigars, in mixed classes of parrot-like species.

During the same period breeders began to specialize in the breeding of Light Yellows that were mainly pure yellow throughout with only faint ghost-like markings.

These strains were known as Buttercup Yellows. At the time of the formation of the Budgerigar Club, Buttercup Yellows were in popular demand, Mr R. J. Watts and Mr Allen Silver being two of their principal sponsors. Light Yellows bred at that time were of high quality, both for type and purity of colour, and were frequently 'Best Budgerigar in Show'. At large shows up to a hundred Light Yellows were exhibited but they are now rare. A few dedicated breeders are attempting to revive this old established variety with a certain amount of success.

Light Yellows are recessive and are therefore more difficult to improve than the dominant kinds of Budgerigars. Selection of the initial breeding stock plays an important part in this. The use of Light Greens as out-crosses for developing Light Yellow strains is a most satisfactory method. The theoretical results of crossing Light Green with Light Yellow (not taking into account any other characters the birds may have), are given below.

(a) Light Yellow × Light Green gives 100% Light Green/Yellow

(b) Light Yellow × Light Green/Yellow gives 50% Light Yellow and 50% Light Green/Yellow.

(c) Light Green/Yellow × Light Green gives 50% Light Green/Yellow and 50% Light Green.

(d) Light Green/Yellow × Light Green/Yellow gives 25% Light Yellow, 50% Light Green/Yellow and 25% Light Green.

(e) Light Yellow × Light Yellow gives 100% Light Yellow.

It must be stressed that these theoretical expectations are not a guide to purity of colour nor to the quality of the offspring.

If the breeder has at least one good-coloured Light Yellow, I suggest that the bird is paired with several Light Greens. The latter should be of a soft, light grass green colour, inclined to yellowish, and of good overall quality (dark hard-coloured green birds showing a bluish tinting should be avoided for crossing with Light Yellows). Such matings will result in Light Green/Yellows and the most promising looking young should be selected and back-crossed to its Light Yellow parent. The remaining Light Green/Yellow half brothers and sisters can then be mated together and should produce 25 per cent Light Yellows of improved quality, some of which will also be of good colour. After taking a nest from the original Light Yellow and its young, the pair should be broken up and the Light Yellow given a further, unrelated, Light Green mate. This pairing will give more Light Green/Yellows to provide partners for the Light Yellows bred from the 'split' pairs. The results of these matings will provide the breeder with enough Light Yellows to found a strain.

There can be Light Yellow forms of all the other varieties and these will show suffusions and markings of various degrees of intensity according to the variety. When Cinnamon is introduced to a Light Yellow strain the resulting Cinnamon Light Yellows show a general reduction in the depth of suffusion and markings but, at the same time, the yellow colour will not be so rich. Light Yellows of different suffusions can be useful in breeding other varieties, particularly Greywings, Clearwings and Whites. As exhibition birds, good Light Yellows are attractive and are well worth more attention by serious breeders and exhibitors.

Lutinos Plates 19, 35
Syn: Red-eyed Clear Yellows
These are more or less clear yellow birds with red eyes and are the Yellow counterparts of the Albinos; the factor is inherited in the same way. Like the Albinos there were at one time two breeding kinds – recessive and sex-linked – but the former seems to have disappeared. The first reported Lutino mutations occurred in Europe in the 1870s, but they were not established. They were next reported in Germany in about 1932, when they were established and soon breeding quite freely. Other Lutino mutations have been observed in Australia, South Africa, America and Great Britain, and all have been sex-linked. Individuals of the different mutations have been paired together and only Lutinos have resulted thereby proving they were one and the same colour break.

It should be noted that there is no such bird as a 'pure' Lutino – it must be a Lutino form of one of the Green series, the colours of which are masked by the Lutino character; thus there are Lutino forms of all green coloured birds: Lutino Light Yellow, Lutino Opaline Dark Green, or Lutino Cinnamon Greywing Green, etc. There is some variation in the depth and purity of the clear yellow colouring exhibited by the different kinds of Lutinos. Those having a single dark character in their genetic make-up, such as Lutino masking Dark Green, can appear a deeper yellow than in the Lutino masking Light Green. A bird having a double dark character (Olive Green series) can be of a slightly deeper colour still. The depth of the yellow colour of Lutinos is no guide to the masked colour since, by careful selective breeding, fanciers have increased the depth of the colour of even the light yellow (Light Green series) shades. In addition to improving the richness of the colour, selective pairings have resulted in a reduction of the suffusion carried on rump and flanks, and the faint ghost markings on wing butts.

However attractive it may seem it is unwise to include even one Lutino hen in a strain of the pure Green series, for breeding Lutinos can easily introduce other colour characters into a strain without the breeder being aware of the fact. The sudden appearance of unexpected colours in a strain can often be attributed to the inclusion of Lutinos (or, for that matter Albinos) at some period.

Good coloured Lutinos can be bred by selective pairings, and careful cross-matings with normally coloured stock. To obtain an overall improvement of a Lutino strain, only first-class Normal birds should be used for outcrosses and of these I find the Dark Greens are most suitable. Such birds carry the useful dark character, are usually of excellent type and quality, and can generally be bought at a reasonable price. However, much will depend on the breeder's own particular selection and the way in which the strain is built up and maintained when green birds are used as out-crosses.

Grey Greens are one of the varieties that have a good effect on type and substance of a strain but they inhibit colour improvement. The presence of the Grey character in the genetic make-up of Lutinos, causes the yellow colour to appear much duller in tone and of much less depth. Grey Greens should not be used in the development of richly coloured Lutinos. However, the breeder may find it necessary to use a single factor Grey Green as an outcross and, if so, the grey-green coloured birds resulting from this cross need not be used for the furtherance of the Lutino strain. Such pairings give both Grey Greens and ordinary Greens and it is the latter that can be usefully employed.

Lutinos, like Cinnamons, have a special use when breeding talking Budgerigars. Young cock birds straight from their parents are best and the breeder can be sure that certain birds are definitely cocks by the use of special matings. When either Lutinos (Albinos) or Cinnamon cocks are paired with any black-eyed hens they will produce only red- or pink-eyed young hens while the young cocks will be black-eyed. In this way the owner can identify young cocks as soon as they hatch.

Mauves (for description see Blue Series, p.77)
Syn: Lavenders, Lilacs
These are Blue series birds that have a double dark character in their genetic make-up and their depth and purity of colour can vary quite considerably. This variation in colour was more noticeable in the early days of its establishment when such birds were often known as Lilacs and Lavenders as well as Mauves. Lilacs and Lavenders were paler and brighter than the Mauves, which were darker and duller. As these birds became more plentiful, breeders realized that the so-called varieties were only shades of the same colour. There are still, of course, differences in their shades depending on how they have been bred.

Mauves originally came from the Blanchard aviaries at Toulouse, France, in the early 1920s, being a further colour evolved from the Dark Greens (see p.80). When they first appeared it was said that the Mauves and their Green counterparts, the Olive Greens, were less substantially built birds than those of lighter colours – an observation that is still true of both birds, whether seen on show benches or in aviaries.

Mauves do not appeal to many modern breeders as their colour is rather dull and patchy, and differs little from that of the more robustly built, and easier to breed, Greys. Nevertheless, Mauves are employed by breeders in the production of birds of the Cobalt and visual Violet series. There can be a Mauve form of all the other varieties. A series of selected matings would probably recreate the much more attractive lilac-shaded Mauves. Even if the right birds could be obtained the re-creation would not be speedy. The violet character could be included in the experiment to produce violet lilac-shaded birds that might be attractive to breeders.

Olive Greens (for description see Green Series, p.83)
Syn: Bronze Greens
In 1916, about a year after the Dark Greens came into being, Olive Greens appeared as a further extension of that mutation. Today we know that when dark green-coloured birds are paired together a percentage of their young will be Olive Greens. Although Olive Greens have never been popular for their colour, their great value for breeding other colour shades has always been recognized. Formerly, when they were known as Bronze Greens, two shades of colour were available – the more sandy Olive Greens, which were comparable to the Lavenders and Lilacs, and the darker, harder Olive Greens, generally known as Bronze Greens.

Olive Greens, like their Blue counterparts, the Mauves, can be created by the breeder without having birds of those colours. When two Dark Greens (or Cobalts) are paired together they do not give all Dark Green (or Cobalt) young. The theoretical expectation from such crosses is 25% Light Green (Skyblue), 50% Dark Green (Cobalt) and 25% Olive Green (Mauve). Olive Greens can also be bred by pairing Dark Greens with Cobalts, or Dark Greens with Mauves. When two Olive Greens are mated they will give only Olive Green young, provided they are not carrying any other colour characters in their genetic make-up.

Experience has shown that the best and most evenly coloured Olive Greens come from the mating of selected birds of that colour. The constant out-crossing to Cobalts or Mauves seems to introduce a considerable amount of flecking on thighs, flanks and rump. Size and quality can be improved and maintained by the periodic inclusion in the strain of a well-balanced and evenly coloured Dark Green. As no sex-linkage is involved it is immaterial whether the Dark Greens are cocks or hens. There can be Olive Green forms of all the other varieties, the Fallow Olive Greens being the most striking – instead of the ordinary olive-green shade the birds are a rich golden-orange tone.

Olive Yellows (for description see Yellow Series, p.95)
Syn: Yellow Olives

These are the deepest coloured birds of the Yellow group and a form seldom seen today. When the Yellow varieties were at the height of their popularity interest was taken in the Olive Yellows and some beautifully coloured specimens were bred. The aim with this Yellow form, like that of the Light Yellows, is to produce birds of a clear colour throughout having as few markings and as little suffusion as possible. Because Olive Yellows have a double quantity of the dark character their colour is deeper and good birds tend to show a distinct orange-tinted shade.

A number of different pairings can produce this attractive colour, the easiest being Dark Yellow with Dark Yellow, Dark Yellow with White Cobalt, and Dark Yellow with White Mauve. To obtain clearness and richness of overall colour, selected birds should be used for each mating, gradually building up pairs that can produce such characteristics. If the cinnamon character is introduced, purity of colour can be achieved more quickly but, of course, with the accompanying loss of depth. Nevertheless, Cinnamon Olive Yellows are pretty and pleasing birds to breed. In my opinion, Olive Yellows are more colourful than their White counterparts, the White Mauves, and are a variety that could be developed.

Opalines Plates 29, 30, 31
Syn: Opals, Marbled, Mottled

The history of this sex-linked colour pattern is interesting in that the mutation occurred in three separate places at about the same time. The first reported Opaline, called Marbled, came from Scotland in the form of an Opaline Cobalt hen; the next report came from Australia, where the bird was a hen of the Green form; and the third report came from Europe but it is not known whether the bird was a Green or a Blue variety. The first British Opaline mutation (first called Piebald and then Marbled) occurred during the 1934 breeding season in the aviaries of Mr A. Brown of Kilmarnock, Scotland. The parents of this bird, an Opaline Cobalt hen, were a Skyblue cock and a Mauve hen, both quite normal looking birds. The hen was the only one of that colour among the pair's young. It was obtained by Mr R. Ashby of Ayr, Scotland, who mated her with a good quality, exhibition Light Green/Blue cock, the result being a Skyblue cock, a Cobalt cock and hen and a number of Green/Blue cocks and hens. It was not known at the time that it was only the cock birds from such a mating that would carry the new mutation. However, from this nucleus the British Opaline strains were founded. An interesting feature of these particular Opalines is that they possessed multiple throat spots of large size – this multiplicity and size of throat spots is still found in a large number of Opalines of all colours, obviously inherited from the original birds.

The Australian mutation, an Opaline Light Green hen, hatched in about 1932 and was noticed by Mr R. J. Byfield of Hobart, Tasmania, in a large batch of wild Budgerigars sent by trappers to the Adelaide bird market. Mr Byfield was attracted to this bird by its vivid colouring even though she was still in nestling plumage. When asked for a name he suggested Opaline, which has now been universally adopted. The offspring obtained from mating this hen with a White Skyblue cock hatched out in 1934, and, as expected, were all light green in colour. In the following year her sons were mated with Normal hens and they gave more Opaline hens among their young. One was also back-crossed to his mother and the first Opaline cocks were raised. Because a White Skyblue had been used in the initial cross with the wild-caught Opaline Light Green hen, other coloured Opalines appeared in the second generation. From these matings it was abundantly clear that the mutation was sex-linked and that it could be produced in all colour shades.

The exact origin of the European Opaline strain is obscure. It is thought that the first birds were bred in Belgium – those I saw were certainly bred in that country.

In due course examples of all three separate Opaline mutations were assembled in Great Britain and test pairings carried out in an attempt to establish whether they were all of the same genetic make-up. The very first cross pairings between these birds revealed that they were indeed the same mutation, although the three mutations did have certain small individual colour differences. The British mutation had heavy multiple throat spots and carried much heavier barring on the head, neck and mantle area; its general colouring was of medium depth and reasonably bright. On the other hand, the Australian version was vividly coloured, showed a clear mantle area and had round, beautifully placed, medium-sized throat spots. The European form was paler than the other two and had well-spaced throat spots although smaller than those of the other two mutations.

When these three kinds were crossed together they blended quite well and their later progeny often carried hidden the characters shown by the original birds. Today we find examples of all three among the Opalines and individual strains have been developed showing certain features more prominently. The original British type has been greatly developed as an exhibition bird. It is many years since I have seen an Australian Opaline and those seen today are similar but do not carry the vivid colour of the first imported specimens. It is possible that in Australia, where they are free from the 'contamination' of other mutations, the Opalines may still retain the original colouring.

Opalines have been introduced into other colours and Opaline forms are now found of all the other colours and patterns. Occasionally, composite types have been evolved which include the opaline character and of these the 'Rainbows' – the Opaline form of Yellow-faced Clearwings – are probably the most vividly coloured. Another interesting type is the Opaline form of the Fallow Grey and Fallow Grey Green which look like the Clearbodies. Although they have red eyes their body colour is almost pure yellow with a grey-green cast, or pure white with a grey cast, and their wings a steely brown colour of the normal opaline pattern. A further offshoot of the 'Rainbows' is the Opaline Clearwings (erroneously called 'Selfs') which have been developed in some strains to show an extra amount of blue colouring on the back and wings. They are handsome birds and make an attractive addition to a mixed free-flying aviary collection.

Because of the sex-linked manner of inheritance Opaline hens frequently appear in apparently pure strains, often caused through the chance addition of a 'split' cock into that strain. As in all sex-linked colour varieties this is very difficult to eradicate from a strain once it has been introduced. The sex-linked method of inheritance is discussed more fully on p.185.

Opaline Blues   The subsequent description applies to all the following colours when these are substituted in the description: Skyblue, Cobalt, Mauve, Slate, and Violet. The Grey (Blue) series are the same, but the body colours are different depths of grey, the cheek patches are light grey to silver, and the dark areas on the tail are jet black.

Mask: white, extending back over the head and merging into general body colour at the level of the wing butts, where the undulations cease leaving a 'V' between top of wings, ornamented by six evenly spaced, large round throat spots, the outer two being partially covered by violet cheek patches. General body colour: mantle, back, rump, breast and underparts blue, not quite the full normal shade. Markings: should be normal with a suffused iridescent effect. Wings: same colour as body. Tail: long feathers light in centre surrounded by dark blue.

Opaline Greens   The subsequent description applies to all the following body colours when these are substituted in the description: Light Green, Dark Green, Olive Green, Slate Green and Violet Green. The Grey Green series are the same, but the body colours are different depths of grey green, the cheek patches are light grey to silver, and the dark areas on the tail are jet black.

Mask: yellow, extending back over the head and merging into general body colour at the level of the wing butts, where the undulations cease leaving a 'V' between top of wings, ornamented by six evenly spaced large round black throat spots, the outer two being partially covered by violet cheek patches. General body colour: mantle, back, rump, breast and underparts bright green, not quite the full normal shade. Markings: should be normal with a suffused iridescent effect. Wings: same colour as body. Tail: long feathers light in centre surrounded by dark blue.

Recessive Pieds Plates 24, 32
Syn: Danish Recessive Pieds, Harlequins
Birds with variegated (pied) plumage are likely to occur in domesticated breeds and generally cause a certain amount of excitement when they appear. When Greens were being bred in their thousands in Europe and large quantities of them were exported to many countries, including Great Britain, birds with a few yellow feathers on back of head, tail, or wings, were occasionally seen in the consignments. These 'mismarked' birds (as they were termed) were frowned upon by serious exhibition breeders even though they did not reproduce their failings. Such birds were not, therefore, true breeding Pieds; it was not until 1933–4 that a true Pied mutation occurred in Denmark. True Green and Yellow Pieds were found in a mixed collection of Budgerigars that had been breeding as a colony, and thus the exact parentage of the Pieds

could not be ascertained. One of the first breeders to realize the importance of this event was Herr C. af Enehjelm, then Curator of the Helsinki Zoological Gardens. It was largely through his efforts that the mutation was developed and produced in the Blue and White forms. It was not until 1948, however, that the first live specimens of these Pieds came to Great Britain, when I was fortunate enough to receive from Herr C. af Enehjelm two Green and Yellow Pieds and a Normal, carrying Pied, from which I founded the first Recessive Pied strain in Britain (by this time it was known that the Danish breed of Pieds was recessive and could be bred in all colour forms).

As in all pied birds the areas of light and dark vary and the colour of individual birds, even from the same nest, can differ considerably. Ideally, the colours in the plumage of the Recessive Pieds should be well distributed and divided in the proportions: 40 per cent dark to 60 per cent light. If two Recessive Pieds are paired there is a strong tendency for their offspring to display areas that are too light. For this reason, and for general physical improvement of the variety, it is usual to mate Recessive Pied to first-cross Normal/Pied. The latter are produced by pairing a good-coloured Recessive Pied with a first-class exhibition-type pure Normal.

At one time it was thought that by constantly mating together Recessive Pieds that had few dark areas, completely clear birds would eventually result. After many such pairings it was realized that although birds with 5–10 per cent dark markings could be bred, completely clear ones could not. The latter can be bred by crossing Recessive Pieds with the Dominant Clear-flighted kind (for details see under Dark-eyed Clears, p.79).

The crossing of Recessive Pieds with the Dominant Pieds in the first stages of their production has resulted in some Dominant kinds that show the pattern markings of the Recessive, particularly the broken-coloured cheek patches and missing throat spots. Although these badly marked Dominant Pieds may look like Recessive Pieds from their body colours they can be easily identified as Dominants by the colour of their eyes. All Recessive Pieds, no matter their colour, have solid deep plum-coloured eyes *without* light iris rings. Dominant Pieds, on the other hand, have the normal dark iris colour but with light iris rings. The dark body-colour areas on Recessive Pieds is much brighter and more metallic than that of their Normal counterparts. This colour was originally linked to a special type of long slender bird that did not reach the requirements for show purposes. It took breeders a considerable time, through the continual use of first-cross

'split' birds, to break this linkage. Because of the efforts of these breeders the many Recessive Pieds now seen show a considerable improvement in their markings and substance. Recessive Pieds are excellent for the new breeder who wants a pretty variety that can be improved.

Recessive Pied Blues The ensuing description applies to the following body colours when these are substituted in the description: Skyblue, Cobalt, Mauve, Slate and Violet. The Grey (Blue) series of these are the same, but the body colours are different depths of grey, the cheek patches are light grey, silver, or a mixture of both, and the dark areas on the tail are black.

Mask; white. Throat spots may be present from one to full quota. Cheek patches: violet, silvery white or a mixture of both. Eyes: deep plum colour without any light iris ring. General body colour: irregular patches of white and blue with the latter mainly on lower chest, rump and underparts. Wings: white with black undulations or spots covering not more than 15–20 per cent of total area, dark feathers in flights are not faults. Tail: can be all light, all dark, or a mixture of both.

Recessive Pied Greens The subsequent description applies to the following body colours when these are substituted in the description: Light Green, Dark Green, Olive Green, Slate Green and Violet Green. The Grey Green series of these are the same, but the body colours are different depths of grey green and the cheek patches are light grey, silver, or a mixture of both, and the dark areas on the tail are black.

Mask. yellow. Throat spots may be present from one to full quota. Cheek patches: violet, silvery white or a mixture of both. Eyes: deep plum colour without any light iris ring. General body colour: irregular patches of yellow and green with the latter mainly on lower chest, rump and underparts. Wings: yellow with black undulations or spots covering not more than 15–20 per cent of total area, dark feathers in flights are not faults. Tail: can be all light, all dark, or a mixture of both.

Silver
This was the name, found in older bird books and magazine articles, used in Australia to describe the ordinary White varieties at the time they were first bred in reasonable numbers.

Silverwings
This was the original name given to the Greywing Blue mutation when it first appeared in Germany. When it was

discovered that they were the Blue form of the existing Greywing Greens, the name was changed to Greywing Blue.

Skyblues *(for description see Blue Series, p.77)*
Syn: Blues, Light Blues, Normal Blues

These are the Blue series counterparts of the Light Greens to which they are Recessive (in fact, Blues of all forms are Recessive to all the Greens). Reports suggest that Blue Budgerigars were first seen between 1880 and 1885 in Belgium and Holland. The two reports probably referred to birds which originated from the same source. The first Skyblues to be exhibited in Great Britain were shown by Mr O. Millsum at the Horticultural Hall, London, in 1910, where their appearance caused quite a sensation. They were said to be descendants of the Dutch 1885 strain. But from the information available it is likely that Skyblues were in existence a long time before they were generally known to the cage bird fancy.

In the early 1920s Skyblues were still quite scarce and only found in the hands of a limited number of European and British breeders. Skyblues were then thought to be more delicate than the plentiful Greens and Yellows and because of this the hens were not used for breeding until their second season. This may have been true as the Skyblues had undoubtedly been closely inbred for many generations because their owners did not wish to lose the colour. With the advent of the Budgerigar Club in 1925, Skyblues began to be circulated more freely and were becoming a regular feature at the larger cage bird shows. In my opinion Skyblues – for that matter Budgerigars – would not have been so popular with bird breeders had it not been for the so-called Budgerigar boom, when the demand for rare-coloured birds was rapidly accelerated by the Japanese. In the late 1920s the keeping and giving of Budgerigars as presents became very fashionable among the higher circles of Japan, led by their Crown Prince, now Emperor. The demand for Skyblues, Cobalts, Mauves and Whites soon outstripped their availability and prices soared to record levels. Bird dealers all over the world were soon offering several hundreds of pounds for rare examples of the blue shades. Many people took up Budgerigar breeding in the hope of quick profits. When the stocks of these colours began to increase prices fell and many breeders abandoned the fancy; many, however, were so intrigued with these delightful little birds that they continued to breed them. Even today with the vast array of colour shades, Skyblues are still considered by some as being the most attractive of the blue colours.

Slates *(for description see Blue Series, p.77, Green Series, p.83)*
Plate 33

The character that causes the slate shades is sex-linked. It causes all the blue and green colours to assume, in the former, an overall slate-blue tone and, in the latter, a slate-green tone. The dark factor influences the individual depths of colour carried by the different varieties. The Mauve form of the Slate is the deepest in colour and probably the nearest to a black Budgerigar.

The mutation occurred in the aviaries of Mr T. S. Bowman of Carlisle, England, during May of 1935, just before the appearance of the Australian Greys. The parents of the first Slate hen were a Cobalt cock and a Skyblue, whose first chicks were a Cobalt hen and the Slate hen. Their second mating produced a further Slate hen and three Cobalt cocks, one of the latter was eventually proved as carrying the Slate character. As one of the young cocks was a 'split' and two hens were produced it would indicate that the original Cobalt cock must have inherited the character from his father, who must have been the source of the original mutation.

Slates were soon being bred in several different colour forms including White and Cinnamon, but before they were established as a popular variety, the Australian Greys were exported to Great Britain and eclipsed the Slates. Although the Slates were similar in colour to the new Dominant Greys, their overall colour was warmer and their long central tail feathers were a deep blue colour as opposed to the jet black of the Greys. Their breeding behaviour was sex-linked which made them fairly easy to reproduce, but not as easy as the Dominant Grey kind. For a number of years, in fact until the late 1960s, only a very small nucleus of Slates was in existence. The efforts of a few keen breeders increased the number and variety of slate colours, and it now seems that the Slates will not die out, as once thought, but will become a small but important part of the Budgerigar colour range of sex-linked shades.

Violets *(for description see Blue Series, p.77; Green Series p.83)*
Syn: Violet Cobalts, Visual Violets

The character known as violet is dominant and can be carried by all members of the Blue and Green Series. However, it is only when the blue and dark characters are combined with the violet that the bright, visual violet shades appear. In other colours, the violet character simply alters their shades. The word Violet is used, like Greywing or Cinnamon, to describe those birds possessing the character in their genetic make-up: for example,

Violet Light Green, Violet Whitewing Skyblue, Violet Skyblue, Violet Yellow-faced Mauve, etc. The character is inherited in the same manner as other dominant characters (see pp. 102–3).

It is possible that at first Violets were thought to be just extremely well-coloured Cobalts. True Violet mutations occurred in Australia, Denmark, and Great Britain about 1936–7; it is not possible to say in which country they first appeared. It was some years after the Australian mutation had been bred that examples came to Great Britain and were established in many varieties. Just before this a Violet form had appeared in an aviary in Lincolnshire, England, and was thought to be a Recessive. The specimens that I saw of this form were similar in colour to the Violet Cobalts seen today. They were not prolific breeders, and unfortunately records of their performances were few; it was thus impossible to reach a definite conclusion concerning their genetic make-up before the strain died out. This left the fancy with the Dominant kind, which has become popular with many breeders, especially those who like brightly-coloured Budgerigars.

Because the violet character is dominant it can be transferred to other varieties with reasonable ease. By careful pairings some lovely birds can be produced such as Cinnamon Violets, Opaline Violets, Whitewing Violets, Pied Violets, etc. in the three Violet forms. When the violet character is combined with the skyblue, the Violet Skyblues resulting have a colour similar to, but much brighter than, a pale Cobalt. The combination of violet and mauve produces Violet Mauves which are of a deep warm mauve shade with a certain amount of violet tinting showing through. The introduction of the violet character to the Blue series can be important in colour breeding.

The Violet Greens, which are birds having the violet and the green characters have an altered shade of green. These shades vary: the Violet Light Greens are a pale dark green, the Violet Dark Greens are a very deep solid dark green, and the Violet Olive Greens a dark hard olive-green shade without any flecking. The various shades are available in all the different Green forms, including the Yellows and Yellow-wings. When the violet character is carried by the Dark-eyed Clears (both White and Yellow), it is not visible in the plumage. Some individual Lutinos show a very faint shading on the rump and thighs, but it is very difficult to put a particular name to it. In the Albinos, however, the suffusion at thighs and rump assumes a rosy pink shade that is most attractive. This can be accentuated by the use of badly coloured Albinos – those that carry a heavy suffusion. Up to the time of writing the Albino

Violets are the nearest approach to the much sought-after pink Budgerigar.

Whiteflights *(for description see Clearflights, p.78)*
Plate 37
Syn: Clearflights
These, and their green counterparts, the Yellow-flights, form a group of Pied birds which are available in all other colours and varieties. Whiteflights are of Belgian origin and were established in the aviaries of M. R. Raymaekers of Brussels during World War II from the original mutation which occurred in about 1942. The inheritance of this colour pattern is of a dominant nature and can be very variable in its visual manifestation. An ideally-marked bird should have all-white primary flights, white tail, and a white patch (spot) on the back of its head, the remainder of the colouring being like its Normal counterpart. The expression of the pattern can vary from just a clear head patch (which, incidentally, is carried by all Clearflights no matter what other markings they have), through the perfectly marked to those with an excess of light areas.

Birds with ideal markings do not appear as frequently as those with the less perfect ones. There does not seem to be an optimum pairing to produce such birds, although some breeders claim that a well-marked cock paired with a 'head spot' hen gives satisfactory results. I have found that a well-patterned cock mated with a good quality pure Normal hen will also produce a high proportion of well-coloured chicks. All-round quality is improved by this latter pairing and is undoubtedly the best from the exhibition point of view.

Over the years I have bred some excellent Whiteflights in several varieties, the best looking being in the Normal series. The bird I liked most was a White-flighted Slate hen, perfect in her pattern markings and of fine exhibition quality. Unfortunately, like many special birds she proved to be an unreliable breeder. Although Whiteflights are not shown so frequently, a good specimen occasionally does find its way to a show.

Whiteflights and, of course, Yellowflights have a very special role in the breeding quarters as they are an essential contributing factor to the production of Dark-eyed Clears. Undoubtedly the appearance of the Australian Dominant Pieds was one of the causes of the rather quick decline in the popularity of the Clearflights. Fashions change in the Budgerigar fancy so perhaps the wheel will turn full circle and Whiteflights will come to the fore once again. There is also an Australian White-flighted form which does not have the head patch like the European kind. Although not many are bred, individuals are occasionally seen in Budgerigar classes at shows. They are dominant in their breeding behaviour and follow the rules given on p.103.

Whites Plates 34, 36
Syn: Silvers, Whites of deep suffusion, Whites of light suffusion
The description given in the next paragraph applies to all the following White forms: White Skyblue, White Cobalt, White Mauve, White Grey, White Cinnamon, White Slate and White Violet.

Mask: white. Cheek patches: silvery white to pale pinkish violet. General body colour: back, rump, breast, flanks and underparts white and as free from colour suffusion as possible; cheeks, back of head, neck and wings should be as free as possible from any markings; tail, white, suffused.

With present-day knowledge of the genetics of Budgerigars, it is surprising that White birds did not appear earlier than they were reported to have done because Blues and Yellows were known to be breeding in the same aviaries. The Whites are not the result of a natural mutation but are the Blue form of the Yellow and can be bred by the following sequence of matings: a Skyblue cock or hen with a Light Yellow, when all the young are light green in colour (and because of their genetic make-up are known as Light Green/Whites); when two such birds are paired they give four different coloured young – Light Green, Skyblue, Light Yellow and White. Although the birds are visually distinct some carry 'split' characters and because of this, they were first known as Light Green/Blue Yellow White. The Whites, of course, carry a double recessive character. As the expectation of a White bird from this last pairing is only one in sixteen (following the Mendelian Rules), a considerable number of young have to be produced in order to provide Whites in any quantity.

The first White Budgerigar to be bred in Great Britain came from a pair of Skyblues (evidently both 'split' for White) in the aviaries of Mr H. D. Ashley at Brinsop Court, England, in September 1920. A White was seen in France in the same year, but particulars of its pedigree were not obtained, and Whites had been reported a little earlier in Germany – again the pedigrees are unknown. Whites (Silvers as they were then called) were bred in Australia in about 1927–8 from green-coloured birds that had known blue and yellow ancestors.

Before the many other colour mutations came into being, the Whites were very popular both as show and aviary birds. For exhibition purposes they were bred in two forms: those with as light a suffusion as possible – the Whites of light suffusion; and those with heavy suffusion – the Whites of deep suffusion. Both forms were obtainable in Skyblue, Cobalt and Mauve suffusions. Of the lightly suffused birds it was mostly those with the Mauve suffusion that had the best colour. Deeply suffused Whites were bred in all three shades, the Cobalts having the deepest suffusion.

Some fine birds were produced in both light and deep suffusions, the latter generally of the best overall quality. Good progress was made with the lightly suffused Whites, some of the individuals bred showing only the faintest traces of undulations and suffusion, the ultimate aim, of course, being pure white. The appearance of the more or less pure white Albinos caused the Whites of light suffusion to steadily decline in favour and today few Whites are seen. Deeply suffused Whites in Grey and Violet forms, as well as the three basic blue shades, are to be found in many aviaries and a few are seen at exhibitions.

Whitewings Plates 37, 38
Syn: Clearwings
This mutation, which includes the Yellow-wings, appeared in Australia in about 1932, at the same time as several other similarly coloured birds were being established. British breeders were trying to get Whites of deep suffusion with very deep body colours and clear wings while in Europe similar efforts were being made, using the so-called Goldwings, to breed Whites with rich body colour. Until live examples of the Australian Whitewings were imported into Europe they were thought to be similar to Whites of deep suffusion. I shall never forget seeing the first arrivals with their solid, deep, bright body shades and almost paper-white wings. The deeply suffused Whites looked quite pale in comparison and it was obvious that there was no connection between the two. There was a great demand for this Australian mutation, especially when it was found that Whites of deep suffusion could be used in their production.

Whitewings are dominant to all the White (Yellow) series and recessive to the Normal varieties. When they are crossed with Greywings the two kinds combine in their colouring forming an entirely new type – the Full Body-coloured Greywings (or Royals as they were first called in Australia). They have the almost full body-colour of the Normals with their wings coloured like their Greywing parents. An interesting breeding point is that when a Full Body-coloured Greywing is paired with an ordinary White (Yellow) their young are either

Greywings or Clearwings. The breeding of this combination is a good genetic programme for those breeders who are interested in Budgerigar genetics and wish to have birds in which the results of their crosses can be immediately seen.

The breeding of Whitewings declined in the 1950s and early 1960s, mainly because of the shortage of suitable breeding stock. Nevertheless, there were a few dedicated enthusiasts in parts of Great Britain who banded together in 1963 to form The Clearwing Budgerigar Breeders' Association, a specialist body catering solely for the development and improvement of this particular mutation. It has done much work in the furthering of Clearwings. Through its efforts the Yellow-wings and Whitewings have once more been established as exhibition birds. At most large cage bird shows, Clearwings are seen in good numbers and examples are to be found in nearly all mixed aviary collections.

Whitewings are one of the necessary mutations for the breeding of 'Rainbows' (Yellow-faced Opaline Whitewings); this, too, has given a boost to their popularity. The production of 'Rainbows' and other composite forms of Clearwings is not encouraged by the Clearwing Budgerigar Breeders' Association, because their production involves the use of Clearwings which they feel should be used for breeding only their own kind. However, 'Rainbows' do have many followers among those who are keen on breeding new and unusual forms of Budgerigars.

Whitewing Blues The subsequent description applies to all the following body colours when these are substituted in the description – Skyblue, Cobalt, Mauve, Slate and Violet. The Grey (Blue) forms have dull silvery grey cheek patches.

Mask: white. Cheek patches: violet. General body colour: back, rump, breast, flanks and underparts, as near as possible to full normal depth of blue. Wings: white, as free from markings as possible. Tail: long feathers blue.

Yellow Series
Syn: Buttercups
The following description applies to all the following Yellow forms when these are substituted in the description – Light Yellow, Dark Yellow, Olive Yellow, Grey Yellow, Cinnamon Yellow, Slate Yellow and Violet Yellow.

Mask: yellow. Cheek patches: silvery white to pale pinkish violet. General body colour: back, rump, breast, flanks and underparts yellow and as free from green suffusion as possible. Cheeks, back of head, neck and

wings should be as free as possible from any markings. Tail: yellowish white.

The information given under Light Yellows applies in principle to the Dark and Olive Yellows. The Dark Yellows are Light Yellows plus a single dark character, which makes them the Yellow counterparts of the Dark Greens and in certain pairings can be used in their stead: for example, if a Dark Yellow is paired with a Light Green, the same result is obtained as if a Dark Green had been used. No records seem to exist of the first appearance of the Dark Yellows, it was probably soon after the appearance of the Dark Green mutation in France. It is possible that the very first specimens passed unnoticed, being thought to be just heavily suffused Light Yellows. The first I saw were in a mixed batch of Light Yellows and Light Greens in a London dealer's shop in 1927 and were part of a consignment imported from France.

Little effort has been made to breed Dark Yellows on the same lines as Light Yellows – that is, to evolve birds showing as little suffusion and faint undulations as possible. The few attempts made were not carried out very seriously and little progress was achieved. Much more enthusiasm has been shown with Olive Yellows (Light Yellows with two dark characters) and some really handsome specimens have been produced. When the greenish suffusion is reduced in the olive-yellow colouring, it gives a rich, warm, orange-yellow shade that is most attractive. The reason Olive Yellows are not more widely bred is probably because they are usually somewhat small, which lessens their appeal to exhibitors.

There can be many tones of the yellow shades and this makes Yellows of interest to colour-breeders and of great value for testing purposes in controlled breeding. It is possible to breed Yellows in all depths of shade in Opalines, Pieds, Greys, Violets, Slates and Cinnamons, and their various combinations. The Yellow forms of the red-eyed Lutinos are difficult to distinguish except from their resultant offspring, but the Yellow forms of the Fallows can be recognized by the varying depths of their colour. The Fallow Dark Yellows and Fallow Olive Yellows show an unusual richness of colour, the latter being of a lovely deep golden shade. Now that more Fallows are available a greater number of the Yellow kinds should soon appear.

Yellow-faced Plates 35, 36
The appearance in 1935 of the first Yellow-faced mutation in the aviaries of Mrs G. Lait of Grimsby, England, surprised the Budgerigar world as, before they appeared, it was thought impossible for yellow and white to occur in

the same bird. It was quickly discovered that the yellow-faced character was dominant to the ordinary blue character and the breeding of birds with this factor went ahead. Breeding was complicated by the fact that Yellow-faced birds were seen to display their colouring in different ways: some had the yellow colour on face, wing butts and tail; others had a yellowish suffusion more or less all over; and there were others in which the coloration was between the two extremes. After much research it was concluded that several different Yellow-faced mutants had occurred in Great Britain, Europe, America and Australia.

Soon after these facts had been established a further anomaly was noticed. When certain normal-looking blue-coloured birds that had been bred from two Yellow-faced parents were mated with pure Blues all their young were Yellow-faced. This unforeseen result only occurred with those Yellow-faced birds which merely showed the yellow on face, wing butts and tail. These have become known as Mutant I. The other kind, which showed the general overlay of yellow colouring, did not give any unusual breeding result and are called Mutant II.

By pairing together two Yellow-faced Blue Mutant I birds, each having a single yellow-faced character, the usual Mendelian expectation would have been 25% pure Blue, 50% Yellow-faced Blue single character and 25% Yellow-faced Blue double character. However, the collated breeding results of a very large number of such pairings indicated that only 50% Yellow-faced birds were appearing. Breeders in America, Europe and Great Britain, pooled their knowledge of this unexpected result and came to the unanimous conclusion that half of the normal-looking Blues were, in fact, birds with a double character that did not show any trace of yellow in their plumage. Once this was known the inheritance of the Yellow-faced Mutant I became clear and, of course, followed the accepted Mendelian Rules.

There can be Yellow-faced forms of all the Blue series and the combinations of characters give rise to numerous strange and unusually-coloured types. Birds of the Green series can also have the Yellow-faced character but because of their overall colouring, it does not show in their plumage. A further extension of the Yellow-faced form is the Golden-faced, which is discussed on p.83.

Yellowflights *(for description see Clearflights, p.78)*
Syn: Clearflights
These are the Green form of the Whiteflights and like them are a dominant breeding kind. It seems possible from facts gathered, that the first Clear-flighted birds were of the Yellow-flighted kind and it was from this form that the Whiteflights were eventually developed. The details given on p.93 for Whiteflights are applicable to the Yellowflights, excepting the colour.

Yellow-wings Plates 36, 37, 38, 39
Syn: Clearwings
These are the Green form of the Whitewings. They originated in Australia in about 1932 and the factor is inherited in the same way (see p.94). The Australian breeders found that by crossing Yellow-wings (or Yellows) with Whitewings (or Whites) the brightness and depth of colour were improved and maintained. I have also found this to be a good method with all other colours.

Yellow-wing Greens The subsequent description applies to all the following body colours when the colour is substituted in the description – Light Green, Dark Green, Olive Green, Slate Green and Violet Green. The Grey Green forms have dull silvery grey cheek patches.

Mask: Yellow. Cheek patches: violet. General body colour: back, rump, breast, flanks and underparts, as near as possible to full normal depth of green. Wings: yellow, as free from markings as possible. Tail: long feathers blue.

HOUSING

Budgerigars can be housed in various ways, according to the purpose for which they are kept. A tame talking Budgerigar is best kept in a fancy, or plain, plated-wire, wire or plastic cage of which there are many excellent designs obtainable at most good pet stores. It should be not only roomy, but well constructed as Budgerigars are forever climbing and poking about. For this reason it is most important to thoroughly wash and brush a new cage in order to remove any loose particles of material that could be dangerous if eaten by the bird.

In addition to the seed and water pots another small pot is required for grit, a clip fitted to the cage for the cuttlefish bone, and a mineral nibble. The perches supplied with the cage will be sufficient as they are spaced apart to give the birds the maximum amount of flying space. It is not advisable to put too many toys in the cage as they only distract the bird, although a small mirror is useful as a plaything. The cage floor should be covered with a sheet of special sanded paper or with loose bird sand (the latter is preferable as it contains extra grits). A

Two types of decorative Budgerigar cages (*Budgerigar Information Bureau*; *Topsy Pet Homes*)

plastic or fabric cover for the outside of the cage bottom will prevent most of the seed husks from littering the area around the cage.

Budgerigars do not like to bathe in the same way as Canaries and other finch-like birds; they prefer to roll in a bunch of wet grass or splash about under a dripping tap. Some birds enjoy using a hang-on bird bath or saucer of water, both of which are easily provided.

The siting of the cage in a room is very important for the well-being of the bird; it should be placed so as to allow the bird plenty of light and, at the same time, it should be free from draughts and the direct rays of the sun. The cage can be hung on a stand, a wall bracket, or stood on a table. Although most birds like the sun they cannot stand long periods in its full rays without being able to hop periodically into some shade. Should there be other animals in the household it is preferable to have the cage on a stand or a wall bracket rather than on a table. Although cats and dogs do become accustomed to a pet

bird there is always a risk. During the summer the bird, in its cage, can be taken into the garden for a change of scenery but, again, it must not be kept for long periods in direct sunlight.

The majority of breeding Budgerigars are housed in box cages (cages having only a wire front, the remainder being made of wood). In my opinion cages housing a single breeding pair should be as large as possible and preferably not less than 36 in (91 cm) long by 18 in (46 cm) deep and 14 in (35 cm) high. These cages can be satisfactorily painted both inside and outside with emulsion paint, which is quite harmless to the birds.

The nest boxes can be fixed either inside or outside the cages according to the breeder's preference; I put boxes inside as I find that the birds like to be able to clamber about their nests. Whenever possible the cages should be constructed in tiered blocks with movable partitions so that when not in use for breeding purposes several compartments can be formed into good long flights.

The perches in the breeding-cages *must* be firmly fixed (otherwise copulation may be unsuccessful and may result in clear eggs). Seed, water and grit pots can be of glass, earthenware, pottery or plastic, and are best placed inside the cage. Special small fountains fixed outside the cages are ideal for supplying drinking water. Cuttlefish bone can be fixed with special clip holders, which can be bought at pet stores.

Flights, pens, or aviaries are used for housing the birds when not breeding and also for the young when they are mature enough. If space is limited the breeding-cages should be constructed in such a way that they can be converted into flights as already described. An additional indoor pen will be of great value in giving the birds extra flying space – particularly when attached to an outdoor flight, which allows the birds to spend some time in the open (one design is shown opposite).

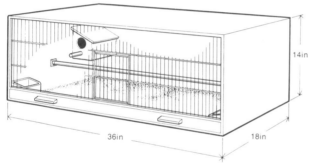

A box breeding-cage, suitable for Budgerigars and other birds, such as Zebra Finches, that will breed in cages

Budgerigar breeding-cages – note that the sliding panels between the cages have been taken out. The trays at the bottom of the cages ensure easy cleaning.

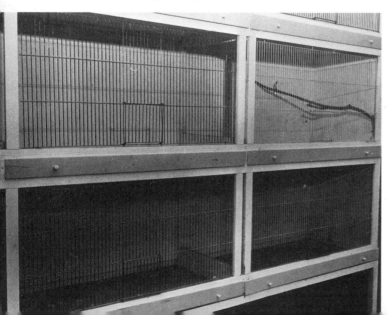

A birdroom or aviary can be built of wood, manufactured boards, sheeting, brick or concrete, or a combination of these materials. Floors can be made of wood, brick, stone slabs, or concrete, whichever is most suitable for the particular structure or site. Every effort should be made to make the buildings and outdoor flights vermin proof. The flights can be covered with small-mesh wire netting or welded square-mesh netting which should be let into the soil for about 12 in (30 cm) and then turned out at right angles for a further 6 in (15 cm). All new wirework should be thoroughly brushed and, if necessary, given a coat of bituminous paint to preserve it.

Flight floors can be covered with grass, sand, small gravel, stone slabs or concrete, or a combination of these. When a number of birds are housed together, gravel (or sand) with stone slabs under the main perches are the most convenient materials. They are easy to clean and replace when necessary and the birds will get great pleasure in pecking over the loose areas. The perching used in the flights can be machined dowelling or branches from fruit, hawthorn, wild plum, hazel, willow, elm or beech trees. Budgerigars always seem to prefer natural wood perches and enjoy gnawing and eating some of the bark – so most perches will need replacing from time to time.

Undoubtedly the most satisfactory way in which to house breeding pairs of Budgerigars is in single-pair flighted pens (opposite). Such structures can be made in ranges of pens of four to twelve or more to meet the requirements of the breeder. They allow the birds plenty of space in which to exercise and an opportunity to get into the open air; at the same time breeding is completely controlled. If there is insufficient space for flighted pens, then unflighted ones make an excellent substitute as they give the birds much more freedom than cages.

Budgerigars are best enjoyed when they are housed in flighted garden aviaries where numbers of different colours can be allowed to fly and breed together (this method is not suitable for colour or exhibition breeding as no control can be exercised over the breeding stock). Such buildings, which can be of many shapes and sizes, can be made attractive and are designed for keeping Budgerigars solely for decoration and pleasure. All kinds of old buildings can be converted for this purpose, or new ones can be specially built (see illustration, below right; the aviaries on p.67 would also be suitable). Such aviaries containing mixed coloured Budgerigars can make a garden bright and cheerful throughout the year.

An outdoor flight can be made decorative if natural perches are used and the floor covered with various grasses. Some brick walling or rockery work and even a small

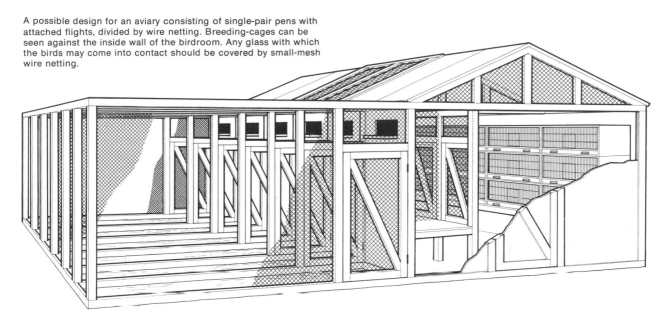

A possible design for an aviary consisting of single-pair pens with attached flights, divided by wire netting. Breeding-cages can be seen against the inside wall of the birdroom. Any glass with which the birds may come into contact should be covered by small-mesh wire netting.

pond can help to create pleasant surroundings. Because Budgerigars like to gnaw, their flights, pens and aviaries should be inspected periodically to see if any woodwork is weak or the wirework is rusting or deteriorating in any way. Any poor areas should be repaired or renewed before any birds escape. It is impossible to grow small trees and shrubs in the flights because the birds soon destroy them by gnawing the buds as soon as they form.

Under certain conditions, it is possible to keep flocks of Budgerigars at complete liberty and have the pleasure of seeing birds of many colours flying freely in the surrounding countryside. Such aviaries must be situated where there is plenty of open space, trees close by, and where there is no disturbance of any kind. Keeping free-flying Budgerigars can only be successfully achieved if the owner has the necessary requirements and therefore only a few people can indulge in this particular facet of the hobby. American readers should note that there is a federal law that prohibits the keeping of free-flying Budgerigars.

FEEDING
One of the special attractions of Budgerigars is that their feeding requirements are few and simple, making them easy to keep. For the owner of a single tame bird, seed mixtures packeted by well-known seed firms are the best.

The mixtures retain their freshness in their ordinary packets but will keep even longer if stored in airtight containers.

Should the owner have more than four Budgerigars it is more economical to buy loose seed, either ready mixed, or in separate kinds blended by the owner to suit the birds' requirements. A good all-year-round mixture can be made up of one part large canary seed, two parts small canary seed, two parts white millet and half part panicum (small yellow millet). During breeding periods, I add a

A portable garden aviary suitable for any small birds

small quantity of oats or groats to the mixture. Some breeders like to give oats in separate dishes after the contents have been soaked for some twenty-four hours. In my opinion, these soaked oats can cause a certain amount of bowel looseness, which is undesirable at any time. Opinions differ on this, so the individual breeder must discover which is the more suitable method of giving oats to his particular stock of birds.

Seeds bought in bulk should be of the highest quality and only obtained from reputable seed firms. All seeds should be polished, sweet and hard and, of course, free from dust, soil, husks, etc. and should be stored in wooden, plastic or metal containers. Plastic bins are easy to keep clean and, with well-fitting lids, the seed will keep in perfect condition for long periods. As each new batch of seed is received the container should be thoroughly cleaned and any seed remaining should be put on top of the new supply. If old seed is allowed to accumulate at the bottom of the container it can go stale and lose its nutritional value, possibly causing stomach upsets. Specially prepared tonic seed mixtures can be offered periodically to the birds with beneficial results. The millet spray (small yellow millet in its seeding heads) is a useful tit-bit at all times and will often tempt a sick bird to eat.

After many years of experience I am convinced that greenfoods are an extremely important part of the diet of Budgerigars, however housed. Some owners state that Budgerigars can live quite well without any greenfood but I am certain that the birds' health is more satisfactory if they receive a regular supply. Budgerigars eat and enjoy many different fresh greenfood, and certain fruits and root vegetables. Chickweed, seeding meadow grasses and the leaves of garden spinach are the best greenfoods. Chickweed is usually plentiful at the start of the breeding season and will be readily eaten by most breeding pairs either in its ripe state (when it is full of small golden seeded pods) or in its lush green state. Seeding grass heads both fully ripe and green are another valuable greenfood acceptable to most Budgerigars. Ordinary meadow and rye grasses should be used, not those with hairy heads. Spinach is easy to grow and whenever possible, a small patch should be constantly growing in the owner's garden. In all cases, care must be taken to ensure that the greenfood is free from insecticides.

Other useful greens that are fairly easy to obtain during much of the year are the leaves and seeding heads of the sow (milk) thistles, seeding heads of shepherd's purse, young dandelion leaves, watercress, seeding heads and leaves of lettuce, chicory, hearts of various cabbages, Brussels sprouts, grated and sliced carrot and sweet apple. When fresh greenfood is difficult to obtain, sprouted wheat, barley or oats, can be used as a substitute. These should be soaked for twenty-four hours in cold water, drained and then stood in a warm cupboard for forty-eight hours, after which it is ready for use. Soaked seed can be given as a change from greenfood at any time of the year.

It is essential that all Budgerigars always have an ample supply of mixed grits which are readily available at seed stores. In addition to grit the birds need a supply of lime, and cuttlefish bone is an excellent source of this important mineral element. Another good source is dried, crushed domestic hen's egg-shells, which are always taken by birds of all ages. Iodine and mineral blocks, pieces of old mortar, lumps of raw chalk, and sea sand all contain various mineral elements needed for the well-being of the birds.

Water vessels should be filled daily with clean water, even though Budgerigars do not drink very much. When young birds are being fed the intake of water by their parents is quite considerable and at this time the pots may need attention twice daily.

BREEDING

Once the kind of breeding accommodation has been decided upon (see pp.97–9 and 101), and constructed, the initial stock should be obtained. If the intending Budgerigar keeper has not had birds before, I suggest that he visit local breeders to see the different colours before buying any birds. Should this not be possible, then the advertisement columns in the Fancy publications should be perused: the weekly paper *Cage and Aviary Birds* in Great Britain and the monthly in the United States, *American Cage-bird Magazine*. Not only do these publications contain advertisements of birds for disposal and all kinds of accessories, but also numerous useful articles on many aspects of bird breeding. It is also advisable to join one or more of the local, national or specialist Budgerigar societies. The breeder will meet others of kindred interests and such contacts will be of value in obtaining good healthy stock.

Opinions on the best time to start the breeding operations vary, but I feel sure it is unwise for the newcomer to proceed before the end of February or the beginning of March, when the days are longer and the weather is more conducive to encouraging the birds to reproduce. However, no matter what time is chosen, the controlling factor must be the condition of the breeding pairs. It is essential that both members of the selected pairs should be fully mature and in the same state of readiness. I am sure that the reason why some pairs are unproductive is that one, and sometimes both of the birds, are not in full breeding condition. Although the birds may be in perfect feather this does not necessarily mean that they are in breeding condition. When cock Budgerigars are in peak condition their ceres are a bright and shiny blue, except those of the red-eyed and Pied kinds, which are a purplish-pink colour. The birds are bright eyed, energetic in their movements, inclined to be quarrelsome among themselves and generally lively. The ceres of all hens in the correct condition becomdough and of deep chocolate colour. Like the cock birds they are inclined to squabble, calling loudly to any nearby cocks and generally searching about for nesting sites in aviary corners. It is not necessary, as it is often thought, to pair all birds on the same day – pairing should be done as and when they are thought to be in the desired condition.

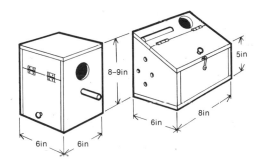

Two designs suitable for Budgerigar nest boxes

A traditional Budgerigar nest box with a removable concave bottom. When this is pushed in, a sliding panel completes the box.

Details of each bird should be entered in a stock book as this will help to ensure that the best possible birds are paired and aid the breeder on any question of pedigree that may arise. It is best to put the newly paired birds into their breeding quarters early in the day so that they have ample time to settle and get acquainted before nightfall.

Nest boxes can be of many shapes and designs but they all have one factor in common: a loose concave bottom. Some designs for the types of nest boxes generally used are illustrated here. Budgerigars do not require any nesting material, but a little coarse pine sawdust in the bottom of the box will prevent the eggs from rolling about and will absorb any surplus moisture from the droppings.

It is preferable to withhold the nest boxes for a day or two so that the birds have an opportunity to mate properly. Otherwise, the hen may go straight into the box, staying there until she lays her eggs, the cock bird feeding her through the entrance holes. If this happens it is inevitable, of course, that the clutch of eggs will be infertile.

The eggs are laid on alternate days and in a clutch of five eggs there will be about ten days between the hatching of the first and last eggs; the incubation period is seventeen or eighteen days for each egg. Although the chicks vary in age the parent birds look after them with equal care. As the chicks grow, the sawdust in the bottom of the nest boxes will need renewing and, naturally, the boxes should be kept clean and dry at all times. The young leave their nests when they are four to five weeks old and are able to fend for themselves seven to ten days later.

The breeding pairs require their usual diet with perhaps some extra oats or groats and, as the young develop, greenfood should be increased gradually. An occasional cube of moistened wholemeal bread or a small dish of soft food will be appreciated by the parent birds. As the chicks begin to emerge from their nest boxes more millet sprays can be given to encourage them to start feeding on their own. Budgerigars, therefore, require very little extra attention whilst they are breeding.

Most breeders ring their birds with closed metal rings (bands) so that they are permanently identifiable. Rings bought through one of the Budgerigar societies carry the breeder's own personal code number as well as a number and year. All birds entered by their breeders in young bird classes at shows must carry these special rings. The method for putting on closed rings is illustrated on p.72. Breeders not belonging to a society can purchase closed rings carrying their initials, number and year, from Messrs Hughes, 1 High Street, Hampton Hill, Middlesex,

in England and in the United States from Red Bird Products Inc., 2786 Fruitridge Road, Sacramento, California 95820 or the Al-Ed Band Company, P.O. Box 202, Opa Locka, Florida 33054. For identifying individual birds or families, split celluloid rings can be used in addition to the closed rings; this will eliminate the necessity of catching many birds to obtain a particular individual.

GENETICS

Should the owner just want chicks from his birds, pair selection is unimportant, except that it is always preferable to choose the best birds. The inhabitants of a mixed aviary can be allowed to breed among themselves, but the results from such indiscriminate pairings cannot be predicted. Controlled breeding is far more interesting, although it does require patience, the keeping of records and a knowledge of the way in which the various characters are inherited.

By careful pairing it is possible to combine several different colour and plumage pattern mutations in a single bird, producing a composite colour effect. The results of such breeding is more exciting than those from the 'straight' colours. In many of the colour forms the markings of the wild birds are present, either in a different shade or a different intensity; in others the pattern of the markings is altered. The mutations giving rise to this great range of pattern and colour variations are inherited in different ways. Before discussing these it is necessary to define the term 'split', which is frequently used in the descriptions of many of the Budgerigar types. A bird is said to be 'split' for a colour when it is visually one colour but has, in its genetic make-up, the possibility of producing offspring of another colour when given the right mate. For example, a Light Green 'split' for Blue is an ordinary looking Light Green bird that, when mated with a Blue or a Light Green 'split' Blue, can produce blue-coloured young. The bird's visible colour is always given first, followed by the hidden colour. The word 'split' is written as an oblique stroke (/), e.g. Green/Yellow, Blue/Cinnamon White.

Dominant Inheritance
Dominant colour characters cannot be carried in 'split' form by birds having any other colour characters; therefore if a bird has a single or double quantity of a dominant colour in its genetic make-up it must show in its plumage. The colour characters that come into this category are grey, violet, Australian pied and clearflight.

Young Budgerigars being reared

RULES OF DOMINANT INHERITANCE

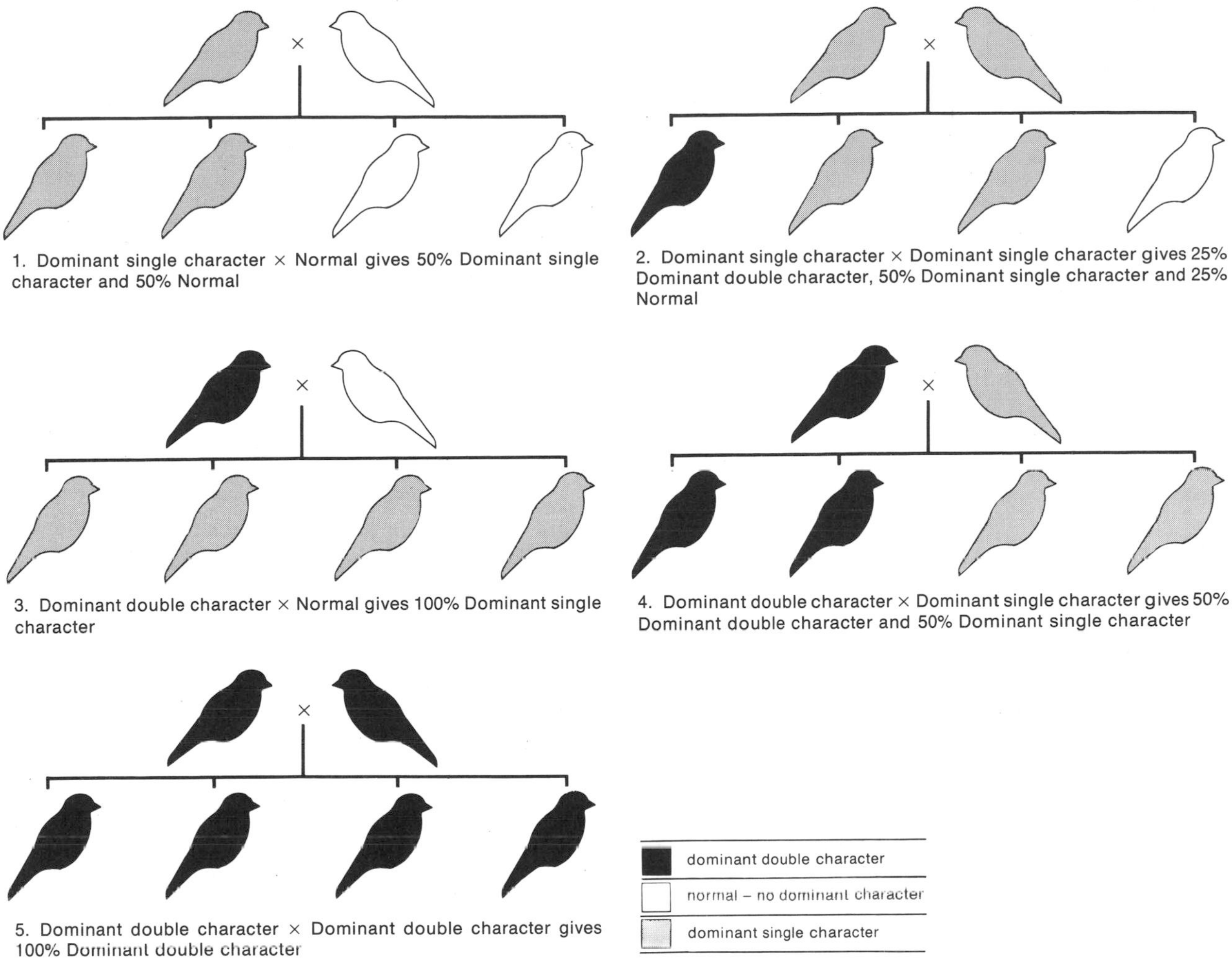

1. Dominant single character × Normal gives 50% Dominant single character and 50% Normal

2. Dominant single character × Dominant single character gives 25% Dominant double character, 50% Dominant single character and 25% Normal

3. Dominant double character × Normal gives 100% Dominant single character

4. Dominant double character × Dominant single character gives 50% Dominant double character and 50% Dominant single character

5. Dominant double character × Dominant double character gives 100% Dominant double character

■ dominant double character

□ normal – no dominant character

▨ dominant single character

The following examples will clarify how the rules work in practice: Grey Light Green single character mated with Light Green gives 50% Grey Light Green single character and 50% Light Green (Rule 1). Australian Pied Skyblue double character to Skyblue gives 100% Australian Pied Skyblue single character (Rule 3) and so on. When two different dominant characters are involved they will both be apparent in the plumage of the progeny depending on the genetic make-up of the individuals. For example, if a Grey Light Green single character bird is paired with an Australian Pied Light Greensingle character bird the young can be Grey Light Green single character, Light Green, Australian Pied Light Green single character and Australian Pied Grey Light Green single character.

Recessive Inheritance

The recessive forms of Budgerigars are Fallows (all kinds), Danish Pieds, Yellows (Whites), Greywings and Clearwings. It is only possible for these colours to be reproduced when the character in question is carried by *each* parent either in a single or double quantity. These recessive colours can be carried in 'split' form by all other colours whether they are dominant, recessive or sex-linked. The peculiar relationship of the yellow (white), clearwing and greywing characters is described under their sections.

Sex-linked Inheritance

We now know that there are five different gene-

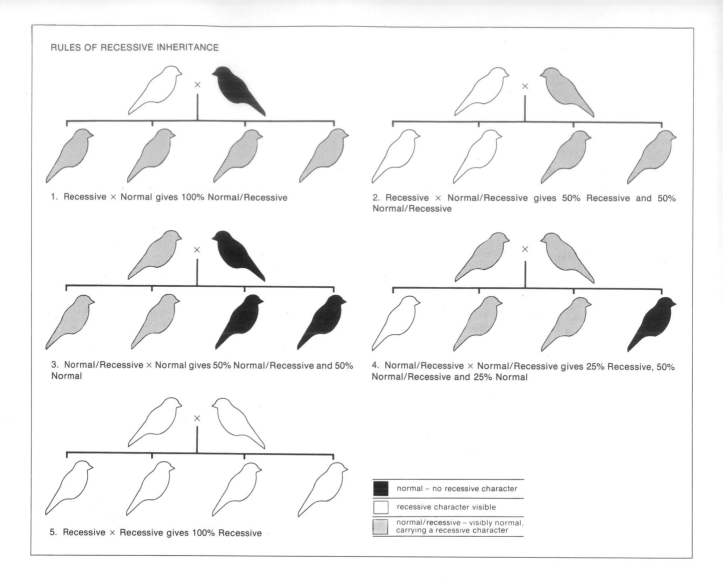

RULES OF RECESSIVE INHERITANCE

1. Recessive × Normal gives 100% Normal/Recessive

2. Recessive × Normal/Recessive gives 50% Recessive and 50% Normal/Recessive

3. Normal/Recessive × Normal gives 50% Normal/Recessive and 50% Normal

4. Normal/Recessive × Normal/Recessive gives 25% Recessive, 50% Normal/Recessive and 25% Normal

5. Recessive × Recessive gives 100% Recessive

normal – no recessive character

recessive character visible

normal/recessive – visibly normal, carrying a recessive character

mutations that are inherited in a sex-linked manner (see p.185) – opaline, slate, cinnamon, lacewing and albino (lutino). When two of them come together in a crossing one acts as though it were a normal character. Cock birds with other colour characters can carry a sex-linked character in 'split' form but hens cannot do so: if hens have one of these sex-linked characters in their genetic make-up it *must* show in their plumage. To obtain cock birds with any of the sex-linked colours the parent hen must always be of that colour. Thus only two matings can give cocks showing the sex-linked colour: 'split' sex-linked cocks with sex-linked hens and sex-linked cocks to sex-linked hens (Rules 4 and 5). Hen birds showing the sex-linked character can be bred when the cock of a pair has the character in either single ('split') or double

(visible) quantity. This gives four possible pairings (Rules 2, 3, 4 and 5).

Dark Inheritance

These three ways in which characters are passed on do not complete the picture – there remains the intermediate dominant behaviour of the dark character. This operates completely independently of any other colour characters that may be carried by the birds as it only affects the depth of colour.

RULES OF DARK INHERITANCE

1. Dark single character × Normal gives 50% Dark single character and 50% Normal.

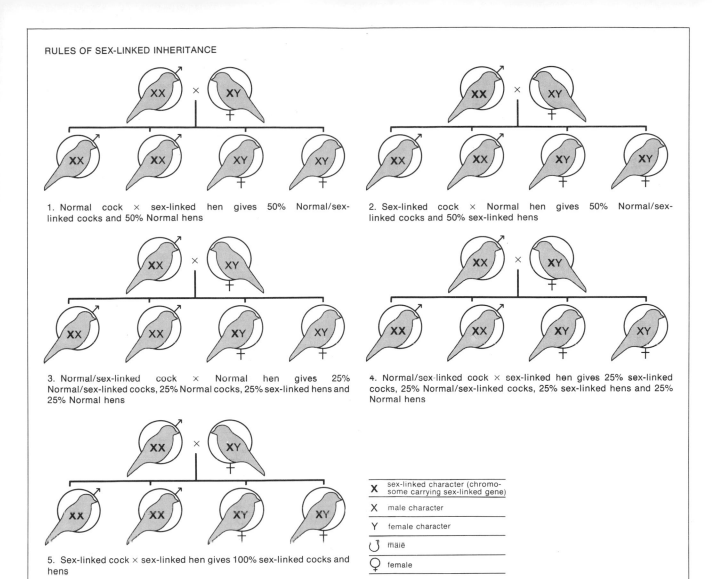

RULES OF SEX-LINKED INHERITANCE

1. Normal cock × sex-linked hen gives 50% Normal/sex-linked cocks and 50% Normal hens

2. Sex-linked cock × Normal hen gives 50% Normal/sex-linked cocks and 50% sex-linked hens

3. Normal/sex-linked cock × Normal hen gives 25% Normal/sex-linked cocks, 25% Normal cocks, 25% sex-linked hens and 25% Normal hens

4. Normal/sex-linked cock × sex-linked hen gives 25% sex-linked cocks, 25% Normal/sex-linked cocks, 25% sex-linked hens and 25% Normal hens

5. Sex-linked cock × sex-linked hen gives 100% sex-linked cocks and hens

X	sex-linked character (chromosome carrying sex-linked gene)
X	male character
Y	female character
♂	male
♀	female

2. Dark single character × Dark single character gives 25% Dark double character, 50% Dark single character and 25% Normal.

3. Dark double character × Normal gives 100% Dark single character.

4. Dark double character × Dark single character gives 50% Dark double character and 50% Dark single character.

5. Dark double character × Dark double character gives 100% Dark double character.

Rule 2 shows that even if both parents have a single dark character they can produce a percentage of Normal young. Sex has no bearing on the inheritance of this character nor does the mixing of any other colour characters influence its distribution in any way.

The sets of rules given above are simplified in that they are concerned with the behaviour of only one character considered in isolation. Budgerigars carry more than one character in their genetic make-up, hence the large range of colour forms described earlier in this section. In fact, some combinations have yet to be bred so there are still opportunities for experimental breeders to produce some of these combinations for the first time. The possibility of producing unusual and perhaps beautifully coloured specimens has encouraged many people in all parts of the world to take up this absorbing hobby.

Zebra Finches and Bengalese

ZEBRA FINCH

Next to the Canary and Budgerigar the Zebra Finch *(Taeniopygia guttata castanotis)* is the most popular fully domesticated species bred in captivity (Plate 40). Their rise to prominence since about 1950 has been phenomenal; before this time they were considered to be just one of many small exotic birds. The success with which they breed in captivity under varied conditions, the appearance and establishment of several new colour phases, their hardiness, and size (they are about 4½ in long), appealed to bird keepers who had limited aviary space and wanted an easy species that was different from the Canary or Budgerigar.

The exact date when the first specimens of these delightful little Australian birds were brought to Europe is unrecorded. Most probably they were introduced to Great Britain in about 1840, at the same time as the Budgerigar. It is known that zoologists were very active in Australia during the first half of the nineteenth century – many other birds and animals were brought from that part of the world to Europe and, undoubtedly, Zebra Finches were among them.

Zebra Finches are still to be found in mixed aviary collections of small exotic birds and in the past, being free breeders, they were often employed as foster parents to the rarer species of Australian and other finches. Their success in this field certainly caused a spread in their keeping and more and more Zebra Finches were raised in captivity.

There are a number of subspecies to be found in different parts of Australia (some ornithologists reckon as many as twelve), all of which contributed to the creation of the present-day domesticated races. The subspecies vary slightly in the depth of their colour, pattern markings and size, and this accounts for the slight variations of the colour mutations of the aviary-bred birds. An interesting feature of the species is that in practically all the colour forms it is quite easy to distinguish between the sexes because the cock birds carry distinctive markings.

The Zebra Finch followed the pattern of other free-breeding species: as colour mutations began to appear breeders all over the world were attracted to them. A group of enthusiasts called a meeting in Birmingham, England, in 1952 and The Zebra Finch Society was formed to foster all aspects of keeping, breeding and exhibiting Zebra Finches. The Society was one of the first to specialize in a single species and it was not long before colour mutations were classified and colour standards formulated. Closed rings were issued to its members, it gave patronage to shows, and issued year books and news letters. In 1958 the Society announced that the wild-type Grey Zebra Finch and its colour mutations would no longer be considered as a 'foreign' bird. This decision was quickly adopted by other countries and the Zebra Finch took its place among the other fully domesticated cage and aviary birds, such as the Canary.

In the 1960s the popularity of the Zebra Finch had increased to such an extent that area societies were formed in Great Britain, and Zebra Finch societies in other countries became affiliated to the original British society. The Zebra Finch Society is now a strong force in the cage- and aviary-bird world with a global membership – because of its endeavours the various colour mutations discussed below have been developed and perfected.

Albino

COCK AND HEN Beak short, conical and coral red, with the hen's being slightly paler. Eyes bright red. Feet and legs pink. The feathers are pure white throughout, showing no trace whatsoever of any colour or shading.

The albino character is sex-linked and was first noticed a few years ago in breeders' aviaries in Australia, where Albino Zebra Finches are now being bred quite freely. Some Albino hens have been reported in other countries, including Great Britain and India, but strains have yet to be developed. Because of a government ban on the export of all Australian birds, live examples of the Australian Albinos have not been seen outside that continent. It is likely that other albino mutations will occur and it is to be hoped that they become fully established. The genetic aspect of this is considered on pp.116–7.

Blues

This is a name occasionally used by British and more often by European Zebra Finch breeders to describe the Recessive Silvers (see p.111) probably to distinguish them from the Dominant form (see p.111). The birds are not a real blue like Budgerigars, but a slate-grey shade, more like that seen in Blue Canaries.

Chestnut-flanked Whites Plates 40, 41

Syn: Marked Whites, Marmosettes, Masked Whites
COCK Beak short, conical and bright red in colour. Eyes dark red. Feet and legs pink. Eye stripes greyish black. Head, neck, back and wings, as white as possible. Underparts clear white. Throat and upper breast zebra striped, with near black lines running from cheek to cheek continuing down to near black chest bar. Cheek lobes orange. Tail white barred with near black side flankings reddish brown decorated with small clear white spots.
HEN as cock but minus throat markings, chest bar, lobe and flank markings. The beak is a little paler in colour and the head may carry some light flecks of grey on top.

This variety was originally called Marked White because it showed markings on a white body; however, as some of the ordinary Whites also carried certain colour areas on their plumage, the name was thought inaccurate. In Europe they are also known as Masked Whites because when in nest feather the whole head and face are sooty black. The Zebra Finch Society decided that the name Chestnut-flanked Whites was the most appropriate and this name was adopted universally. The character of the Chestnut-flanked Whites is sex-linked (see pp.116–7).

There can be a Chestnut-flanked White kind in the other varieties but with the Fawn and Silver kinds the markings appear far too pale. There cannot be visual examples of the Chestnut-flanked White forms of Albinos and normal Whites. Opinion varies among breeders as to which pairings produce the best coloured birds, some say selected Chestnut-flanked Whites and others insist that normal Greys must be used periodically to maintain the depth of the markings. I have found the latter method the most satisfactory in the majority of cases, but a great deal depends on the quality of the Chestnut-flanked Whites used in the initial crosses. The method I would suggest is to use first-cross normal Grey/Chestnut-flanked White cocks to Chestnut-flanked White hens. If first-cross birds are used for each pairing the depth of the markings on the resulting Chestnut-flanked Whites can be maintained and improved.

Originally the body colour of this variety was more or less pure white but in recent years birds have been appearing which show an almost cream shade on their neck, mantle and back. It is possible that there has been a further Chestnut-flanked White mutation which has given rise to these cream-coloured birds, or they may be the result of selective breeding for certain show points. As we do not know when the first cream-coloured birds appeared, it is difficult to be sure whether they are the result of another mutation or of selective breeding.

Cinnamons

This name was first used to describe the darker form of the birds we now call Fawns. The old name was discarded when it was discovered that the so-called Cinnamons and Fawns were in fact the result of the same mutation. White-ground birds such as Zebra Finches are usually called Fawns whereas yellow-ground ones are called Cinnamons but they both owe their existence to one mutation. Probably the birds were called Cinnamons at the time in order to distinguish a rich dark fawn shade from some of the existing lighter fawn colours.

Creams (Dominant) Plate 41

COCK Beak short, conical, and red in colour. Eyes dark red. Eye stripe dark fawn. Feet and legs pink. Head, neck, back and wings pale to deep cream. Throat and upper breast zebra striped, pale grey with darker grey lines running from cheek to cheek and continuing down to chest bar which is pale greyish brown. Underparts white with slight cream shading towards the vent. Cheek lobes silvery to pale orange. Tail pale greyish brown with white bars, and side flankings bright reddish fawn decorated with small clear white spots.

HEN Like the cock, but without throat markings, chest bar, lobe and flank markings. The beak is a little paler in colour.

The Dominant Creams appeared shortly after the Dominant Silvers and were the direct result of experimental cross-pairings. It is thought by some breeders that the Silver is of European origin and there was certainly a great deal of activity after 1946 in the breeding of rare coloured varieties. Creams are in fact Fawns with either one or two dominant dilute characters in their genetic make-up. There is no visual difference in the colour of the single- and double-character birds and the only way to distinguish between them is by breeding. They are interesting birds from the colour point of view as they are the visual manifestation of sex-linked and dominant characters.

As would be expected there can be quite a variation in the depth of colour of different strains and even individuals. The best coloured specimens should be of a good clear light cream shade but with the characteristic markings clearly visible. If the specimens are too pale they appear insipid and if too dark they are too close to the colour of the lighter Fawns. Creams probably show the widest colour variation of all the mutations; because of the dilution, the shades carried by the original subspecies mixing are shown up quite clearly. Nevertheless, whatever shade Creams may be they are an extremely attractive addition to a mixed collection as they set off the darker colours to the greatest advantage.

Creams (Recessive)

These are the same as the Dominant form but of a deeper shade of colour throughout. The shade is between that of the Dominant Creams and the Fawns.

It seems that the Recessive Creams (and Silvers) appeared before the Dominant kind but had passed more or less unnoticed for a considerable time because of their nearness in colour to the already established light Fawns. The reasons the Recessive Creams have not been so well received as the Dominants are that they are more difficult to produce because of their recessive nature and because the colour is so close in colour to that of the pale Fawns. However, this should not deter breeders from keeping strains of Recessive Creams – by selection a delightful pure colour shade can be evolved. Unfortunately only a few of these excellently coloured birds are ever seen on the show benches, the majority of specimens being in communal aviaries. If more breeders would take up production of Recessive Creams they would be rewarded by the excellent colour of the birds ultimately produced.

Crests

Birds with small head crests like the Gloster Fancy Canary have been reported as being seen at a bird dealer's in Spain and there was also a report in 1972 from Paris, France, that a Crested Zebra Finch had appeared as a mutation in a mixed-coloured breeding flock. It seems, therefore, that the mutation has occurred but, as yet, no breeding stock has been established.

Dilutes

This is a group name sometimes used to include the cream and silver mutations. Because the name Dilute is not particularly descriptive of the birds' colour but of their genetic make-up, it is only used when describing the group; the individual colours are given more descriptive names such as Dominant Cream, Dominant Silver, Recessive Cream and Recessive Silver. The fact is mentioned because it is often easier for fanciers to use the group name when speaking of the different varieties.

Fawns Plate 40

Syn: Cinnamons in Great Britain; Isabels in Europe
COCK Beak short, conical and deep red in colour. Eyes dark red. Eye stripes dark brown. Feet and legs pink. Head, neck, back and wings a deep even fawn shade. Throat and upper breast zebra striped, grey with darker lines running from cheek to cheek continuing down to the chest bar which is blackish. Underparts white, shading to a very pale fawn towards the vent. Cheek lobes dark orange. Tail dark with white bars, and side flankings reddish brown decorated with clear white spots.
HEN Like the cock but without throat markings, chest bar, lobe and flank markings. The beak is a little paler in colour and there is generally more fawn tinting on the underparts.

The first reported mutation of the fawn character came from Adelaide, Australia, in about 1936. Since then it has been reported from Europe, America, again from Australia, and South Africa. The early breeding results soon made it quite clear that the mutation was sex-linked and the first of its kind in the species. Reports of other mutations indicate that these are genetically the same as the original one. The fact that the mutation is sex-linked and the pleasing soft warm brownish colouring meant that Fawns were soon in great demand in most countries. Because of the sex-linkage the majority of the first birds available for breeders were hens and for a little time true pairs were in short supply. Once this was remedied Fawns became, and still are, the most popular Zebra Finch colour mutation.

There are many matings that will give varying percentages of fawn-coloured young, but the aim of all breeders is to maintain and improve the general quality and the colour of the birds. There is a considerable difference in the colour shades of various Fawn strains. It has been my personal experience that to obtain good colours, Normals of even shade must be used periodically in the breeding programme. If Fawns are continually mated together the colour tends to become less intense and more smoky in appearance. The inclusion of an occasional well-coloured pure Normal, either cock or hen, in a Fawn strain will be beneficial to the clarity of the colour and to restoring the colour. By pairing a Fawn cock to a Normal Grey hen the resultant hens will be all Fawns and the cocks all Normal Grey/Fawns (see p.117). These are of great value to mate with Fawn hens that have been bred from two Fawn parents. As with all other colours the use of first-cross 'split' birds is always preferable – a point that cannot be over emphasized. There are, of course, good Fawns bred from other matings, but in order to maintain and improve a strain a definite programme must be followed.

Greys Plate 43
Syn: Normals, Normal Wild Type; in Australia, Chestnut-eared Finches
COCK Beak short, conical and coral red in colour. Eyes dark red brown. Eye stripes black. Feet and legs reddish. Head dark grey, lightly patterned with deeper grey; neck, back and wings grey. Throat and upper breast zebra striped, grey with dark grey lines running from cheek to cheek continuing down to chest bar which is jet black. Underparts white, shading to a pale fawn towards the vent. Cheek lobes deep orange. Tail black with white bars, and side flankings rich reddish brown decorated with small clear white spots.
HEN Like the cock but minus throat markings, chest bar, lobe and flank markings. The beak is a little paler in colour.

Because of the inter-breeding of the numerous sub-species in the course of domestication there are slight variations in the depth of the colours carried by individual birds and different strains. These slight colour differences are reflected in most of the Zebra Finch colour mutations but they do not create separate varieties. Each mutation can be separated roughly into light and dark forms; between the two extremes there is a range of shades. For exhibition purposes it is important that both members of a pair are of the same shade of colour throughout, thus forming a matched pair.

Understandably, Grey Zebra Finches have been much used in the development and improvement of other colour mutations. This cross-pairing has resulted in a deterioration of their colour and it is now difficult to find normal Grey Zebra Finches that are of a good colour and that do not carry other colour characters. Undoubtedly, the best way in which to consistently breed good quality birds is to make selective pairings of Grey to Grey, always discarding the poorly coloured and 'split' birds. The word 'split' is used to describe Zebra Finches in the same way as Budgerigars (see p.102).

If selective pairings are not made odd colour discrepancies creep into the various strains. One of the most noticeable during the past decade is the extra light tips to the secondary feathers. In some cases this fault has spread to Fawns, Silvers and Creams, and if allowed to continue would spoil the general colour picture. Perhaps the production of large exhibition birds has played a part in these small colour failures as breeders aiming for size have often neglected colour, but fortunately the emphasis has now shifted from size to quality, both of colour and type.

Grizzles
COCK AND HEN Beak short, conical and red in colour. Eyes dark red brown. Eye stripes dark grey. Feet and legs reddish. General colouring is the same as their Normal counterparts except that their dark areas are liberally sprinkled with small white flecks giving a pepper and salt effect.

This mutation is another that first appeared in Australia in the late 1960s in the normal Grey form, from which other coloured kinds showing the same grizzling effect have been developed. It was first thought that the character was dominant but a later investigation of the results of the first breeding, and some experimental crosses carried out in Great Britain, point strongly to the character being recessive. When Grizzles become more plentiful they should make a useful addition to both show bench and mixed aviary.

Penguins Plate 41
Syn: Blue-wings, Silver-wings, White-bellied
COCK Beak short, conical and red in colour. Eyes dark red. Feet and legs pink. Head, neck, back and wings an even silvery grey with flights, secondaries and coverts edged with a paler shade of grey producing a laced effect; this lacing does not show to advantage until after the second full moult. Underparts from beak to vent pure white without any trace of barring. Cheek lobes pale cream to

pale orange to match body colour. Tail silvery grey barred with white, and side flank markings reddish brown decorated with clear white spots.

HEN Like the cock but minus flank markings and with the cheek lobes white. The beak is a little paler in colour.

This interestingly coloured recessive Australian mutation was reported as breeding in Europe about 1948–9 in its normal form, and from these the Fawn version appeared somewhat later. One of the first names given to this mutation was Silver-wing and originally it seemed to be satisfactory, but then the name Blue-wing began to supersede it, probably because of a difference in the depth of the wing colouring. When it was discovered that there could be other variations of this mutation a more practical name was sought. As these birds have completely white throats, chests and underparts set off by dark coloured wings the name White-bellied was suggested and used for a time but was rather cumbersome. The colour resemblance to penguins was noticed and hence the present name, which is now used as an affix to describe all forms having the character visible in their plumage, e.g. Normal Penguins, Fawn Penguins, Silver Penguins, etc.

Penguin Zebra Finches have something in common with the Danish Recessive Pied Budgerigars: they both have their colour closely linked with a slender type of bird. It took breeders of Recessive Pied Budgerigars many years to break the link between type and colour and the breeders of Penguin Zebra Finches have run into the same difficulty. It is only by the constant use of first-cross 'split' birds that breeders can develop in the Penguins more substance and the desired cobby shape. Pairing good normal Grey hens to the best Penguin cocks gives excellent quality first-cross 'splits' (both cocks and hens) as no sex linkage is involved. Some good quality Penguins have been bred by pairing two first-cross 'splits', such pairings giving 25 per cent Penguin cocks and hens. The only drawback to this type of mating is that a large proportion of the young have a genetic make-up that can only be ascertained by further pairings to Penguins; this is known as 'wastage'. The actual Penguins raised from these 'split' crosses are invariably of vastly improved quality and I think well worth breeding for future mating with other good quality normal birds to obtain further first-cross 'splits'.

As I have already stated Penguins can be bred in colours other than normal Grey and Fawn although to my mind these two are the most attractive. Penguin Pieds have areas of white that are too large and Penguin Chestnut-flanked Whites are far too pale in colour; the same faults also apply to the Silver and Cream Penguin forms. Despite their visual faults, their raising is useful for the breeder to gain a general knowledge of genetic behaviour, which increases the interest in breeding Zebra Finches.

Pieds Plates 40, 42

COCK Beak short, conical and deep red in colour. Eyes dark red. Feet and legs pink. Dark colour broken with white approximately 50 per cent of each colour, white underparts not to be included in this 50 per cent. Cock markings to be retained in broken form on cheeks, chest and flanks. Eye stripes distinct but can be broken.

HEN Like the cock but minus ear lobe, chest and flank markings. Beak is a little paler in colour.

Quite often one of the first breaks in colour of a domesticated species takes the form of variegation (pied) and for many years a few birds were bred with some white feathers in their plumage. It was not until 1936 that a true breeding Pied Zebra Finch mutation appeared in Denmark. These Pied birds were found to be Recessives after their first trial crosses with normal Greys, and followed the usual recessive manner of inheritance. Like all pied species the amount of light areas on individual birds can and does vary considerably. Ideally, Pied Zebra Finches should be as described above, but breeding them often poses problems. Generally, if Pieds are paired together indiscriminately for any length of time their young can become either too light or too dark, usually the former. For exhibition purposes, therefore, both members of a pair should be matched for substance, type and colour pattern. Breeding pairs should be matched so that they are likely to give the greatest number of well-marked young. I have found the matings that produce the best coloured results are well-marked Pieds to first-cross Normal/Pieds. The 'split' birds should be bred from good quality pure Normals paired with well-marked Pieds.

Some breeders have used normal Whites as out-crosses for Pieds and in some cases have been quite successful in producing good coloured Pieds. However, I believe that it is not a sound plan to use Whites for crossing with other colours except to breed Whites: if Whites are used, a number of the second generation birds are white in colour, masking the desired colour, and thereby reducing the number of birds of that colour.

Pied Fawns are often thought to be the most handsome pied variety – they are certainly attractive, with their warm cinnamon-brown colour broken with irregular white areas. In addition, Pied Fawns are more exciting to breed because of their sex-linked inheritance. Although the lines of demarcation on the Pied Silvers and Pied Creams are not too distinct, breeding them can be interesting as the dominant dilute character which produces them is easy to combine with the Normal types.

Saddlebacks

From time to time white birds with grey- or fawn-coloured saddles have appeared among stocks of White birds breeding in uncontrolled mixed-colour aviaries. Birds with such markings do not appear to breed true to type – this is not unexpected as their colour must be due to chance selection and not to a mutation. This does not detract from their interest, however, and if pairs with the same saddle markings can be found they will make unusual exhibition birds. Evidence received from Australia and Europe in 1973 shows that true breeding races of Saddle-backed White Zebra Finches have been established. It has not yet been determined whether these birds are the result of a mutation and thus the genetic behaviour is unknown. Until a standard is laid down by the Zebra Finch Society, Saddlebacks must be exhibited as 'Whites' in Great Britain and their marking will be a fault.

Schwarzling

A variety produced in Germany, in which the pied markings are black instead of the usual white. I have only seen coloured drawings and transparencies, and believe that it has yet to be seen outside Germany. The colour of these birds is a little darker than the normal Grey and the chest bar is an intense black. There are black markings at the back of the head and mantle and black feathers around the joints, where the legs join the body. The amount of black carried by individual birds can and does vary.

Silvers (Dominant) Plate 44

COCK Beak short, conical and red in colour. Eyes dark red brown. Eye stripes grey. Cheek lobes deep cream to pale orange. Breast bar dark grey, throat and upper breast zebra striped, grey with darker lines running from cheek to cheek and continuing down to chest bar. Head, neck, back and wings silvery grey. Underparts white. Tail silvery grey with white bars. Side flankings reddish brown to pinkish fawn.
HEN Like the cock but without chest barring, lobe and flank markings. Beak a little paler in colour.

During the development of a fully domesticated variety a dilute mutation invariably occurs, and this has been the case among Zebra Finches. It is believed that the first Dilutes to be bred were the Dominant Silvers, followed by the Dominant Creams. The Dominant Silvers were once thought to be of European origin, but later it was ascertained that they first appeared in Australia like many other Zebra Finch mutations.

When Dominant Silvers were distributed in Great Britain they rapidly became popular, firstly because they were quite new and secondly because, being dominant in character, they were easy to breed and improve. However, when the Creams appeared they steadily replaced the Silvers because of their appealing colouring, and partly because it is far more difficult to produce evenly-coloured Silvers. This may be due to breeders paying too little attention to the colour quality of the normal Greys used in the initial production of their Silvers.

It is possible to obtain Silvers with an even colouring by the use of selected parent birds. Only pure Normals that have a solid clear grey colour should be chosen for crossing with Silvers. The Silvers should be of the best colour the breeder can produce, avoiding those showing a distinct fawnish tinting on the back and wings. Such matings will give half Silvers and half normal Greys; the Silvers with the most desirable colour should again be selected and paired with further good normal Greys. If this selected mating is carried out for a number of generations the resulting Silvers should be of the desired colour. If a good even silver colour is required Fawns, Creams, and Normal/Fawns should, whenever possible, not be used in the production of this variety. Like all dominant characters that of the Dominant Silver can be carried in either a single or double quantity without a visual difference in the colour of the birds.

Silvers (Recessive)
Syn: Blues
These are the same as the Dominant form only of a deeper shade of colour throughout. The grey colour is more bluish than the silvery grey of the Dominant form. So different was the colour shade that these birds were first called Blues and, I believe, still are by some European breeders. I am sure that the bluish tone of the Recessive Silvers could be improved upon if they were more selectively bred than at present. There are far more Recessive Silvers (Blues) being produced in Europe than there are in Britain, where support is limited. For experimental purposes Recessive Silvers should be most useful and, with a little forethought, some interesting composite forms could be evolved.

Unestablished kinds
Periodically an odd colour form is reported, and sometimes specimens appear in bird shows, probably the most

frequent being birds that have an excess of black on their plumage or that, in a few instances, are completely black. I have seen, bred, and examined a number of such birds but in all cases they have been unable to reproduce these characters. Most examples have, after their second or possibly third moult, become more or less normal Greys. This indicates that their abnormal colouring has been due to a temporary and not an hereditary pigment disturbance. These birds are quite distinct from the German Schwarzling variety and the reported Black-masked kind. The latter are said to have a completely black mask and are slightly darker grey in colour than normal Greys. (As this book goes to press it can be stated that this variety – also known as Black-breasted and Black-fronted – has been established in Europe. It has black colouring from chin to breast bar; its ear lobes are larger, its flankings are marked with white bars instead of white spots and its rumps are washed with beige.) A true breeding race of Black Zebra Finches may eventually be evolved.

Other variations appear from time to time: for example I saw some very attractively patterned birds a few years ago, which had dark markings on their wings somewhat in the style of the Opaline Budgerigars. Although there were several examples in both sexes the race was, unfortunately, not established and appears to have vanished.

A few white birds with dark grey spots or dots on head, neck and back have been seen but again after several moults they became ordinary grey-flecked Whites. Also, white birds with red dots have been reported, but on investigation these spots could only be described as a pleasing shade of fawn. The genetic inheritance of these variations is not known; if they were recessive the character would be hidden in normal-looking birds and could, of course, reappear. Whenever a colour change, even a small one, is noted, every effort should be made to preserve it in case it should be a true colour mutation.

Whites Plates 40, 41, 42

COCK AND HEN Beak short, conical and red in colour, with the hen birds being slightly paler. Eyes dark red brown. Feet and legs pink. Body feathers should be pure white without any ticking or flecking of grey, silver, fawn or cream.

Whites were the first colour mutation known to be established from the normal Greys and they were first reported in 1921 in the aviaries of A. J. Woods of Sydney, Australia, where they were developed and soon spread to many countries. I have examined all known references to the early Whites but can find no mention of their purity of colour. It is uncertain, therefore, whether the original

Whites carried any signs of flecking or if the flecking was introduced later into the strains by crossing them with Normals. Today we know that Whites with perfectly pure white plumage can be bred by selective pairings and that many good strains are in existence throughout the world.

A large number of Whites bred under uncontrolled circumstances do show flecking to a lesser or greater degree but nevertheless are still classified as Whites. Their vivid red beaks and white plumage make them a striking contrast to all other patterned forms of the Zebra Finch. Together with the Albinos, the Whites are the most difficult birds to sex having no visual sexual markings; there is, however, a difference in the beak colour when the birds are in full healthy breeding condition. The beaks of the adult cock birds are bright red and those of the hen birds are a shade lighter. A slight difficulty can occur when young cocks are examined beside two- or three-year-old hen birds whose beaks may be a deeper red. Fortunately, healthy young cocks will give their characteristic courting display and song when in the presence of hens and can thus be identified.

To maintain the pure white colour of the variety, Whites should always be paired together except when it is necessary to improve the overall quality. The best out-cross for a White is a Fawn, which gives a beautiful feather texture and can minimize the visibility of any flecking. Fawn cocks to White hens are the most useful matings, the Fawn/White hens that result should then be back-crossed to further Whites. The Whites from this second generation should be of improved quality and can be paired back into the strain. It is advisable to keep the number of 'split' Whites as low as possible and to use the White to White cross when developing a strain.

Yellow-beak

The general colour is similar to the normal Greys and to all other mutations except that the beaks of both cocks and hens are of varying shades of yellow, the cocks having the richer colour.

Yellow-beaked Zebra Finches have been known for a number of years and it is only recently that the variation was discovered to be a separate mutation and not just poorly-coloured normal red-beaked birds. They have been accepted by the Zebra Finch Society as a distinct mutation and are exhibited in Any Other Colour classes. Their overall colouring is perhaps a little less bright than that of the Normals but their yellow beaks make them quite distinctive. They can be bred in all varieties and examples seem to exist in most countries. It is unlikely that they will ever become very popular although they do add another Recessive variety to the list and make the field for experimenting greater.

Zebra Finch Hybrids

Being such free breeders and mixing well with other members of the finch family it is not unexpected that Zebra Finch Hybrids have occurred unaided in mixed aviary collections. Young have been raised from Zebra Finches and such other birds as Bengalese, Silverbills, Diamond Sparrows and various mannikins. When Zebra Finches are crossed with a fairly closely related species it is possible that some of the young hybrids will be fertile. There is a strong possibility of new colours or colour patterns being introduced into Zebra Finches by the use of such fertile hybrids. Zebra Finches will mate quite easily with birds of similar and slightly larger size if given the opportunity. Hybridizing is an interesting field of investigation and one that could have fruitful results.

HOUSING

One of the many attractions of Zebra Finches is that they can live happily and reproduce quite freely when housed under very varied conditions both in- and out-of-doors. They can even be kept in relatively small cages but invariably do much better if provided with a good space in which to fly. A normal sized Budgerigar single-pair breeding-cage will make a roomy home for a breeding pair or about eight to ten young or non-breeding birds. There are three types of housing in which Zebra Finches may be kept – cages, already mentioned, indoor flights or pens and aviaries.

A large proportion of Zebra Finches bred for colour or exhibition purposes are now produced in cages, because of a general lack of space for keeping birds of any kind. Such cages should not be less than 30 in (76 cm) long, by 12 in (30 cm) deep, and 15 in (38 cm) high, and constructed wherever possible in tiers divided by slides, so that when not required for breeding they can be quickly converted into flights by simply removing the slides. Housing the birds in cages is, of course, essential for colour and exhibition breeding where the exact ancestry must be known. See p.98 for suitable cages.

The normal type of cage fronts suitable for all kinds of small birds are obtainable in varying sizes at bird stores. Should these fronts have drinker holes they should be wired up as it is both better and safer to put the seed and water vessels inside the cage. The fronts designed especially for Budgerigar cages have a large door which is most useful for putting in and examining the nesting boxes. Zebra Finches are very quick on the wing and the owner must be cautious when opening the cage doors lest a bird escapes. The sliding partitions used to divide the cages can be made of wire, plywood or hardboard, according to the owner's preference. The seed, water and grit vessels can be made of glass, metal, plastic or earthenware and in all cases should be shallow. It is most inadvisable to use deep water pots as newly fledged young Zebra Finches can easily drown in less than 2 in (5 cm) of water. Water pots should be 1 in (2·5 cm) deep. Zebra Finches like plenty of water as they are keen bathers at all times of the year and in the hot weather the water vessels may need refilling several times a day.

The materials which can be used for making tiers of cages are varied but the most suitable are wood, plywood, or manufactured boards. Metal or asbestos sheeting should be avoided because of its coldness, condensation and ensuing dampness which can be detrimental to the health of the inmates. White emulsion paint is ideal for decorating the cages, both inside and out. Emulsion paint dries quickly, is washable, can be easily renewed and, above all, it is quite harmless if any chippings should be eaten by the birds. It is essential to see that all paintwork is thoroughly dry and hard before the birds are allowed access to the cages.

To ensure that the feet of all cage and aviary birds are maintained in a healthy condition sound perches of varying thicknesses are needed. The difference of perch size helps to keep the muscles of the feet and legs strong and pliable and thereby prevents the development of stiff toes. These perches can be made from machined dowelling of different diameters or light branches cut from fruit trees, hawthorn, wild plum, elm, beech trees. The manufactured perches are of course easier to keep clean but the natural ones are simple to replace if necessary. Excellent perching can also be made from the long stems of herbaceous plants such as the Michaelmas daisy and goldenrod. In the autumn the stems can be stripped of leaves, cut into lengths and left in a dry place until they become hard and ready for use. Such perches will be of different diameters and can be used in cages for most species of birds except, for obvious reasons, those of the parrot-like families.

The floors of cages are best covered with bird sand – sawdust, unless it is very coarse, gets blown about too much by the rapid flight of the Zebra Finches. Seed husks will also get fanned about and for this reason it is necessary to have a front cage rail of not less than 3 in (7·6 cm). In addition to absorbing moisture, the sand supplies the birds with another source of grit.

If the breeder has the necessary space for the construction of indoor pens this is a much better way of breeding Zebra Finches because the extra space invariably means the production of more vigorous young. In fact the majority of breeders who use cages for breeding also have indoor and sometimes outdoor flights for housing their young, growing stock. The size of these pens will of course be governed by the accommodation available and the number of breeding pairs required by the owner. A standard size pen is about 4 ft 6 in (1·35 m) deep by 6 ft 6 in (2 m) high and 30 in (76 cm) wide. Pens of this size will house one or two breeding pairs, or about twenty young or non-breeding birds. Emulsion paint can be used for the woodwork; the seed, water and grit vessels are as described above. Again the best floor covering is bird sand, fine gravel, or a mixture of both.

Should Zebra Finches be required only for pleasure and decorative purposes then outside flighted aviaries are ideal. Often existing buildings can be converted into attractive aviaries, or new ones can be built to suit the individual owner's taste and requirements. Zebra Finches

will certainly breed much more readily in aviaries but the owner cannot exercise complete control over the breeding pairs. A colony of Zebra Finches can be most attractive if a number of the different colour mutations are included. When breeding under such conditions it is necessary to remove the young birds as soon as they are seen feeding on their own. This is to prevent young Zebra Finches from breeding before they are fully developed. New birds will be needed in the breeding flock from time to time to maintain its stamina and correct any colour deficiencies.

If the aviary has an outside planted flight the birds may build their own nests in shrubs, but they will still need some wooden nest boxes to allow a choice of nesting sites. A fast growing shrub suitable for flights which provides excellent sites for Zebra Finch nest building is *Lonicera nitida*, a shrubby honeysuckle. The large varieties of lavender are also good for this purpose. An outdoor flight can be made most attractive with a little ingenuity on the part of the owner.

Without outdoor aviaries every precaution must be taken against the intrusion of vermin, especially mice which will soon disturb nesting birds. Small-mesh wire netting should be used to cover the flights and this should also be set into the ground all round the aviary. If mice do get into the flight, mouse bait should be laid under cover to eradicate the intruders. Examples of pens and aviaries will be found on pp.67 and 99.

A lean-to aviary with the shelter built inside the enclosure. Note the finch-type nest box in the top right-hand corner.

FEEDING

Zebra Finches are extremely easy to feed and require very little in the way of extras when breeding. This feature together with their simple housing needs makes them particularly attractive to newcomers. The principal food of all Zebra Finches is a small yellow millet seed called panicum and they can live happily on this seed alone. It is usual however to add some small canary and white millet seeds to the panicum to give variety to the diet. During the colder weather a small quantity of niger, a high oil-bearing seed, can be offered and it will be eaten by the majority of the birds. Because of its rather fattening nature the niger seed should only be given in limited quantities especially to those birds housed in cages.

Millet sprays, the complete seeding heads of the Indian millet, are enjoyed by Zebra Finches of all ages and provide an excellent means of getting young birds to feed on their own. Although some breeders give millet sprays that have been soaked for a time in water, I prefer to give them in their dry state. Dry millet sprays will not go mouldy in

Aviary suitable for small finch-like birds. The area nearest the birdroom can be given a waterproof cover to afford the birds protection from adverse weather. The birdroom itself can be adapted to the owner's requirements for his stock.

warm weather as they will if they have been soaked. An occasional dish of mixed wild flower seeds not only provides a change of diet but is useful because of the vitamins contained in the mixture.

Parent birds can be given a little soft food or cubes of moistened wholemeal bread to feed their ever demanding chicks. The soft food can be either a plain Canary feeding food or a mixture of that and a fine insectivorous food. A mixture of just over one third insectivorous food to just under two thirds of Canary soft food makes an extremely good blend. Although soft food is not absolutely necessary for rearing young it is a great help and both young and adults will benefit from it. During warm weather any uneaten soft food or moistened bread should be taken from the cages, pens, or aviaries to prevent it becoming stale and causing upset stomachs.

A regular supply of various fresh greenfoods plays an important part in the health of Zebra Finches. There is a large range of both wild and cultivated greenfoods that will be eaten by the birds and it is best to offer a variety of these to accommodate their changing tastes. Zebra Finches have two main favourites – seeding grass heads and chickweed. Both are easily obtainable for most of the year and like all other forms of greenfood must only be gathered from uncontaminated sources. They like chickweed in its fresh juicy green state and also when it is loaded with seed pods containing tiny golden seeds. Seeding grasses in their semi-ripe condition seem to attract Zebra Finches more than when they are fully dry and ripe. Among the other wild greens eaten by Zebra Finches

are sow thistles (milk thistles), complete with seeding heads and green leaves, shepherd's purse, especially when the heart-shaped pods are full of seeds, plantains, both large and small, and new tender dandelion leaves. Of the cultivated greens, spinach is their favourite; they will also take chicory, lettuce and tender cabbage leaves, and some birds will eat a little grated carrot. Germinating seeds are useful sources of greenfood during the winter when other supplies are hard to get. The seed, which can be canary seed, millet, oats or wheat, should be soaked in water for about twenty-four hours and then left to sprout in a warm place. The young leaves usually appear after about forty-eight hours, and are then ready to be given to the birds. During breeding periods it is best to tie the greenfood into small bunches so it cannot be used as nesting material or to make sandwich nests, that is, one nest on top of another.

Even if Zebra Finches have ample supplies of food, water and greens, they will not thrive unless they have access to plenty of grits and other minerals containing trace-elements throughout the year. The birds use grits to break down their food so that it can be absorbed into their systems and the elements – an essential part of the birds' diet – are needed to build feather, bone and muscle. Suitable grits can be obtained at bird stores, as can pieces of cuttlefish bone – a good source of calcium. Cuttlefish bone should not be given in lieu of grit but in addition to it. Sea sand, crushed dried hens' egg-shells, crushed raw chalk and old mortar rubble, are all excellent sources of minerals.

BREEDING

The work of preparing the housing quarters for the stock of Zebra Finches is usually done during the autumn or early spring so that everything is ready for the birds when they arrive. The birds should only be purchased when the cages, pens and aviaries are completed, painted and fitted with all the necessary utensils. New fanciers can make enquiries about birds from local breeders of Zebra Finches. If this is not possible then the advertisement columns of *Cage and Aviary Birds* (the British weekly bird paper) or the *American Cage-bird Magazine* should be scanned, or the secretary of the nearest cage bird or Zebra Finch society contacted for help and advice on where to obtain the necessary stock. Joining a society is a most useful step as it brings new bird keepers into closer association with experienced fanciers whose help and guidance will be invaluable.

The time when breeding should commence is always difficult to decide as so much depends on such factors as the construction and siting of the aviaries, the weather, the age of the stock, the experience of the breeders, and above all the condition of the birds themselves. The end of February to the middle of March is the best period to pair the birds and settle them in their breeding quarters. It is a waste of time to attempt breeding from stock that is not ready for the task; it is far better to wait a week or two and get successful results.

The birds should only be put together when both members of the pair are seen to be in the necessary condition. Hens usually look heavy around the vent area and start to look round the flight or pen for nesting places; they may carry anything that could be used for nest building in their beaks. Cocks will also be active with pieces of nesting material and will constantly utter their strange little bubbling courtship song.

Only one nest box need be given to each pair, but in a

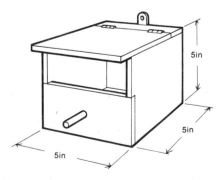

Nest box suitable for Zebra Finches and other finch-like birds

mixed colony more boxes than pairs should be supplied. The extra boxes will help to prevent undue squabbling for nesting places. The nest boxes are best made of wood in the form of 5 in (13 cm) cubes with a half-open front or a circular entrance hole like a Budgerigar box (see p.101). If possible a hinged top should be made so that inspection for ringing or other purposes is made easy. Usually, I half fill the boxes with soft dried grasses and then give the birds a further supply of grasses, a little moss, and a few feathers, so that they can finish constructing their nests. As soon as the nests are completed and egg laying has started, all surplus nesting material should be removed. If this is not done there is always the possibility of the birds making sandwich nests (one nest on top of another), and if this happens the eggs are spoiled.

Egg laying starts about ten to fourteen days after pairing. The clutches vary from two to seven in number but generally average about five. The eggs are laid on consecutive days and the incubation period of twelve days usually begins after the second or third egg, thus one or two chicks hatch a day or so later than the others. Both parents share in incubation and feeding the quickly growing chicks, which are ready to leave their nesting boxes when about twenty days old. A few days before the chicks are due to hatch the parent birds should be given a little soft food so they are ready to feed them when they arrive.

Colour and exhibition breeders ring their young Zebra Finches with closed coded metal rings when they are about seven days old (see p.72). The ring numbers are entered in the breeding register under the heading of the individual pairs together with any other relevant details. Split coloured celluloid rings can be used in conjunction with the closed metal ones for marking individual families or special birds.

To maintain the vigour of the stock it is advisable to take no more than two full nests of young from each pair per season. Should a clutch fail to hatch, however, then it is quite in order to have a further clutch from that particular pair. Chick rearing can weaken the adults – not just the egg laying, but the constant demands of an ever hungry brood.

The usual rules of Mendelian inheritance apply to the colour mutations of Zebra Finches; examples of sex-linked, recessive and dominant inheritance are set out below.

There are three sex-linked varieties of Zebra Finches now being bred – the Fawns, the Chestnut-flanked Whites and the Albinos. The following rules for the Fawn character apply to all three:

RULES OF SEX-LINKED (e.g. FAWN) INHERITANCE

1. Normal cock × Fawn hen gives 50% Normal/Fawn cocks and 50% Normal hens

2. Fawn cock × Normal hen gives 50% Normal/Fawn cocks and 50% Fawn hens

3. Normal/Fawn cock × Normal hen gives 25% Normal/Fawn cocks, 25% Normal cocks, 25% Fawn hens and 25% Normal hens

4. Normal/Fawn cock × Fawn hen gives 25% Fawn cocks, 25% Normal/Fawn cocks, 25% Fawn hens and 25% Normal hens

5. Fawn × Fawn gives 100% Fawn cocks and hens

It will be seen that with Rule No. 3 both Normal and Normal 'split' cocks appear among the young; unfortunately there is no way of distinguishing between the two genetic kinds except by test pairings.

The rules of recessive inheritance are also simple: they follow the usual pattern and are applicable to all the following mutations – Whites, Pieds, Penguins, Yellowbeaks, Recessive Creams and Silvers, and, it is thought, Grizzles and Saddlebacks, although the mechanics of breeding the last two forms is not yet fully understood. When two different recessive varieties are paired all the young produced are normal in colour but recessive kinds are 'split'. For instance, if Pieds are paired to Whites their chicks will be normal in colour and will carry the characters for both Pied and White in their genetic make-up. See p.104 for Rules of Recessive Inheritance.

Apart from the normal Grey which is a natural domin-

ant there is at present only one other kind with a dominant character: the Dominant Dilute which embraces the Silver and Cream forms. The dominant character can be carried in either single or double quantity and both genetic kinds give the same visual result. Other Dominant breeding kinds may occur in the future and all will be covered by the rules found on p.103. The dominant dilute character works quite independently of any other colour characters that may be involved in any particular pairing.

The three sets of rules of inheritance are, or course, only applicable to the *colouring* of the birds concerned and have no bearing on their other physical attributes. However, all these characteristics are also subject to fixed hereditary patterns, which are very complex and can only be interpreted by the skilful breeder. For this reason it is important that the breeder has a thorough knowledge of the breeding potential of the stock. Years of careful observation and recorded evidence have given breeders the information enabling them to match their breeding pairs so that the best qualities are evident in the progeny.

Most Zebra Finches are reliable parents and quite free breeders under all kinds of management although, like all livestock, they will vary in their individual performance. Healthy stock that is well housed and fed on a good, wholesome diet will, with the minimum amount of attention, be a delight to the owners and give the most satisfactory results.

BENGALESE

The Bengalese (*Lonchura domestica*) is about 5 in long and sometimes known as the Society Finch because of its peaceful and friendly nature. It is the oldest known domesticated cage bird. Breeding extends so far back that records of its development, if they ever existed, have vanished. One sure fact is that the Bengalese belongs to the mannikin group of species and is the result of hybridizing several species, one of which is thought to have been the Sharp-tailed Finch (*Lonchura striata acuticauda*). The late Allen Silver, a great authority on all bird matters, was of the opinion that Striated Finches, Silverbills and Sharp-tailed Finches were all involved in its development. Indeed, Bengalese cross readily with these birds and a number of other mannikins to produce hybrids, many of which are fertile.

It is said that the Japanese originally developed

the Bengalese and by careful selection from the original hybrids obtained the different kinds we see today. Other authorities quote the Chinese as the originators, and say that the Japanese obtained their first stocks from China and then developed them further. Both countries are known to have good bird breeders, so perhaps both can claim to have had a hand in their development.

Although they have been domesticated for a long time Bengalese are available in comparatively few colour forms. The Chocolate Selfs and Chocolate and Whites are the most plentiful and from them usually come the best quality exhibition birds. Pure Whites are more difficult to produce and are generally a smaller type of bird. It is thought that some strains of Whites carry a gene for blindness but this has not yet been proved. The Fawn Selfs and Fawn and Whites are, because of their soft fawn shades, the most pleasing to the eye. Dilute forms of the darker colours also exist. It is possible that other colour forms appeared during the early development of this domesticated bird but were never established. It is equally possible that enthusiastic breeders may, by crossing the fertile young of Bengalese with mannikins, produce other coloured forms.

Besides their pleasing ways Bengalese are excellent foster parents and most pairs will accept the eggs or chicks of other small birds and some will even take and mother half-grown youngsters. In a mixed collection of waxbills and small finches it is not unusual to see Bengalese helping to feed the young of the other inmates of the aviary. Because of centuries of cage-breeding they are not always particularly strong on the wing although after a spell in a flight they rapidly gain wing power.

One of the few difficulties new breeders find with the Bengalese is that they are rather difficult to sex as they possess no sexual differences in colour as do Zebra Finches. However, the cock birds do have a distinctive courtship song which is usually accompanied by neck stretching movements. The best way to sex them is to place each bird in a separate cage and keep them well apart for several hours. When the two cages are then placed facing each other a cock bird will invariably start his song and can be identified as a male and marked as such with a coloured split ring. If nothing happens this procedure should be tried several times. If after, say, three attempts no song is uttered by either bird it can be assumed that both birds are hens. If both birds are cocks, they will 'sing' one against the other. Generally speaking, cock birds are more plentiful than hens and thus a so-called 'pair' is far more likely

Two pairs of matched Bengalese – Chocolate and White (left) and Fawn and White

to consist of two cocks than of two hens.

There are two small but enthusiastic specialist societies in Great Britain and New Zealand concerned solely with the improvement of every aspect of the Bengalese. They issue individual ring code numbers to their members and encourage them to closed-ring their birds; this should be done when the chicks are about seven days old (see p.72 for details). The matching of the breeding pairs is particularly important with the Pied kind so that the greatest number of young can be produced with matching plumage. The broken plumage colour pattern is, to a certain extent, inherited and after a period of selective pairings the desired patterns are reproduced fairly regularly.

Chocolate Selfs Plate 45

Beak thick and dark grey brown in colour. Head well rounded from the top of the beak to the nape of the neck, the neck itself is thick. Eyes dark and set well back from the base of the beak. Back and body nicely rounded to give a look of cobby substance. Tail straight and wings carried in line. Feet and legs dark brown.

Chocolate Selfs together with the Chocolate and White forms are the most robust of the colour mutations. Only by careful selective pairing can true Chocolate Selfs free from foul markings be bred. Selfs should always be paired together to eradicate all foul-marked birds. It takes a long time to build up a free-breeding strain of Chocolate Selfs.

The overall standard for Chocolate Selfs is the same for all colours except of course the Crested birds that carry a small head crest. The general colour should be a good rich dark chocolate with the appropriate lighter chocolate markings on wings and back.

Chocolate and Whites Plate 46
In all respects these are the same as the Chocolate Selfs except they have a broken colour pattern of approximately 50 per cent white to 50 per cent chocolate areas. The white areas should be well distributed and as even as possible in pattern with each bird of a pair carrying the same pattern. The amount of white carried by individual birds can and does vary a great deal in all Pied birds.

Crested Plate 46
Birds with a small flat circular head crest, their colour and markings the same as those of non-crested kinds. They are exhibited in pairs consisting of one Crest and one non-Crest, the sex is immaterial, but both birds must be of the same colour form. When breeding for Crests it is essential that a crested is paired with a non-crested bird – the reasons for this are explained in the Canary section under Crests, pp.50-1.

Dilutes Plate 45
Dilute forms of the darker colours are shown at approximately half strength. A comparatively recent development, the results from breeding this form in the rather restricted numbers available indicate that the dilution is a sex-linked character.

Fawn Selfs
These are the same as the first two colour forms mentioned with the exception of their basic colour which is a warm shade of fawn. Beak pink horn; feet and legs are pink brown. There can be a variation in the depths of the fawn colouring and members of pairs should be selected so that they both have the same tone of colour.

Fawn and Whites Plates 45, 46
These, like the Chocolate and Whites, should have approximately 50 per cent white and 50 per cent fawn areas, the fawn of the same shade as that of the Selfs. Because of the lighter tone of the dark areas, the lines of demarcation may not always be as clearly defined as in the Chocolate and Whites. Every endeavour should be made to mate Fawn and Whites so that they produce young with clear-cut colour lines.

Whites Plate 46
These should be pure white throughout without any trace of foul dark feathers. They have pink beaks, feet and legs. Whites are generally smaller in build than the other colour forms and offer much scope to the breeder who wishes to develop a special colour form. In Asia the production of Whites was considered to be the highest achievement in the breeding of the Bengalese.

HOUSING, FEEDING AND BREEDING
The general management of the Bengalese is very similar to that of Zebra Finches (see earlier). There is, however, a small though important difference in feeding: the seed, soft food, greens, grit and minerals are the same as those given to Zebra Finches but Bengalese should have white millet and canary seed in their standard seed mixture.

The Bengalese have the same breeding habits as the Zebra Finches and they use the same kind of wooden nesting boxes. They do differ from Zebra Finches in that they do not have the habit of making sandwich nests when there is a surplus of nesting material in the cage or aviary.

I have found that they will breed equally well in aviaries or cages although some breeders find that when several pairs are housed together they are inclined to have communal nests which does not help with satisfactory hatching. Being bred especially for cage life they naturally breed extremely well in Zebra Finch and Budgerigar breeding-cages and small indoor pens. See pp.98-9 for diagrams. For colour and exhibition breeding the matched pairs must be kept strictly on their own so that the exact pedigree of each bird is known and can be recorded by the breeder.

Parakeets

This book is concerned with those species that can be bred without too much difficulty in captivity and, therefore, some parakeet species and subspecies do not come within its scope. It is only within the last few decades that the parakeet fancy has really developed, though aviculturists in many countries had taken an interest during the past hundred years in breeding many of the species with varying degrees of success. There was until recently no difficulty in obtaining fresh supplies should anything happen to existing stocks. It was not until supplies of the wild Australian parakeets ceased with the ban on their export that aviculturists saw that many species might disappear from their aviary collections. This has led to a world-wide revival in their breeding, particularly the Australian species, which take so kindly to captive conditions. Outside Australia the main centres of parakeet breeding are in Europe, America and Great Britain, where fine ranges of aviaries have been built and are now in full use with many hundreds of parakeets being raised each season. In fact, certain species are now more numerous in captivity than in the wild. Breeding parrot-like birds, and other species for that matter, is extremely important to the aviculturist because with advances in civilization and mechanization, many of the rare species are losing their hold in their native areas and their existence needs to be safeguarded. Conservationists and aviculturists should be encouraged to work together for the preservation of any species of bird and other animals threatened with extinction – indeed it is hoped that the information given in this book will contribute towards this end.

During the past few years a number of parakeet species have become domesticated and new colour forms have been evolved through mutations, thereby increasing the interest in those particular varieties. With this surge of enthusiasm in parakeet breeding more species will doubtless become domesticated and mutations may occur, adding further interest to this group of birds.

Because of their wide distribution, species are grouped according to area: first, those from India and surrounding areas (Asian parakeets); second, the Australian kinds; finally, the South American.

ASIAN PARAKEETS

The main group of parakeets that live in the forest areas of the Indian subcontinent and surrounding countries are the long-tailed ringneck family of which there are some thirty-five species and subspecies. Some of the species are extremely rare while others are plentiful and are to be seen in aviaries all over the world. One of the disadvantages of these birds is that they do not come into breeding condition and full adult plumage until they are three years old. This makes their breeding a long term project; nevertheless, there are many aviculturists who have been breeding the ringnecks and their mutations for many years, thereby building up their own domesticated strains. Because of their comparatively large size, these birds require plenty of flying space and reasonably big aviaries if they are to breed successfully. Each breeding pair will need their own aviary since, during the breeding period, the birds become pugnacious and it is most unsafe to mix them.

Alexandrine Parakeet (*Psittacula eupatria nepalensis*)
Syn: Alexandrine Ringneck, Indian Rock Parrot, Large Indian Parakeet
COCK Overall length about 21 in (53 cm) of which about 12 in (30 cm) is the tail. Eyes light yellow. Beak dark red. General colour pale green, brighter on forehead and dull on underparts. Small red patch on upper part of each

wing. Cheeks and back of head bluish. Black stripe running from eye to nostril and wide black moustache bands. Deep collar at back of neck rosy pink. Feet and legs greyish.

HEN Shorter and without pink collar or black markings.

These are the largest of the ring-necked parakeets and at first sight appear rather heavy at the top end, but this is offset by the fine long tail. Alexandrines are hardy birds and survive in outside aviaries in most countries. Being sizeable birds they need a large flying area, although the aviaries need not be wide providing they have plenty of length, 20 ft (6·1 m) to 25 ft (7·6 m) being ideal. Once a pair has settled down and started to breed they will do so for many years and successfully rear their young. There are several colour mutants: Lutinos, Blues and, on rare occasions, Albinos have been raised. A number of variegated birds are also seen and it is thought that one or two strains of these pied forms are in existence. The Lutinos and Albinos are sex-linked; the blue colouring is recessive. The Lutinos are lovely birds with a golden body colour and a light, rosy-red ring around their necks. Because the birds do not become fully adult until their third year, it takes a considerable time to produce a strain (see p.193).

Derbian Parakeet (*P. derbyana*)
Syn: Lord Derby's Parakeet
COCK Overall length including tail about 20 in (51 cm). Eyes light straw coloured. Beak red. General colour bright grass green. Head and breast a beautiful shade of soft lilac, which is tinted with blue on the forehead. Wings have a soft bright yellowish-olive patch and the thighs and vent area are olive coloured. A black stripe runs from eye to nostril and wide black moustache bands (bluish below) stand out clearly against the soft colouring of the breast. Feet and legs greyish.

HEN Beak black; shorter and lacks black markings.

These are among the rarer ringnecks and, unfortunately, do not breed too readily although there are some pairs that have taken more kindly to captivity and produce numerous young. If strains were to become well established in aviaries, I feel sure they would reproduce as freely as other members of the group. The Derbian Parakeets are most attractive in colour – probably the most colourful of the whole group.

Indian Ring-necked Parakeet (*P. krameri manillensis*)
Plate 47
Syn: Bengal Parakeet, Green Parakeet, Rosy-ringed Parakeet
COCK Overall length about 16 in (40 cm). Eyes light yellow.

Beak red, dark at tip. General colour soft greyish green with a strong bluish tint on nape; underparts dull and yellowish on underwing coverts. A black stripe runs from eye to nostril and a broad black band runs downwards from the beak across sides of neck, under which is a rosy-red collar. Feet and legs yellowish grey.

HEN Shorter than cock, without the pink collar or black markings, the collar being replaced by a pale emerald-green band.

Mutations occur in wild Indian Ringneck populations and captured specimens are now breeding well in captivity. The mutants are Pied, Blue, red-eyed Yellow (Lutino) and normal-eyed Yellow. From Blues crossed with Lutinos, Albinos have been produced. By crossing Blues with normal-eyed Yellows it should be possible to breed normal-eyed Whites (as in the Budgerigar). The golden-yellow Lutinos seems to be most numerous of the colour mutations.

Indian Ringnecks are the most widely kept and bred of all parakeets. They make good single pets, excellent aviary birds, and are ideal for the beginner. They are hardy, like all members of the group, once acclimatized or aviary bred. Ringnecks are susceptible to frostbite which affects their nails and toes and therefore they must not be allowed to sleep on the aviary flight-wires during the winter months in northern temperate countries subject to hard frosts.

Ringnecks are early breeders and it is the general practice to leave nesting boxes or nesting logs in position all the year. Most pairs are first-class parents and hatch and rear their young without trouble. Breeders do not agree as to whether inspection of the nesting boxes is detrimental or not; I think inspection should be severely limited. The hens incubate the eggs, which take about twenty-one days to hatch; both sexes share in feeding and rearing the chicks.

African Ring-necked Parakeet (*P. k. krameri*) is as its common name suggests, is a subspecies from Africa. It is slightly smaller than its Indian relative and lacks the rosy colour on its ring and its beak is blackish instead of red. No colour mutations have been recorded for this subspecies but they may have occurred. The same management is applicable.

Malabar Parakeet (*P. columboides*) Plate 48
COCK Overall length about 15½ in (39 cm). Beak red above, yellow tip and black below. Eyes yellow. General colour bright green, more yellowish below. The head, neck, breast and mantle grey with a greenish-blue band on forehead. The narrow neck ring is black edged with a

wider band of bright green. Central long tail feathers blue tipped with whitish yellow. Feet and legs grey.

HEN Similar to cock but without green neck band, shorter tail, all black beak.

Closely related to the Plum-headed Parakeet this species is a little larger, less colourful, and not quite so timid. Malabars are not easy to obtain and therefore in demand when stocks are available. They are reasonably good breeders and need the same general management as other members of the genus. At breeding time, which is early in the year, they are somewhat quarrelsome with each other but settle down when the eggs have been laid. They are fond of all kinds of fruit throughout the year but rarely eat greenfood.

Moustached Parakeet (*P. alexandria fasciata*) Plate 49
Syn: Banded Parakeet, Red-breasted Parakeet
COCK Overall length about 15 in (38 cm). Eyes light yellow. Beak red, paler at tip with underparts blackish. General colour bright green with head, cheeks and throat lilac. Breast rosy lilac with underbelly green. Shoulder spots yellowish green. A black stripe runs across the forehead from eye to eye. A wide black band runs from base of beak across base of cheeks (hence their common name). Feet and legs greyish yellow.

HEN Beak black. Generally duller in colour than the cock with breast a more pinkish hue.

Moustached Parakeets are smaller than the Derbian and thought by some breeders to be just as colourful. Both sexes have the characteristic moustache markings. They are fairly easy to obtain in Great Britain and Europe but not in America. They are usually a little more difficult to acclimatize than the Indian Ringnecks although once pairs have settled down they are quite hardy and most of them will breed and rear chicks. Secretive and nervous at breeding time they like to be left undisturbed as much as possible. Otherwise their treatment is like that of the Indian Ringnecks.

Plum-headed Parakeet (*P. c. cyanocephala*) Plate 50
COCK Overall length about 14 in (36 cm). Long narrow tail. Beak horn yellow on top and black at base. Eyes orange. Overall colour bright yellowish green. Head rose red at front changing to purplish plum at back with a narrow black collar edged with bright pale blue. Throat black. Wings washed with bluish green. Shoulder patches bright maroon. Feet and legs yellowish grey.

HEN Beak more yellowish. Head slaty grey blue without black collar but with yellow band in place of the blue edging of the cock. Shoulder patches absent.

These birds are often confused with the Blossom-headed, or Rosy-headed, Parakeet, a smaller subspecies (*P. c. rosa*), which has a paler head colour, both sexes having the red shoulder patches. Both forms make ideal aviary birds and have been crossed producing young believed to be fertile. The courtship song of the cocks, used quite freely during the breeding, is pleasing. They are among the most gentle of the ringnecks although when their chicks appear they can become very savage towards other species. In a reasonably sized aviary a breeding pair will generally appreciate the presence of a few other birds such as Zebra Finches, or quails on the aviary floor. They have the same feeding and breeding habits as the ringnecks but usually nest a little later. Plumheads are rather unpredictable breeders in captivity and success, to a great extent, seems to depend on their housing, which should be spacious. Lutino forms of the Plumhead with heads of a beautiful plum shade and a pure golden-yellow body colour are known. A pair of Plumheads are a pleasing addition to any collection of parakeets.

Young birds of all members of the ringneck group are coloured more or less like the hens until their full adult plumage is assumed at about three years and so it is a gamble when buying young in nest feather for a 'pair' can prove to be of the same sex. Nevertheless, it is wise to obtain young aviary-bred birds if possible, to allow time for them to settle down in their new home well before they are required for breeding.

AUSTRALIAN PARAKEETS

Australia is extremely rich in beautifully coloured parakeets, many species of which are now breeding successfully in captivity in many parts of the world. If this were not so aviculture would be the poorer because of the export ban on all Australian birds. Of the species discussed below most are fairly easy to obtain, hardy, and breed well provided the stock is fit, healthy and vigorous.

Closely related species have been crossed, the resultant fertile hybrids being useful in 'strengthening' both of the pure kinds. Some species contain one or more subspecies and the existence of these and the results from cross-breeding account for some of the small differences in colour and size found in aviary-bred birds. The best example of this is seen in the domesticated Budgerigar, where the subspecies and mutant colour forms have been crossed giving the large variations discussed elsewhere in this book.

Australian parakeets can be divided into three main

groups – the grass parakeets, the rosellas (broadtails, large and small), and the other smaller families.

GRASS PARAKEETS

These are among the more popular species because of their beautiful colouring, their convenient size, 8–9 in (20–23 cm) and the freedom with which most will reproduce in captivity. Like all birds, however, some pairs and strains will do better than others in breeding quarters.

Grass parakeets are double-brooded and when fully-matured birds fail to hatch a clutch they will frequently produce a third nest. They usually lay four to six eggs in a clutch, which takes about eighteen days to hatch. Grass parakeets do not seem to be particular about what type of nesting boxes they are given provided they are of the long upright kind, about 8 in (20 cm) square and 18 in (46 cm) deep, with 4–5 in (10–13 cm) of well-packed rotting wood and/or peat at the bottom. It is useful to cover the front and sides of the boxes with strips of bark as the birds like to climb about their nests and to make an entrance that way.

As all the species are now more or less fully domesticated, colour mutations might appear among the breeding stocks. A few Lutinos and Pied specimens have already been reported but I have not yet heard of any strains actually being established. It will be seen from the species described below that grass parakeets are ideal aviary birds. Should species other than those mentioned, such as the Rock Grass Parakeet (N. petroplela) and the Orange-bellied Grass Parakeet (N. chrysogaster), be obtained they will need the same management.

Blue-winged Grass Parakeet (Neophema c. chrysostomus)
Syn: Blue-banded Grass Parakeet, Blue-winged Parrot
COCK Overall length about 9 in (23 cm). Eyes dark brown. Beak greyish horn. Main colour of upper parts olive green. Head washed with yellow, lower belly, flanks, undertail coverts and thighs creamy yellow. Sides of neck, throat and upper breast bright pale green. Bar across forehead and wing patches brilliant dark blue. Tail blue, yellow and green. Feet and legs yellowish grey.
HEN Generally duller in colour with less blue on forehead and wing patches.

This species is delightful both in its colouring and temperament; it agrees with other non parrot-like birds which is a useful asset in an aviary. Some breeding pairs have been reported as very prolific (one breeder informed the author that his pairs produce young with the regularity of Budgerigars) and as being good parents, tending their young long after they have left their nests.

Some breeding failures have been due to the use of very closely related stock. This is always a possibility with parakeets, more especially with those species that are in short supply. Breeders should make every effort to record and pass on all relevant details of the breeding of every parakeet sold. This would help to minimize close inbreeding. Split, numbered and year-dated metal rings (leg bands) should be used to mark the stock.

Bourke's Parakeet (N. bourkii) Plate 51
Syn: Blue-vented Parakeet, Pink-bellied Parakeet
COCK Overall length about 8½ in (21·5cm). Eyes dark brown. Beak dark horn. Head and back of neck suffused with rose pink and forehead with eye stripe light blue. Cheeks pink with feathers edged with brown. Upper parts brownish and the upper chest and stomach rosy pink. Under tail and wing coverts, thighs and sides of rump pale blue. Tail slaty blue marked with white. Feet and legs grey brown.
HEN A little smaller and duller in colour throughout with the upper breast marked with greyish brown and without the blue eye stripe.

Bourke's must be the most widely bred of the grass parakeets and their quiet ways make them particularly attractive to aviculturists. The eyes of this species are quite large considering the size of the bird – an indication of the bird's semi-nocturnal habits. They can be observed moving about quite freely in aviaries during the dusk of summer evenings. They do not seem to require so much flying space as some related species and, on numerous occasions have been bred in large flight cages. Good fully matured healthy pairs will rear young consistently and can almost be described as the 'Budgerigars' of the parakeets.

For the breeder with limited aviary space, Bourke's are ideal and because of the freedom with which they reproduce, pairs can be bought at reasonable prices. Although coloured much like their mother, young birds are fairly easy to sex since the cocks usually show some traces of blue on their foreheads and the hens have smaller, more rounded heads. This is another point in their favour as it means that any young not required can be disposed of early. It is becoming rare in its native habitat but is fortunately common in captivity.

Elegant Grass Parakeet (N. e. elegans)
COCK Overall length about 9 in (23 cm). Eyes light hazel. Beak greyish horn. General colour an unusual shade of golden olive green. Frontal band deep blue edged with light blue and the leading edge of the wings are likewise

two shades of blue. Throat and thighs greenish yellow. Stomach deep yellow. Two long central feathers bluish green. Feet and legs greyish yellow.

HEN General colour more olive green; blue areas duller and not so clearly defined.

This lovely golden-olive shade is seldom seen in parakeets. This species is a reliable breeder and pairs are good parents. Although Elegants are not plentiful a small but steady supply of young birds seems to be available each year. Like all grass parakeets they are quite hardy if they have dry, draught-proof sleeping quarters and are shut in at night during the winter. They do best in small aviaries with medium length outdoor flights (about 6 ft (2 m) long, 3 ft (1 m) high, 3 ft (1 m) deep). Some pairs, however, have been known to produce young in large flight cages, although this is not recommended, as the lack of flying space must be detrimental to young birds, particularly those of the second generation. The lack of exercise leads to over-fat parakeets which become prone to other ills. Wherever possible, long narrow flights are preferable to wide short ones, each flighted aviary accommodating a single breeding pair. Although young and non-breeding birds can be housed together quite safely, breeding pairs do not like the presence of other parrot-like birds, even their own species, in the same enclosure.

Splendid Grass Parakeet (*N. splendida*)

Syn: Scarlet-chested Parakeet, Scarlet-breasted Parakeet, Splendid Parakeet

COCK Overall length about 8½ in (21 cm). Eyes dark brown. Beak black. Upper parts grass green with facial area deep iridescent sapphire-blue turning to black at beak. Leading edge of wings deep blue with turquoise blue above. Lower part of chest and underparts of tail rich yellow. Upper part of chest vivid scarlet with a few bright green feathers at sides. Long tail feathers bluish green. Feet and legs brownish black.

HEN Upper parts more brownish green with underparts olive green. Sides of head and wings lack blue. Breast greenish and without scarlet.

Compared with the soft beauty of the Elegant Grass Parakeet discussed above, it is hard to find adequate words to describe the vivid colouring of this species. It is certainly quite an experience to see for the first time living examples; I remember, for example, how my conception of Australian parakeets changed after I had first seen a male bird about twenty-five years ago.

There are two forms of the Splendid Grass Parakeet, one in which the scarlet is more or less limited to the throat area and the other in which it extends well down the chest. These may be two subspecies or different varieties. The two forms are sometimes paired which makes it hard to come to a definite conclusion.

Formerly the main centres for breeding Splendid Grass Parakeets were in Europe, where many of these birds are still raised, but other countries are now increasing the supply. Some of the early breeders used other species, such as Bourke's, to hatch the eggs and rear the chicks from the Splendids fearing that the latter would fail in their domestic duties. However, present-day breeders invariably find that their Splendid pairs make most attentive and attractive parents.

Turquoisine Grass Parakeet (*N. pulchella*) Plate 52

Syn: Beautiful Parakeet, Chestnut-shouldered Parakeet, Turquoisine Parakeet

COCK Overall length about 8 in (20 cm). Eyes dark brown. Beak horn. General colour bright green. Front of head, facial mask and edges of wings deep turquoise blue of two shades. Underparts golden yellow, deeper in centre. Shoulders have a band of reddish chestnut. Long tail feathers green. Feet and legs yellowish grey.

HEN Duller colours throughout with less blue on face, and chestnut missing from wings.

These birds have been consistently bred in captivity longer than other members of the family. They were well known in European aviaries as good breeding birds in the 1870s since when they have been produced in varying quantities. Like Bourke's and kindred species they have nocturnal habits. Before the ban on exporting parrot-like birds from Australia, wild stock was readily obtainable and consequently the vigour of the aviary birds could be maintained without any difficulty. Now breeders should be, and, indeed, are, careful when obtaining new 'blood' thus avoiding the complications of close inbreeding. The care exercised has resulted in first-rate, vigorous and reasonably free-breeding strains of this and related species.

Some strains of Turquoisines have been bred with a much richer breast colouring than the normal birds and are called Orange-breasted Turquoisines.

The first mutant to be recorded in this species is the Dilute. In 1968 a pair of unrelated Orange-breasted Turquoisines in the aviaries of Professor A. F. Posnette of Maidstone, Kent, England produced a mutant hen and the following year a cock of the same colouring appeared. This was a recessive dilute mutation in which the normal Turquoisine colouring is expressed at the same intensity of tone as the shade carried by the Yellow Redrumps. About twelve Dilute Turquoisines have so far been bred and, therefore, the mutation seems firmly established.

A second mutation, a Pied cock, was bred in 1974 by Mr A. Hacker of Cambridge, England from a normally coloured pair.

Turquoisines can be rather temperamental with each other – even apparently contented breeding pairs will suddenly squabble. In spite of this behaviour they rear their young well. It is very important, however, that immediately the young are seen to be feeding on their own they are removed from their parents' aviary to prevent them being attacked by the adult birds.

ROSELLAS (BROADTAILS) *Platycercus* species
Many species in this group of parakeets, which range in size from 11–15 in (28–38 cm), are now domesticated and in some species colour varieties have been established. A number have been bred regularly in captivity for many decades, particularly in Europe. They are all extremely handsome birds of bright and pleasing colour arrangements and, as in the grass parakeets, related species can be crossed resulting in fertile hybrids. Such hybrids have often been extremely useful in strengthening stock that has been inbred and increasing the numbers of those that are in short supply. Broadtails appear to settle down very well in most countries and generally reproduce with considerable freedom. For aviculturists who like large brightly coloured parrot-like birds, the broadtails provide a fine range of about twenty-two species and subspecies from which to select. Those described are reasonably easy to obtain although other rarer kinds appear on the market from time to time.

To obtain satisfactory breeding results it is essential to house all the breeding pairs singly in flighted aviaries with a good length of flying space, from 16 ft (4·88 m) to 20 ft (6·5 m). If the breeder has not had any previous experience with broadtailed parakeets it is best that an inexpensive variety of parakeet is first obtained. The Red-rumped Parakeet is probably the most suitable (see p.128).

Adelaide Rosella (*Platycercus elegans adelaidae*)
Syn: Adelaide Parakeet
COCK Overall length about 15 in (38 cm). Eyes dark brown. Beak horn. General colour orange red which varies in depth and shade, some yellowish red at sides of breast. Back and upper parts blackish edged with yellow and shoulder patches black. Cheeks light blue and some blue on wing edges and tail. Feet and legs blackish.
HEN Generally a little duller and smaller in the head than the cock. Tail more greenish.

The colouring of this species varies more than most of its related species, so individual aviary strains differ considerably in their colour shades although the general pattern is the same. It resembles the Crimson Rosella to some extent and the young obtained from crossing the Crimson and Yellow-naped Parakeets are similar to the Adelaide in colour. It has been suggested that the Adelaide is a natural hybrid of these two species, but this has yet to be proved.

Adelaide Rosellas were first bred in Great Britain during the early part of this century although they had already been bred a number of times in Europe. Some pairs reproduce extremely well but, as a captive species it is more difficult to persuade it to take up domestic duties than others in the genus. There are usually four eggs to a clutch and the chicks are mainly deep green with some brick red on crown and throat. The cheeks and wing edges are blue like those of their parents but their tails are green. Even in nest feather, the young cocks can be distinguished from the hens by their bolder and larger heads.

Barnard's Parakeet (*P. zonarius barnardi*)
Syn: Bula Bula, Mallee Parakeet, Mallee Parrot, Mallee Ringneck
COCK Overall length about 14 in (36 cm). Eyes dark brown. Beak light horn with lower part darker. General colour shades of vivid green. Forehead band deep red with crown vivid green. Cheeks, throat and wing edges bluish green. Nape banded with dull brown with yellowish band around back of neck widening at sides. Wings deep turquoise green with dark blue surrounding the area. Chest, wide band of orange yellow. Tail greenish blue. Feet and legs dark grey.
HEN Duller and a little smaller than the cock.

These delightful parakeets and their closely related species – the Cloncurry, Bauer's (Port Lincoln Parrot) and Yellow-naped Parakeets – are sometimes thought to form a separate genus. However, the present consensus of opinion is that although they differ slightly from the rosellas they should still be included in the genus *Platycercus*.

Barnard's Parakeet and its related species do not have the spangled mantle that is a characteristic feature of the rosellas, but their shape and tails are the same.

The majority of Barnard's Parakeets are kindly disposed towards other birds with which they can be kept quite safely, except during the nesting period when quarrels may occur. Some breeders find that they will even tolerate the presence of grass parakeets and Cockatiels. Immature birds, which are duller in colour than the adults, are most docile. Barnard's and their near relatives will survive in most climates, provided they are well housed and free from draughts and dampness during cold weather. They are reasonably early nesters; on average there are five eggs in a clutch laid by a fully mature hen. Pairs become very attached to each other and they look after their young with scrupulous care.

Barnard's Parakeets are a useful and colourful addition to any collection of broadtails.

Common Rosella (*P. eximius eximius*) Plate 53
Syn: Eastern Rosella, Red Rosella, Rose Hill Parrot, Rosella
COCK Overall length about 13 in (33 cm). Eyes dark brown. Beak greyish horn. General colour crimson red. Cheek patches white; wing edges and tail blue. Shoulder patches black. Mantle feathers black, edged with greenish yellow. Lower breast yellow with underparts yellowish green. Tail dark blue washed with green. Rump yellowish green. Feet and legs dark grey.
HEN Nearly as brightly coloured as the cock but having a smaller and flatter head.

Although this species is generally called the Common Rosella this does not accurately describe the startling beauty of its colouring. This delightful species is one of the easiest to obtain and it breeds with great regularity. Keepers of broadtails often start their collections with Common Rosellas and become so intrigued with them that it is not long before other species are added when the opportunity arises. The colour differences between the sexes are not particularly marked, but they can be sexed quite easily by the bolder and larger heads of the cocks both in adult and immature plumage. Young birds in nest feather are quite different in colour from their parents, being mainly dark green with some red on top of head, throat and under tail and there is a great variation in the colour of both individual birds and strains. In the wild there is a slightly darker subspecies (*P. e. cecilae*), see right, and it is possible that some of the colour variations may be due to the inclusion of this darker race in with the normal birds during the course of their breeding in captivity. Another subspecies, *P. e. diemensis*, is also recorded.

Like most members of their group, Common Rosellas are quite affable to other species. At breeding times they are inclined to be somewhat fussy and may be nervous of anything unusual happening in the vicinity of their aviary. When the eggs appear and the hens start incubating, they settle down to their normal routine. It is better not to inspect the nesting boxes of sitting hens if this can be avoided; when the chicks have arrived they do not mind a short periodic visit. They are particularly fond of greenfoods, fruit and green twigs, especially during the breeding period.

Crimson Rosella (*P. elegans elegans*)
Syn: Mountain Lowry, Pennant's Parakeet
COCK Overall length about 15 in (38 cm). Eyes dark brown. Beak horn. General colour deep rich crimson red. Cheeks and upper wing coverts deep vivid blue with some blue on tail also. Back feathers black edged with crimson. Shoulder patches black. Feet and legs blackish grey.
HEN Similar in general colour to cock but with a smaller head.

The Crimson Rosella is slightly larger and even more vividly coloured than the Common Rosella and it makes good aviary bird. It is hardy and thrives well in most countries but does not like draughts or dampness. If supplied with natural branches for perching in the flights it will delight its owner with its playful habits. The supply of Crimson Rosellas is fairly constant as they breed with reasonable freedom in most countries. Like all species of their group their musical call notes are usually heard in the mornings and evenings.

Although they are thought by some aviculturists not to breed quite as well as the Common Rosella, they perform their domestic duties freely when suitably housed and if the birds are from vigorous stock. Individual pairs will, of course, vary in their reproductive powers but this is true of all the different species. The average clutch of eggs is five and the chicks are coloured dark green with a varying amount of red on the head. They have been known as aviary breeding birds for nearly a century and all strains available are now well domesticated.

Golden-mantled Rosella (*P. eximius cecilae*)
Syn: Yellow-mantled Rosella
COCK Overall length about 13 in (33 cm). Eyes dark brown. Beak dark greyish-horn. General colour crimson red with more of a vermilion shade on head. Cheek patches, wing edges and tail deep blue. Shoulder patches black. Mantle feathers black edged with deep golden yellow. Lower breast deep yellow and underparts reddish yellow. Rump bright bluish green. Tail dark blue with some green. Feet and legs dark grey.
HEN Similar in colour but not quite as bright as cock, head smaller.

There is a difference of opinion as to whether this is a variety of the Common Rosella or a subspecies. The hybrid results of crossing the two forms suggest that it is, in fact, a subspecies as indicated in the heading.

When the hybrids are back-crossed to the individual forms the offspring only show minor colour differences.

It is a delightful bird with the same features and needing the same treatment as its close relation.

Mealy Rosella (P. adscitus palliceps)

Syn: Blue Rosella, Pale-headed Rosella

COCK Overall length about 13 in (33 cm). Eyes light brown. Beak pale horn. Head light yellow deepening in shade at nape. Cheeks white with blue at base and on breast and underparts. Vent red. Wings blue. Shoulder patches black. Mantle feathers black edged with bright yellow. Rump bluish. Tail greenish blue. Feet and legs dark grey.

HEN Usually shows a more greyish-blue shade on breast. Not so easily distinguished by size and shape of head as most other members of the genus.

This species has the same arrangement of pattern as others in its genus but the more usual red areas are replaced by blue (hence one of its common names, Blue Rosella). Mealy Rosellas were first bred in Europe around the turn of the century and they are now breeding freely in many countries, especially America where some very fine strains exist. They are striking birds and look particularly nice in aviaries that house a collection of other broadtails. In nest feather the young are pale counterparts of their parents. Although the birds originally imported were said to be rather difficult to acclimatize, the present-day strains appear to be hardy, vigorous and breed well. Most pairs make attentive parents and are of a placid nature.

Western Rosella (P. icterotis)

Syn: Stanley Parakeet or Rosella, Yellow-cheeked Rosella

COCK Overall length about 11 in (28 cm). Eyes dark brown. Beak horn. General colour of crown, nape of neck, breast and underparts bright red. Cheeks and thighs yellow. Mantle feathers black edged with greenish yellow. Rump golden green. Shoulder patches deep blue. Tail dull blue. Feet and legs brownish grey.

HEN Generally duller in colour, with more pale green in the upper parts, and usually a little smaller.

One of the smaller species, in spite of slightly less vivid colouring, it still makes a pleasing aviary bird. It is one of the more costly species and much sought after; fortunately, it is an excellent breeder and being double brooded can multiply quickly. I know of a pair that reared thirty-five young in five seasons – a good record. When not breeding they mix well with other birds, but during the breeding period they should be separately housed. Most pairs resent inspection of their nest boxes and certainly should not be disturbed while nesting. Young birds in nest feather

resemble their mother but show more green and less red, and are without the yellow cheek patches. The young should be removed from their parents as soon as they are seen to be feeding on their own, allowing the adults to proceed unhampered with their second brood.

The species of Rosellas described above are those most frequently met with – should other species, such as Brown's, or the Northern Rosella (P. venustus), the Green Rosella (P. caledonicus) or the Yellow Rosella (P. flaveolus), come into the hands of breeders they should be managed in the same way. The various species have been crossed from time to time and some interesting hybrids have been produced, many of which have been found to be fertile.

OTHER AUSTRALIAN PARAKEETS

Cockatiel (Nymphicus hollandicus) Plate 54

Syn: Cockatoo Parrot, Quarrion

COCK Overall length about 13 in (33 cm). Eyes dark brown. Beak grey horn. General colour grey with some brownish shadings, silvery on rump and tail coverts. Wings dark grey with white bar down centre. Long pointed curving crest on head and sides of head lemon yellow with bright orange-red ear patches. There is some yellow wash on wings. Tail grey. Feet and legs blackish grey.

HEN Duller in colour. Crest shorter with brownish suffusion. Ear patches less bright than cock. Tail speckled with white.

Like the Red-rumped Parakeet, the Cockatiel is a free-breeding species and because of its gentle ways it is a universal favourite among parakeet lovers. Cockatiels breed in colonies in the same way that Budgerigars do. They are harmless to both smaller parrot-like birds and to members of the finch family and so all may be kept together. Cockatiels breed successfully in Budgerigar-type aviaries and they will, in fact, nest successfully in large cages. They are excellent parents and rear several nests each season. The young are similarly coloured to the hen and thus accurate sexing is difficult until they have achieved adult plumage.

All the attributes mentioned above make this species a first-rate bird for the new parakeet breeder, and experienced breeders have successfully used them as foster parents for rarer parakeet species. A single Cockatiel will make a good household pet – they become very tame and even learn to mimic a few short words.

There are several colour mutations: albino, pearled (a new variety with patterned markings on a light ground), pied and cinnamon. Albinos are sometimes mistaken for

Lutinos because some specimens show a strong yellowish wash over parts of their plumage. In fact, normally-coloured birds also have a yellow wash which varies in its area and intensity of shade. The albino factor is sex-linked, as is the pearled. The pied factor is recessive and the amount of white varies considerably. It is thought that it may be possible over a period of time, by careful selective pairings, to evolve pure white birds with normal eyes. With regard to the reported Cinnamons, these should really be called Fawns in keeping with the naming of white-ground birds. No details of this mutation is available. As in all Cinnamon (Fawn) birds this factor is likely to be sex-linked.

King Parakeet (*Alisterus s. scapularis*)
Syn: King Lory, Red Lory
COCK Overall length about 15 in (38 cm). Eyes yellowish. Beak orange red above, darker below. Head, neck and underparts bright scarlet. Wings deep green with light green stripes. Rump and narrow band at back of neck a deep blue. Tail black. Feet and legs grey.
HEN Head and upper parts green. Throat and top part of breast green shaded with red. Stomach bright red. Rump blue. Tail greenish black.

These birds are more heavily built than the rosellas, with long wedge-shaped tails and vivid colouring. They are rather slow as breeders and need time to settle down in new quarters, which should be spacious for these rather clumsily-flying birds. King Parakeets are reasonably hardy but should have some extra protection during cold weather. Their life expectancy is quite long, about 15 to 20 years, and this counter-balances their slow breeding potential. Nesting boxes should be of the log type and large in size and it has been found beneficial to provide the breeding pairs with a choice of sites. The first breeding in Britain was recorded in 1876 and, although a few examples are produced each year in various countries, the demand is always greater than the supply.

Princess Alexandra Parakeet (*Polytelis alexandrae*)
Syn: Princess of Wales Parakeet, Queen Alexandra Parakeet
COCK Overall length about 17 in (43 cm). Eyes light brown. Beak bright red, lighter at tip. Forehead, top of head and nape pale blue. Back of neck and mantle olive green. Cheeks and throat rosy pink. Breast and stomach greyish green with pink at thighs. Wing coverts yellowish green. Rump violet. The two long central tail feathers are olive green and the others washed with pink. Feet and legs dark grey.

HEN Paler in colour and a little smaller in size.

This is a large, beautiful pastel-shaded parakeet that looks rather spectacular when part of a large flight. Although the soft colouring makes it appear rather delicate, healthy, well-bred specimens are quite tough. It belongs to the same genus as the Rock Pebbler and should be managed in the same way (see p.129). Being such graceful aviary birds they are always in demand and fortunately, although fairly rare, most pairs reproduce quite freely, and thus the stocks are steadily expanding. Clutches of eggs vary from four to six and the hens start incubating usually after the second egg and sit for about three weeks. The cocks are most attentive in feeding their incubating mates. Care must always be taken to avoid close inbreeding which will quickly weaken the strain.

Red-rumped Parakeet (*Psephotus haematonotus*) Plate 55
Syn: Blood-rumped Parakeet, Red-backed Parakeet
COCK Overall length about 12 in (30 cm). Eyes dark brown. Beak blackish horn. General colour vivid green, lighter on head and darker on back. Underparts green turning to yellow towards vent. Rump deep red. Wings blue green with yellow and blue edges. Tail dark blue, lighter on underside. Feet and legs greyish.
HEN Much duller than cock with green of a brownish shade. Red on rump is absent.

Two subspecies, *P. h. caeruleus* and *P. h. haematonotus*, are known in the wild and the two forms have been blended to give the domesticated race. One of the most widely kept of all parakeets, they were first bred in Britain in the late 1850s. A few years later they were reported as breeding in a number of establishments in Europe and since then have gradually spread to aviaries all over the world. Their popularity is understandable as they are pleasingly coloured, simple to sex even in nest feather, very hardy, and reproduce well in a much smaller aviary space than many other species of the same size. I have a pair that have given me forty-six young in the last five years and this is by no means a breeding record for the species. When breeding they must be kept in single pairs as they do not allow other parrot-like birds in their enclosure. They do not object to other small birds in their aviary and in fact they seem to enjoy their company. I usually keep a pair of Zebra Finches with my Redrump breeding pairs and it is amusing to see one of the former sidle up to a Redrump and cheekily pull out a small feather for its nest. This behaviour does not seem to annoy or trouble the larger birds and they do not even punish the liberty with a peck.

A few years ago a dilute mutation occurred, now universally known as Yellow although it is not the same yellow factor known in Budgerigars, but a pastel form of the normal Redrump. The original hen from which all Yellow Redrumps have descended was a wild bird imported into Britain by the late Duke of Bedford. This bird was loaned to Keston Foreign Bird Farm, England, where the strain was fixed and developed. There are reports that a cinnamon form has been bred. In such a free breeding domesticated species as the Redrumps, other mutations may occur.

There are several related species but at present stock is not often available.

Rock Pebbler Parakeet *(Polytelis anthopeplus)*
Syn: Black-tailed Parakeet, Regent Parrot
COCK Overall length about 16 in (40 cm). Eyes light hazel. Beak red. General colour rich deep yellow with head washed with olive green and olive green on back. Wings blackish with some yellow and deep red. Tail dark blue black. Feet and legs blackish grey.
HEN More olive brown than yellow. Tail green with light rose-pink edging.

A sturdy, plump looking, long-tailed parakeet with a rather unusual, but most attractive colour pattern. They are quiet in temperament and quickly settle down in an aviary, which should be spacious enough to accommodate these rather large birds. Rock Pebbler Parakeets have been breeding in captivity for a very long time and most pairs make excellent parents. The clutches of eggs are five or six, only one clutch per season being laid. These birds are desirable additions to an aviary in all respects, and blend in with the vivid red colours of the broadtails. There is a subspecies in which the cock birds are greener and the hens are lighter. The two kinds have been crossed a number of times and the young hybrids raised successfully.

SOUTH AMERICAN PARAKEETS
These parakeets, which are not all confined to South America – some ranging to Central America and Mexico – are generally known as conures and conurine parakeets.

CONURES
There are a considerable number of species and subspecies of conures, all needing the same kind of treatment. Some are quite common in captivity, others rare, and some practically unknown in private collections. Hybrids between species have been bred from time to time. They differ in several ways from both Asian and Australian parakeets; their heads are large and their beaks quite big and powerful but their bodies are slender and they have long tapering tails. Their voices are, in most cases, rather loud and harsh. When acclimatized they are very hardy, take extremely well to cage and aviary life, are easy to feed, and generally make fine individual pets although most species do not seem to breed freely in captivity. They vary in size, with the largest being about 20 in (51 cm) overall length and the smallest about 9 in (23 cm). The main colourings are various shades of green decorated with white, yellow, orange, red or blue, with a few species having golden yellow as their basic colour.

Brown-eared Conure *(Aratinga pertinax ocularis)*
Syn: Veraguan Conure
COCK Overall length about 9½ in (24 cm). Eyes dark brown. Beak dark horn. General colour green, darker on upper parts. Forehead and top of head washed with blue and face, cheeks and throat brownish with the feathers having a yellow centre. Flight and tail feathers dark with blue tinting. Feet and legs dark grey.
HEN Coloured as cock so difficult to distinguish from it.

This is the most popular of a small group of closely related species and comes from Panama, where it is reasonably common. Although birds of this species are inclined to be nervous when first acquired, with gentle handling they will quickly become tame and friendly. Their call notes are not as harsh as some of the other conures and thus are rather more suitable for aviary collections. Brown-eared Conures have been bred on a number of occasions in both Europe and America, but they cannot be described as free breeders.

Golden-crowned Conure *(A. a. aurea)*
COCK Overall length about 11 in (28 cm). Eyes golden brown. Beak dark horn. General colour greenish olive on upper parts, yellowish green below. Forehead and crown yellow orange with yellow around the eyes. Wings and tail green and blue with some blackish shading. Feet and legs dark grey.
HEN Similar to cock but a little paler in colour throughout.

This Brazilian species is slightly larger than the Brown-eared Conure and a trifle more colourful. They do well in outdoor aviaries, being hardy and of a contented nature; a single young bird will make an excellent pet and with patience many have been taught to mimic a few words. Golden-crowned Conures breed well in large

Jenday Conure, cock

and small aviaries and when pairs have settled down they will rear young for a number of years. They were first bred in Germany in 1880 and since then young have been produced in many other countries including North America. Breeding pairs should be housed in enclosures on their own. They make first-rate birds for those starting a collection of parakeets.

There is a subspecies (*A. a. major*), which is a larger bird. It too has been bred on a number of occasions in Europe and America although it is not such a free breeder.

Jenday Conure (*A. jendaya*)
Syn: Yellow-headed Conure
COCK Overall length about 12 in (30 cm). Eyes light brown. Beak very dark horn. Head, neck and throat deep bright yellow tinted with reddish orange on forehead, around the eyes and throat. Underparts and lower back

deep orange yellow. Wings and tail green and blue. Feet and legs dark grey.
HEN Same colouring but a little smaller than the cock.

A medium sized and quite colourful conure. It is not pugnacious towards others provided it has sufficient room and is not overcrowded. Jenday Conures are probably the most popular of the more common conure species and are widely kept in most countries. Like the Golden-crowned Conures they have been bred in aviaries for over eighty years. Some breeders are known to have several generations of aviary-bred birds. When nesting the birds must be housed in separate pairs as they will not tolerate other birds near their nesting boxes. Although they are good parents, it is a wise precaution to remove the broods of chicks as soon as they are seen to be feeding on their own.

Nanday Conure (*Nandayus nenday*)
Syn: Black-headed, Black-hooded, Black-masked Conure
COCK Overall length about 12 in (30·5cm). Eyes dark reddish brown. Beak black. General colour a pleasing mixture of greens, black and some vivid red. Head and upper throat soft black. Back of head dark chocolate brown. Upper parts bright green with some blackish shading on chest. Wings blue and black and tail black on the underside and dark bluish green on the top. Thighs vivid red, set off advantageously by blackish-grey feet and legs.
HEN Similar in overall colouring and slighter in build.

This species is well established as a fairly reliable breeding bird once acclimatized and settled in permanent quarters. They have been bred in Great Britain, Europe and America for many decades and these aviary-bred stock are easier to handle than imported specimens. In an aviary they are cheerful birds with reasonable voices and they obtain much enjoyment from climbing about perches and wirework. Their general elegance is an attraction to many bird keepers.

Patagonian Conure (*Cyanoliscus patagonus byroni*)
Syn: Greater Patagonian Conure
COCK Overall length about 20 in (51 cm). Eyes medium red brown. Beak black. General colour soft olive green with some blackish shading and darker green on the upper parts. Forehead and crown almost black which makes the white ring around the eyes very prominent. A band of white runs across the chest; white patches on the wing butts. Stomach yellow with red in the centre. Thighs red. Feet and legs dark grey.

Nanday Conure, cock

HEN Similar to cock in general colouring but head not so bold.

A large, well-proportioned bird which, with its pleasing general colouring, looks quite striking in aviaries where it soon settles down. The availability of this subspecies is variable for it is scarce in its native land of Argentina. For this reason captive pairs should be encouraged to breed. Although it has been bred a number of times in various countries, no serious attempts have been made to develop aviary-breeding strains, which is a pity for it would be a loss to aviculture if this attractive subspecies was allowed to disappear from aviaries. Another subspecies, *C. c. patagonus*, is much like it in colour, but smaller and rather more common.

In the wild state, Patagonian Conures nest in holes made in soft sandstone cliffs, but in aviaries they will use a rotting log or wooden nesting box (see p.151).

Petz's Conure (*Aratinga canicularis*) Plate 56
Syn: Half-moon Conure
COCK Overall length about 9½ in (24 cm). Eyes yellowish brown. Beak dark on the underside and light horn on the upper. The general colour is bright green, deeper on the upper parts and more of an olive shade on the lower. The forehead is barred with orange yellow (hence one of its common names), the crown washed with dull blue and there is dark blue on the flights. Tail greenish, lighter on the underside. Feet and legs greyish.
HEN Of similar colour to the cock, but the orange forehead is slightly duller.

This is an attractive species both as a single household pet or in pairs in garden aviaries. Because single birds soon become tame and friendly and because they are not expensive to buy, this is another popular parrot-like pet in America. Their one failing is that when excited their voices are apt to be raised and become somewhat harsh. When being trained as a pet, it is preferable to obtain a young bird as the adults are difficult to teach – this is so of most species of parrot-like birds.

In aviaries Half-moon Conures are excellent and settle quickly in new quarters. They are active birds, preferring long flying areas, where they are shown to advantage. They have been bred on numerous occasions in Britain, America and Europe, although they do not nest quite as freely as other conures. This may be partially due to the difficulty of ensuring that the breeding pairs are true pairs. I know of one particular pair that have reared young for several seasons in a nest box that was designed for Cockatiels.

Quaker Conure (*Myiopsitta m. monachus*) Plate 58
Syn: Grey-breasted Parakeet, Quaker Parakeet
COCK Overall length about 12 in (30·5cm). Eyes brown. Beak dull pinkish. General colour green, much more yellowish in tone on the flanks and underparts. Forehead, face, throat and breast, a pleasing shade of warm grey; feathers edged with a lighter shade giving a scale-like appearance. Wings green with blue flights. Feet and legs greyish yellow.
HEN Coloured like cock but is a little heavier in head and neck with a stouter and more powerful beak.

Although the colouring of this species is not so bright as that of some conures its quiet shades and scale-like feathers make it rather attractive. Their breeding habits are different from those of the majority of parrot-like birds: instead of building in holes they construct large two-compartment domed nests of twigs and branches. Obviously in an aviary they will need suitably arranged branches on which to build these clumsy nest structures. A breeding pair will need a considerable quantity of different sized twigs and branches, and some stiff grasses. They are reasonably free breeders if given a good sized flighted aviary and a suitable nesting site. In some countries they breed quite well as free birds and for a number of years there has been a small flock of Quakers breeding at liberty in the gardens of Whipsnade Zoological Park, England. In America there are flocks of Quaker Parakeets breeding freely at liberty not only in sub-tropical Florida but also in the quite cold northern states of Wisconsin and Michigan.

The records of Quakers breeding in captivity in Europe go back more than a hundred years and recently many more breeding successes have been reported from other areas. There is a blue form but whether the mutation occurred in captivity or whether it was evolved from a wild blue mutant does not seem to have been recorded. A yellow variety has also been known.

Quaker Conures are the only members of the genus but they do show some variation in the size and distribution of their markings. In the wild they live in very widely separated areas of South America and several subspecies (*M. m. luchsi*, *M. m. cotorra* and *M. m. calita*), all varying slightly, are known. Without doubt domesticated strains of both free-flying and aviary birds could be established by several breeders working in cooperation.

Queen of Bavaria Conure (*Aratinga quarouba*)
Syn: Golden Conure, Yellow Conure
COCK Overall length about 14 in (35 cm). Eyes golden brown. Beak pinkish. The overall colour is a beautiful brilliant rich golden yellow set off by bright green flight feathers. Feet and legs greyish.
HEN Similar to cock.

This is one of the rarest and most sought after species of conure and, like the Sun Conure (*A. solstitialis*), another predominantly orange-yellow species, it is considered to have the most striking colouring. It is very rare for either of these handsome species to be kept as pets because of their scarcity – most available specimens go to aviculturists. Those fortunate enough to have true pairs endeavour to get them to breed and indeed young have been successfully reared on a number of occasions. Because of their desirability and their rarity, both in the wild and in aviaries, concerted efforts are now being made in several countries to establish aviary breeding strains. It is to be hoped that these ventures will be successful, as they do reproduce quite well, and then these beautiful birds will be seen more frequently.

Red-bellied Conure (*Pyrrhura f. frontalis*) Plate 57
COCK Overall length about 10 in (25·5 m). Beak blackish. Eyes orange red. General colour green, chin and breast pale grey green, darker at tips. Narrow chestnut band on forehead, ear patches brownish; patches of red brown on lower back and centre of underparts. Wing coverts washed with blue. Tail copper red at base and tip, underside brownish red. Feet and legs dark grey.
HEN Coloured as cock and therefore difficult to distinguish sexes.

It is difficult to distinguish between this and two other subspecies – Azara's Conure (*P. f. chiripepe*) and Krieg's Conure (*P. f. kriegi*). With colouring that is quietly attractive this species and others of the genus *Pyrrhura* are popular with the aviculturists who specialize in conures. They have been bred in Great Britain, Europe and America, and appear to make good and attentive parents. Breeding is more likely to be successful if the pair is housed on its own in a quiet sheltered aviary. They require the same general management as other conures.

White-eared Conure (*P. l. leucotis*)
COCK Overall length about 9 in (23 cm). Eyes light orange brown. Beak black. Head dark brown with ear coverts white. Forehead and cheek stripes reddish brown. Nape and throat blue. Breast green, striped with black and white. Stomach green, red brown in centre. General colour of upper wings, flanks and vent dark green with a deep maroon patch on rump. Wings green with some blue. Tail brownish. Feet and legs black.
HEN Coloured as cock; bolder head and beak.

Because of its friendly nature this is one of the most favoured of the smaller conure species. There are four other races (*P. l. pfrimeri, P. l. griseipectus, P. l. emma* and *P. l. auriculares*) that have slightly different colour patterns according to the area from which they come. They make good aviary birds and once settled in flighted aviaries, even quite small ones, they will usually breed. They are of a docile temperament and make conscientious parents, even after the young are able to fend for themselves. As household pets they are easy to train, will learn to repeat a few words and some become extremely tame and will let their owners handle them freely. I know of one cock bird which after being a house pet for some years, was given a mate and put into an aviary and in due course the pair raised young on several occasions. The first pair I owned were wild-caught birds but after a few weeks they were completely finger tame. Although they did not breed while I had them, later they did so.

CONURINE PARAKEETS

There are about sixteen species and subspecies in this group. They are smaller than the conures to which they are closely related, ranging from 6–9 in (15–23 cm) in overall length and like their relatives, are mainly green in colour. Although their plumage is not particularly brilliant they are popular in America, where they are kept as pets, as well as in other countries. This popularity is because of their docile nature, the ease with which they can be fed, the fact that most can be quickly tamed and some can be taught to mimic a few simple words. When acclimatized they are hardy and have a life expectancy of 12 to 15 years. They are amusing to watch in aviaries and some pairs will breed satisfactorily. Although reasonably friendly towards other birds, breeding pairs should be kept in separate enclosures.

Bee Bee Parakeet (*Brotogeris jugularis*)
Syn: Bee Bee Parrot, Orange-chinned Parakeet, Tovi Parakeet
COCK Overall length about 7½ in (19 cm). Eyes brown. Beak horn coloured. General colour green, lighter on the underparts. Wings green with some brown shading and blue on flights. Chin has bright orange spot. Feet and legs greyish.
HEN Coloured like the cock but generally a little larger.
There are two subspecies, *B. j. exsul* and *B. j. apurensis*, of this extremely popular little parakeet which vary slightly in colour shades and size, but all have the same endearing ways. The vast majority of Bee Bee Parakeets are kept as pets, either as single birds or pairs. Although the pairs

may not always be a cock and a hen they are compatible, but it is rather difficult to make two birds equally tame as there is a jealousy factor. A single bird or pair enjoy the liberty of a room and provide their owners with much enjoyment. However, it is not really safe to leave free-flying birds on their own for any length of time as they may have the urge to gnaw some prized possessions!

They have been bred in aviaries for many years but because of the ease with which they could be obtained and their rather sombre colouring, parakeet breeders have not been attracted to them. They are equally at home in aviaries and cages and they like to sleep in a box or hollow log. The provision of such a sleeping place is essential with newly acquired birds as it takes time for them to become fully acclimatized. When a pair does go to nest they are mostly successful in rearing their young.

Canary-winged Parakeet (*B. versicolorus chiriri*) Plate 59
COCK Overall length about 9 in (23 cm). Eyes brown. Beak pale horn colour. General colour green, lighter on the underparts and darker on the wings which also have some blue shading. Primary wing feathers bright rich yellow. Tail greenish with some blue. Feet and legs pale pinkish.
HEN Similar to cock and difficult to sex.

This is a larger species than the Bee Bee Parakeet and has a correspondingly louder voice, which is one of their minor failings. In spite of the noise they can make when excited or frightened many owners find that they can be trained to become very friendly if kept singly and become much attached to their owners, who can teach them to perform simple tricks. Most of these tame birds will learn to repeat a few simple words in a quiet clear tone.

Their bright yellow wing colouring is seen to its best advantage when the birds are flying in outdoor aviaries. They like to climb about the highest perches and the top of the wire flights. Canary-wings have been bred for a number of years in Britain, Europe and America, and they are said to make most satisfactory parents but this attribute can vary considerably.

Tui Parakeet (*B. st thoma*) Plate 60
COCK Overall length about 7 in (18 cm). Eyes brown. Beak dark horn colour. General colour mainly green, paler on rump and underparts. Forehead bright yellow with yellow stripes behind eyes and surrounding areas washed with blue. Wings and tail shaded with blue. Feet and legs greyish.
HEN Similar to cock in colour but without yellow stripes behind eyes.

These are generally thought by aviculturists to be the most pleasing in colour of the whole group. The Tui Parakeet has a delightful temperament, living harmoniously with other birds, but it is rather pugnacious towards related species. As aviary birds they are hardy, and amusingly playful. Young have been raised on a number of occasions but this species is not considered to be a free breeder. A single bird as a household pet will quickly settle and become very friendly and tame. Tui Parakeets can be obtained at reasonable cost.

White-winged Parakeet (*B. v. versicolorus*)
COCK Overall length about 9 in (23 cm). Eyes brown. Beak horn colour. General colour dark grass green on upper parts, yellowish green on underparts. Forehead and cheeks washed with bluish grey. Wings, outer flights black with blue at tips and on edges, inner flights green and blue. Secondaries white with some yellowish tinting. Major wing coverts yellow. Tail greenish, lighter on underside. Feet and legs brownish.
HEN Similar to cock in colour and difficult to sex.

This is another quite friendly species but it has not become as popular as other conurines perhaps because, unlike the Canary-winged, which can be sexed at a glance, it is rather difficult to distinguish between the cock and the hen. In other respects the White-winged is similar to the Canary-winged and requires the same general management.

HOUSING

Most pet parakeets should be housed in either large wooden wire-fronted box cages or all-wire, traditional parrot cages. The type used depends largely on the species and on the siting of the cage. The box type should be of a stouter construction than those commonly used for Canaries or Budgerigars. Specially made wire fronts can be purchased from bird stores or made from heavy gauge, welded square wire mesh. The box cages should be painted, inside and out, with white emulsion paint.

The seed, water and grit pots should be heavy and firmly fixed to the cage so as to prevent the birds from turning them over. The perches are best made of natural bark-covered wood and fixed so that they can be easily replaced when necessary. The best covering for the cage floors is washed sand or fine gravel. All cages should have a large door to facilitate cleaning and for training the birds to become finger tame.

As noted in the separate descriptions, most species need to be housed in separate enclosures during their breeding season. This means that parakeet-breeding aviaries are best built in blocks of four, six, eight or even more, according to the requirements of the breeder. An important element in all such breeding aviaries are the flights, which need not be wide provided they are long (see illustrations). For the species of the grass parakeet size, the width can be 2 ft 6 in (76 cm) to 3 ft (91 cm) and about 9 ft (2·75 m) to 12 ft (3·7 m) long. Of course, all types of buildings can be adapted to make flighted aviaries and the best way to convert such buildings must be left to the ingenuity of the individual breeder.

The shelter areas of the aviaries can be made of brick, manufactured blocks, reinforced fibre glass, manufactured sheetings, wooden boards, or a mixture of these materials. All windows on the flight side of any aviary must be covered with wire screens to prevent the inmates from damaging themselves or escaping. A safety porch (see illustration) should be fitted to all outside entrance doors to prevent the birds escaping. Many valuable birds have been lost by flying over the heads of their owners as they entered the aviaries. Where it is not possible to erect such a porch, all entrance doors should be low, with about 2–3 ft (61–91 cm) of wire netting between the top of the door and the flight roof.

I have observed that a greater degree of success in breeding Asian parakeets is achieved if their aviaries are somewhat higher than normal structures. The conures, too, always seem to prefer being in the highest parts of the aviaries. On the other hand the Australian parakeets do not appear to need height provided the flights are long. Flighted aviaries used for Budgerigars may, in many cases, be adapted for breeding parakeets.

Seed, water and grit vessels should not be kept on the floor, but placed on a small shelf or table situated in the sheltered part of the aviary. The perches, which should be made of heavy dowelling or tree branches, must be firmly fixed and clear of all vessels. If the floors of the flights are covered with grass (which should always be kept trimmed), strips should be cut away from beneath the main perches and filled with sand or fine gravel. This prevents the grass becoming messy and looking unsightly from the droppings. The same considerations apply in the larger aviaries used for housing young or non-breeding birds. In such communal aviaries large rotting logs placed in the centre of the flight floors will create a more natural habitat, giving them much pleasure and their owners amusement from watching their antics.

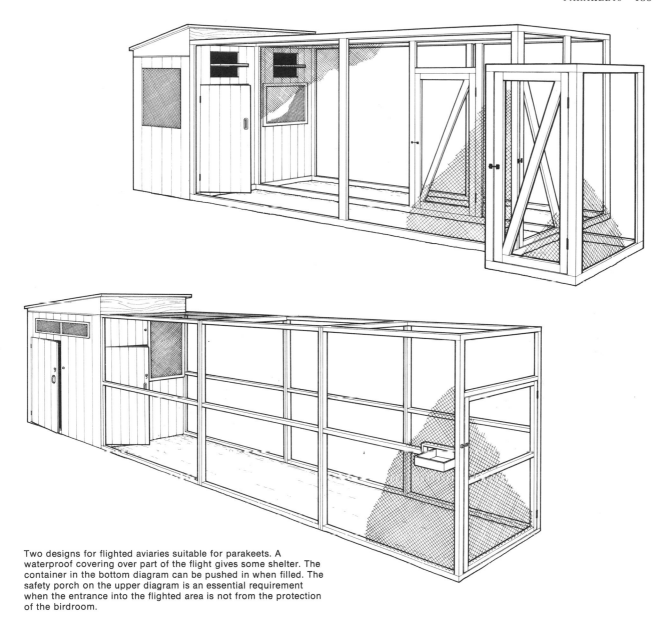

Two designs for flighted aviaries suitable for parakeets. A waterproof covering over part of the flight gives some shelter. The container in the bottom diagram can be pushed in when filled. The safety porch on the upper diagram is an essential requirement when the entrance into the flighted area is not from the protection of the birdroom.

Invariably, when young parakeets leave their nests they will, for a time, be uncertain of their surroundings and fly rather blindly about their aviaries. Should any of them fly into a sharp flight corner-support or strike a flight cross-member serious casualties can occur. To lessen the likelihood of this danger (which exists for adults too should they be suddenly startled by unaccustomed sounds or lights) the corners of all projecting woodwork should be rounded. This danger can, however, be virtually removed by fixing the wire mesh to the inside of the supports instead of to the outside.

The sheltered sections and the flights themselves should be cleaned regularly throughout the year except when the hens are laying and rearing their young. It will not matter if these areas get untidy during that period; it is more important that the birds are not disturbed. Any decorating and repair work is best carried out during the early part of the winter so that breeding birds can settle down in their clean quarters before the breeding season starts.

FEEDING

The seeds used in the mixtures that form the basic diet of all parakeet species are the same, but the proportions vary. For the owners of several different species it is best to buy the seeds loose in their separate kinds. This will allow mixtures to be blended to the requirements of each species and the quantities of each seed adjusted when necessary. For instance, if it were found that a certain pair of birds were continually rejecting one particular variety of seed it could be removed from their mixture and thus avoid waste. Most seed stores supply loose parakeet seed mixtures for general use and for the owner of a single bird this is the best way to obtain the seed. Should any special ingredient be needed in the blend, the seed stores will add it at the owner's request.

When the seed is bought in bulk it should be carefully stored in metal, plastic or wooden containers that have tightly fitting lids. To prevent an accumulation of stale seed it is essential that the containers are emptied completely before adding a new supply. It is most important that only good fresh seed is available to the birds at all times, if they are to be maintained in a fully healthy condition. Stale seed loses some of its nutritious value and, of course, stale or sour seeds, if eaten by the birds, can quickly cause upset stomachs. All vessels used for holding seeds, whether in cages or aviaries, should be emptied and cleaned regularly.

The chief seeds used in blending are sunflower, which is available as white, black or striped, canary seed (the large type is best), various millet seeds, oats and other cereals. Other mixtures contain hemp, paddy rice, dari and buckwheat. A good mixture for Asian parakeets can be made up of four parts sunflower, two parts large canary, one part white millet and one part a mixture of hemp, oats, large yellow millet, safflower and panicum millet. The proportions can be varied to suit individual pairs, different species, and the time of year. Additionally, the birds require a regular supply of soft fruits, such as sweet apples, pears, grapes, small ripe tomatoes, etc. The birds will also eat the bark and chew the wood of thin branches from fruit and willow trees.

When the pairs are breeding they will need some form of soft food in addition to the diets described. A good soft food can be made by mixing one of the patent Canary

rearing foods and a medium grade insectivorous mixture in equal proportions. This should be fresh and given daily in a crumbly, moist state. This part of their diet can be varied by giving moistened wholemeal bread, or freshly sprouting seeds of canary, grass, oats, maize (corn), wheat or barley. None of these foods should be allowed to become stale – any left uneaten should be removed from the aviary or cage at the end of the day. Although parakeets eat greenfoods they generally prefer fruits. Some breeders also give their breeding pairs, when they are feeding their chicks, a few mealworms or gentles (maggots). I have not given these to my birds but it is likely that they would be a very useful addition to the diet.

Mixed grits consisting of crushed limestone, flint and oyster shells should always be available in cages or aviaries. Pieces of cuttlefish bone, large prepared mineral blocks, and lumps of soft wood complete with bark will all help to keep the birds occupied and prevent their beaks from getting overlong. Although parrot-like birds do not drink very much, a fresh clean supply of water must always be available. The water will be used for both drinking and bathing and, to prevent newly fledged young from drowning, should be provided in shallow dishes. When young are in the nest boxes the consumption of water is greatly increased and the pots must not be allowed to become dry.

The Australian parakeets mostly eat the same kinds of seeds as the Asian species, although the mixture is slightly different. I have found that Australian birds do well on mixed sunflower seed and large canary seed, together with hemp, oats, white, yellow and panicum millets. A good mixture is: two parts mixed sunflower, two parts large canary, and one part mixed hemp, oats and millets. The Australian species are especially fond of millet sprays and, if allowed to do so, will consume large quantities. Some breeders, myself included, give the seeds in separate dishes – sunflower in one, canary in another, and the other mixed seeds in a third. Other breeders supply all the seeds in one dish on the basis that the birds have a better chance of a more balanced diet. I find that with separate pots the birds eat only what they want and form their own balance; there is no indication that they eat only one kind and reject the rest. Whichever method is used, they will often eat the hemp seed first and then go on to the others.

Unlike the Asian parakeets, the Australian species are not particularly partial to fruits, their preference being various fresh greenfoods. They like seeding grasses, chickweed and spinach best, but they will also eat shepherd's purse, sow thistle, lettuce, Brussels sprouts, cabbage, chicory and watercress. Sprouted seeds are a good winter standby and are also a useful addition during breeding time. Mixed grits, cuttlefish bone, mineral blocks, and dried crushed domestic hens' egg shells should always be provided. Australian parakeets enjoy bathing and the necessary facilities for this should be provided in addition to their drinking vessels.

The conures and conurines also eat most of the seeds that the Asian and Australian parakeets do but with some additions. The chief mixture is made up of two parts mixed sunflower and safflower, one part canary seed and one part mixed yellow and white millets, oats, rye, corn (maize) and hemp. They like most soft fruits and some greenfoods, such as cabbage, lettuce and chicory, carrots, garden peas and beans. At breeding times some species like boiled carrots and potatoes mixed with insectivorous or Canary soft food. They will also eat wholemeal bread moistened with fresh milk. These soft foods must be fresh, any left uneaten being removed at the end of the day.

They need the same grits and minerals as other parakeet species together with some bark-covered branches from fruit trees for gnawing. Most species do not seem very keen on bathing but they do enjoy an occasional fine spraying. Fresh clean water must always be provided. Whereas Asian and South American parakeets spend much of their time climbing about and gnawing the branch perches, the Australians spend a great deal of time on the floor of the flight pecking about in the grass, sand or gravel.

The diet of all species should be as varied as possible to ensure the intake of vitamins and mineral elements necessary for good health.

BREEDING

The main principles for the successful breeding of all parakeets in captivity are much the same. Certain details differ according to the location and design of the aviaries, and the types of birds housed in them. The breeding pairs should consist of only fully matured, well-developed, healthy stock that are fully acclimatized to outdoor aviary life. Poor quality, defective, or ailing birds should not be used as this will only frustrate and disappoint the owner. Should there be any doubt about the age of a bird it is more sensible to wait a further season than risk using an immature specimen. Relationships must be carefully recorded to avoid close inbreeding. The deterioration of many aviary breeding strains in the past has been traced to close uncontrolled inbreeding.

If the birds, both adult and young, are not already closed-ringed this can be rectified by the use of split metal rings. Split rings do occasionally come off but most are retained by the birds all their lives, giving a reasonably permanent mark of identification. Closed metal rings put on the legs of young birds are better but it may not always be possible to achieve this; should the adults be unduly disturbed by the opening of their nest boxes it is much more practical to use split rings. Some species of parakeets such as the Red-rumped, the Cockatiel and Bourke's are quite domesticated and do not object to the inspection of their boxes by their owners provided it is not done too often. I have always found that the best time to close ring any species of bird is when they are being given their morning feed. The owner is expected at that time of day and a quick inspection and ringing will pass almost unnoticed by the birds. All numbers, year dates and codes on the rings, both closed and split, should be carefully entered in a stock record book with particulars of the birds carrying them. When any parakeets are sold the relevant details and ring numbers should be given to the new owner.

The siting of the nest boxes for the individual breeding pairs is extremely important and is controlled to some extent by the type and situation of the aviary. For the Asian parakeets it is usual to hang the boxes as near to the top of the flights as possible. These, with weatherproof coverings such as bitumenized felt, can be hung in the all-wire sections or at the partly covered ends of the flights. The nest boxes can be left in position all the year and, after any chicks have been reared, cleaned, repaired if necessary, and returned to their original position. The reason the boxes are hung outside is to allow the wood to absorb moisture, which helps the eggs to keep in a good condition and not become too dry, thereby preventing them hatching. Over-dryness of eggs is the cause of a large number of hatching failures (this is so in all species of birds). Nest boxes are heavy and must be fixed securely.

Experience has shown that the long grandfather clock type of wooden nest boxes are the most practical for the aviary breeding of parakeets. If old rotting logs are used it is almost impossible to inspect the nests and they cannot be cleaned when this is necessary. The boxes are best made of thick unplaned boards with some bark on them, with a 4 in (10 cm) entrance hole at the top and an inspection door at the front or side of the lower part. See illustration on p.151 for design.

Concave nest bottoms like those used for Budgerigars are not necessary for parakeets; instead they require a good thick layer of peat, rotting wood, small wood chippings, coarse sawdust or a mixture of these. The turf, 2 in

(5 cm) thick should be cut to fit and put in first, soil side up, followed by the peat, rotting wood, etc., to a depth of about 5 in (13 cm), and the whole packed well down. The birds can then dig out their own nest hollows where it suits them. To ensure that the adult birds and later their young can easily climb in and out of the long-necked grandfather clock nest boxes, wooden slats or wire netting should be fixed on the inside.

Most Asian parakeets start their breeding operations early in the year and their clutches vary from three to five and are laid on alternate days. The incubation period is about twenty-one days with the hens doing all the sitting. The cock birds feed their hens during this time and continue feeding them and their young until the hens think it safe to leave their chicks and feed themselves. Young birds leave the nests when forty to fifty days old – the time varies in individual nests and in different species. After they have left the nest boxes the young are fed by their parents for several weeks. As soon as the young are able to fend for themselves they should be moved so as not to upset their parents. As soon as the chicks are hatched the adult birds will need soft food and an increased amount of fresh ripe fruit in addition to their normal seed mixture.

The smaller Australian parakeets require a nest box different from that used for Asian parakeets: about 9 in (23 cm) square and about 15 in (38 cm) high with a 3 in (8 cm) entrance hole near the top. A piece of rough wood or bark can be fixed just below the hole to serve as an entrance perch. The larger parakeets such as rosellas need boxes of similar design with a bigger all-round measurement and a 4 in (10 cm) entrance hole. Some breeders give their rosellas the grandfather clock nest boxes with a 30 in (76 cm) tunnel entrance. Whichever type is chosen the bottom should be covered in the same manner as described for the Asian parakeets.

Most Australian parakeets are double brooded and their clutches of eggs range from four to six with an incubation period of eighteen to twenty-one days according to species. Both parents share the feeding of their chicks and need extra greenfoods as well as their normal seed diet. Most species will appreciate a certain amount of soft food during this period. It is much safer to take the young away from their parents as soon as they are seen to be feeding on their own.

Conures are usually given the rectangular wooden nest boxes similar to those used by the Australian parakeets. The birds seem to prefer having them hung high in the sheltered part of the flights. Sometimes a pair will refuse to go near a wooden nest box but if a large piece of rotting

Parent Cockatiel outside a nest box of the kind that can be used for Australian parakeets

log is offered they will at once dig out a nest and proceed to lay. Their incubation period, the feeding of their young, etc., are similar to that of the Asian parakeets.

In certain domesticated species colour mutations have arisen and have been perpetuated by breeders. All lutino, albino and cinnamon forms and the Yellow Redrumps are produced by sex-linked characters which are inherited following the rules given on p.105 in the section on Budgerigars. The characters that give the yellow, pied or blue mutations are inherited recessively, following the rules on p.104.

Colour breeding in the ringnecks is a slow process because the birds do not come into breeding condition until they are three years old. If several breeders owning similar mutations cooperate and pool their resources results can be obtained much more quickly. Australian parakeets mature far earlier and are usually ready for breeding in their second season – another reason for their popularity.

Parrots and Allied Species

The princes and nobles of the Indian subcontinent were among the first people to keep and breed parrot-like birds in captivity. Indeed, the enthusiasm for parrot-like birds dates back to some of the earliest civilizations (it is known that the Romans and Ancient Egyptians kept birds, probably ringnecks). South America is rich in parrot-like species and some of them must have reached Europe soon after the Spanish explorations. They quickly became extremely popular in Europe as single household pets – for obvious reasons: their great gift of mimicry (shared only by mynahs), their beautiful colours, and their longevity. Members of the parrot family are usually more expensive to buy than many other species but their life expectancy compensates for this. It is not unusual for a parrot to be a pet through three generations of owners (I know of an African Grey Parrot that was bought as an adult in 1912, and is now owned by the grandson of the original purchaser). At a cage bird exhibition in the winter of 1972–3, a Sulphur-crested Cockatoo which was about fifty years old was shown. The larger parrots take even longer to mature than the Asian parakeets discussed in the previous chapter, and thus the formation of aviary breeding strains is a slow process.

Although parrots have been kept as pets for hundreds of years it is only in the last few decades that the breeding in captivity of the larger members of the family has been seriously attempted on a world-wide scale. In the latter part of the nineteenth and beginning of the twentieth centuries a few successful breedings of a limited number of species were recorded in Britain and Europe. Since the end of World War II interest in parrot breeding has steadily multiplied and this has resulted in a marked increase in the number of individuals and species bred. In Britain, the Parrot Society was formed in the early 1960s to encourage the breeding of parrots and parrot-like birds in captivity.

The following members of the parrot family are discussed below: parrots, cockatoos, lories and lorikeets, macaws, and lovebirds (the latter are true parrots in spite of their smaller size and should not be confused with Budgerigars which are grass parakeets). There are a great many species of seed-eating parrot-like birds other than the groups mentioned above – all of which need the same treatment. Also, there exist a considerable number of nectar- and fruit-eating kinds including the lories, lorikeets and the hanging parrots. These species should be acquired only by bird lovers who have had considerable experience with the seed-eating kinds as they need specialist care and treatment to maintain them in good feather and health.

PARROTS

African Grey Parrot (*Psittacus erithacus*) Plate 61
Syn: Grey Parrot, Red-tailed Grey Parrot
COCK Overall length about 13 in (33 cm). Eyes light yellow. Beak black. Large white area of skin around the eyes. Basic colour soft shades of grey, darker on the upper parts and wings and paler on the underparts; the breast feathers have light edges giving a scaly effect. Tail short and bright red. Feet and legs dark grey.

HEN Like the cock, less heavy in build; difficult to sex.

Of all the large parrots the African Grey makes the most desirable pet. The prowess of African Greys as talking birds has been known for hundreds of years, indeed their ability to accurately mimic the human voice and other sounds is quite astounding. With sensible management they will become attached to their owners and allow themselves to be handled quite freely. They can become friendly with other family pets, such as cats and dogs, and it is not unusual to see them playing happily together.

For training purposes it is always best to have young birds since fully adult specimens take far more time and patience to tame and train. Young birds can be identified by their dark grey eyes – fully adult birds have eyes of a pale straw colour. When first obtained most birds will have had their flight feathers clipped on one or both wings to prevent escape. These cut feathers will fall out and be replaced by new ones when the birds moult, approximately every twelve months. Newly imported birds need special care until they are fully acclimatized, but after this period (six to eight months) they will give no trouble.

Most birds kept as household pets are housed in either round or square traditional all-wire parrot cages although they can be kept on a 'T' stand.

Reports of African Greys nesting and rearing young in captivity have become more frequent, no doubt due to the attention being paid to breeding in order to conserve and increase its stocks. Breeding pairs must of course be suitably housed and given the right kind of nesting receptacles (see p.151). Parrot aviaries must be made of very strong materials, including heavy gauge wire, nesting boxes of stout boards or large hollow logs (see Breeding, p.151). Once a pair have started to nest in an aviary they will do so regularly for many years and produce fine healthy young. Aviary-bred birds are ideal for training as tame, talking household pets.

A subspecies of the African Grey is the Timneh Grey Parrot (*P. e. timneh*) which is darker grey with a maroon coloured tail. It is about 1 in (2·5 cm) shorter than the African Grey. Individuals are occasionally offered for sale in bird shops – they need the same treatment as their near relatives.

Blue-fronted Amazon (*Amazona a. aestiva*)
Syn: Turquoise-fronted Parrot
COCK Overall length about 14 in (36 cm). Eyes medium brown. Beak blackish. General colour grass green, lighter on the underparts. Forehead bright turquoise blue. Throat and sides of head pale lemon yellow. Shoulders scarlet. Flight blue, red and green. Tail green with some red markings. Feet and legs grey.
HEN Similar to cock in colour with a little less scarlet on shoulders and a smaller head.

This is a popular member of the large Amazon genus which has a wide distribution in South America. The amount of blue and yellow on the head of this species varies according to the age of the bird and its original location. Although this species is quite commonly kept in Europe it is less frequently found in North American homes. Its talent for mimicry is excellent and it is often claimed to be a serious rival to the African Grey. When taken as young birds Blue-fronted Amazons can be tamed very quickly and allowed out of their cages for exercise. Most specimens have a gentle nature that makes them ideal as family pets. During the last forty years records of their breeding in aviaries have been reported periodically, but they cannot be described as free-breeding in captivity.

Double Yellow-headed Amazon (*A. ochrocephala oratrix*)
Syn: Double-fronted Amazon, Levaillant's Amazon, Mexican Double Yellow-headed Amazon.
COCK Overall length about 15 in (38 cm). Eyes light yellow. Beak pale horn. The general colour is bright green, a little darker on the upper parts. Head yellow, neck yellow and yellow flecked green. There are red areas on shoulders, wings and tail and also blue in the wings. Tail shades of green. Feet and legs greyish.
HEN Similar to cock in colour, usually a little smaller but with a broader beak. Difficult to sex.

These attractively coloured Amazons are great favourites in America, undoubtedly because their natural home is in Mexico. Examples of Levaillant's Amazons, as they are sometimes called, are quite rare in Europe although they are highly regarded as pets. Their ability to mimic is excellent and although they are large, strongly built birds they are docile once their full confidence has been gained. Young birds show much less yellow on the head area than fully adult specimens and until they are about ten or twelve years old the amount of yellow increases annually. The price of young, untrained birds is reasonable and stock is particularly plentiful in America. It would appear that because of the ease with which these birds can be obtained extremely few attempts have been made to breed them. However, some fine specimens have been bred in Californian aviaries during the past few years and the results indicate that the birds are satisfactory parents.

Festive Amazon (*A. f. festiva*)
COCK Overall length about 14 in (36 cm). Eyes light greyish. Beak horn. General colour green, deeper on upper parts and slightly paler on underparts. Forehead rich plum red. Eye stripes and chin blue. Lower back and rump red. Wings green with some black shading, flights blue. Tail dull green with yellow at tips. Feet and legs greyish.
HEN Similar to cock in colour but a little smaller in build.

This is a popular species among European parrot lovers but does not find a great deal of favour in North America. The birds are liked not so much for their power of mimicry as for their exceedingly friendly and amenable natures. They mimic clearly but the number of words and phrases they can learn is limited. When taken into the household as young birds it is usually only a matter of days before their owners can start handling them freely. Fully adult birds take longer to tame though they too quickly respond to gentle treatment. Because of their friendly disposition it would be reasonable to assume that Festive Amazons would make suitable birds for breeding purposes, but this is not the case – breeding pairs are rare. For owners who prefer tame friendly birds to colourful ones this species is highly recommended.

Grand Eclectus Parrot (*Lorius r. roratus*) Plate 62
Syn: Eclectus Parrot, Temple Parrot
COCK Overall length about 16 in (41 cm). Eyes dark brown. Beak, upper part red with yellow on tip, lower part black. General colour bright rich green on the upper parts, paler towards the head. Breast, patches of red at sides. Underwing coverts red. Upper side of tail green with blue and white tips, underside bluish black tipped with yellow. Feet and legs greyish.
HEN About the same length as cock but more powerfully built. Eyes dark. Beak black. Head and breast bright red. Stomach and nape of neck blue. Wings rich maroon with undersides shaded with maroon, blue and green. Flight feathers blackish. Vent red. Tail, upper side maroon, shaded to orange at tips. Feet and legs greyish.

This species is unusual in that the hens display brighter, richer and more varied colours than the cocks. Because of the great difference in their colouring, the two sexes were thought at one time to be two separate species. There are some twelve subspecies all having this unusual richness of colour in the hen birds. A further strange feature of this species is that the feathers have the appearance of animal fur that has been combed.

Because Grand Eclectus Parrots are scarce and expensive they are not often kept as single pets although on a few occasions they have proved themselves to be very amenable to the ordinary household life of pet parrots. This aptitude applies to all species in the *Lorius* genus. Most specimens, if housed in fair-sized flighted aviaries, will nest and rear young. A number of successful hatchings and rearings have been recorded in various parts of the world. Before breeding is attempted the birds must be fully adult and well acclimatized to their surroundings. They eat ordinary parrot seed mixtures but also consume far greater quantities of fruit than most parrots, particularly while breeding.

Maximilian's Parrot (*Pionus m. maximiliani*) Plate 63
COCK Overall length about 11 in (28 cm). Beak yellowish horn, darker at base. Eyes yellowish brown. General colour bronze green with the head feathers edged with dark grey and the forehead dusky black. Breast and underparts grey at edges. Chin and band on upper breast purplish blue. Tail feathers marked with brown, blue and red, under tail coverts red. Feet and legs dusky grey.
HEN Coloured like the cock, difficult to sex.

This is a pleasingly coloured member of a genus that is closely related to the Amazons but the species are mostly smaller and stockier in build. Many of the imported specimens are adult birds and take a considerable time to settle down, but once they have become fully used to captivity they are tame and confiding. Although a few true pairs have been kept under breeding conditions they do not appear to have produced any offspring. Another species, the Blue-headed Parrot (*P. menstruus*), has raised young in captivity on several occasions.

Mealy Amazon (*Amazona f. farinosa*)
Syn: Blue-crowned Amazon
COCK Overall length about 16 in (41 cm). Eyes light yellow. Beak pale horn. General colour dull green with a powdery appearance. Head and shoulders green. Crown and back of neck bluish-lilac tint with a patch of dull yellow or orange yellow on the crown. Large red patch on wings. Tail green. Feet and legs pale grey.
HEN Similar to cock.

This species is sometimes confused with a slightly larger species, the true Blue-crowned Amazon (*A. f. guatemalae*), and there are certainly many similarities. Mealy Amazons are more commonly kept in Europe than the Blue-crowned but, interestingly, it is the reverse in America. They are not very brightly coloured, but their soft shades are pleasing. They are easily tamed and most birds make good talkers. In their native Brazil they are very popular as talking pets. Records of Mealy Amazons being bred in captivity do not seem to be available although it is probable that such an amenable species has been bred.

Red-fronted Amazon (*A. v. vittata*) Plate 64
Syn: Puerto Rico Amazon
COCK Overall length about 12 in (30·5 cm). Beak yellowish brown. Eyes yellow. General colour bright green with neck and head feathers edged with black. The

forehead has a narrow red band and there is some red at the base of the outer tail feathers with blue on primary coverts, secondaries and outer flights. Feet and legs brownish.

HEN Coloured like the cock, difficult to sex.

Now threatened with extinction, this subspecies is unlikely to be exported, but many specimens are still to be seen in collections. They need the same treatment as the Blue-fronted Amazon.

Vernal Hanging Parrot *(Loriculus v. vernalis)* Plate 65

COCK Overall length about 6½ in (16·5 cm). Beak red. Eyes yellowish. General colour green, brighter on head with throat deep blue. Rump and upper tail coverts red and tail greenish blue. Feet and legs yellow.

HEN Coloured like the cock but with less blue on the throat.

This species belongs to a group of small, fruit- and nectar-eating parrots that spend a great deal of their time head downwards. They are brightly coloured and are amusing but, because of their copious loose droppings frequently voided, they are rather messy birds to keep. They need some form of heating during cold weather. Owners have found them quite harmless to other birds – even small ones like waxbills; in fact, they are the only parrot-like species that can be safely kept with smaller aviary birds. They would make ideal inmates for a mixed collection of Exotics were it not for their unfortunate excretory habits.

Yellow-bellied Senegal Parrot *(Poicephalus s. senegalus)* Plate 66

Syn: Senegal parrot

COCK Overall length about 10 in (25 cm). Eyes light yellow. Beak blackish. Head and cheeks grey. Neck darker grey. Upper chest and upper parts green. Lower chest yellow shading in centre to rich orange yellow. Flights and tail brownish black edged with green. Feet and legs blackish.

HEN Paler on head, lacking the orange tones on the underparts.

This is a delightful little parrot and, apart from the African Grey, is the most widely kept of all the African parrots in Europe. It is popular in America but it has strong competition from the more easily obtainable Amazon species. There are two other subspecies, the Orange-bellied Senegal Parrot *(P. s. mesotypus)* and the Scarlet-bellied Senegal Parrot *(P. s. versteri)* which are occasionally imported with batches of the more common Yellow-bellied. The differences among the three kinds are confined mainly to the colour of their underparts. Occasionally some specimens show extra yellow areas on neck and back, but it is not known whether this is an individual variation or an inherited pied character.

Senegals are considered by many parrot keepers to be the most gentle and docile of all those that are kept as pet birds. My own experience with them endorses this view. Generally, their talent for imitating the human voice is limited to a few clearly articulated sentences. As with all parrot-like species, the young are best for training, although with patience fully adult birds will become tame. Pairs kept in the same cage will give their owners much amusement by their playful antics.

If given fairly large, strongly built aviaries all three subspecies of Senegal Parrots will breed and raise young. They have a strong inclination to gnaw woodwork so it is essential that thick wood and heavy gauge wire is used in the aviaries' construction. Senegals like to climb and appreciate plenty of thick bark-covered branches placed high in their aviary flights. Being comparatively small they do not require very large nest boxes or nesting logs (see p.151).

Yellow-fronted Amazon *(Amazona o. ochrocephala)* Plate 61

Syn: Colombian Amazon, Single Yellow-headed Amazon, Yellow-headed Amazon

COCK Overall length about 15 in (38 cm). Eyes red. Beak light horn dark at tip. Upper parts bright deep green with dark edging to feathers and lighter green on the underparts. Forehead blue. Crown, cheeks and chin yellow. Wings green. Shoulders red and yellow. Flights blue. Tail yellowish-green on underside. Feet and legs greyish.

HEN Similar to cock in colouring but usually slightly paler.

A fine large colourful bird, strong but docile, hardy, a good mimic of the human voice, with a great capacity for learning sounds. Yellow-fronted Amazons become very attached to their owners and can be allowed long periods out of their cages without any damage being done to the furniture. Like some of their related species they become friendly with domestic cats and dogs and take great delight in calling them in imitation of their owners. Many tales are related by owners regarding the varied exploits of their pets.

Yellow-fronted Amazons have been bred from time to time for a number of years both in Europe and in America. These large birds require big aviaries in which to breed but not many fanciers have such facilities, thus the number of breeding pairs is always limited; those that do breed invariably prove themselves to be good and attentive parents. They are excellent birds either as single pets or for aviary collections.

COCKATOOS

This spectacular family of birds consists of some fifty species and subspecies, all originating from Australia and the South Pacific Islands. All cockatoos have one thing in common – a head crest that can be raised to show either fright, pleasure or anger. They are generally white in colour but a few birds are black or grey, and they vary in size from 12–30 in (30–76 cm). In general they are noisy birds, their natural calls being interspersed with 'human speech' and other noises which they mimic. The same word or words are repeated again and again, particularly when the birds are excited. At such times and when angry they will dance up and down on their perches, flap their wings, or go into all kinds of acrobatic contortions. Whatever else they may be, cockatoos cannot be described as inactive or dull.

Cockatoos are popular in bird gardens and zoological establishments and once acclimatized to such conditions they enjoy the constant stream of visitors to whom they show off. They can be housed in large all-wire parrot cages, on 'T' stands or in very strongly built aviaries. Undoubtedly cockatoos look most striking when kept in aviaries large enough for them to fly freely, with room for a number of different species. The largest species are more suitable for aviary life than as household pets. Individuals of most kinds have been trained as talking family pets. They are intelligent and live to a great age – a hundred years has been reported. Most cockatoos make first-rate breeding birds in captivity.

Great Black Cockatoo (Probosciger aterrimus)
Syn: Palm Cockatoo
COCK Overall length about 30 in (76 cm). Eyes dark brown. Beak black. General colouring smoky black with a greenish tint. Crest large and curving backwards with a spine-like appearance to the feathers. Bare skin areas on cheeks pale pink to red. Feet and legs black.
HEN Similar to cock. Slightly more slender.

This is a massive, soberly coloured species with a large fearsome looking beak and a magnificent crest. The smoky colouring is due to a fine powdery substance formed by the feathers as a waterproofing agent, a feature peculiar to all cockatoos. As would be expected these fine birds are expensive and are far better as aviary birds than as household pets. A few individuals have been hand tamed and have learned to repeat a few words in a rich and clear tone. Their fearsome appearance belies their peaceable and docile nature. This species is specially mentioned because of its unusual colouring and size in comparison with the more common smaller white species such as Leadbeater's and the Sulphur-crested Cockatoo. There are five subspecies (P. a. alecto, P. a. aterrimus, P. a. goliath, P. a. intermedius, P. a. stanolophus) that vary slightly in their mainly black plumage. No records of breeding in captivity are available.

Greater Sulphur-crested Cockatoo (Kakatoe g. galerita)
COCK Overall length about 20 in (51 cm). Eyes black. Beak black. General colour white with yellow suffusion on ear patches and under tail coverts. Long recurving crest of sulphur yellow with white first feathers. Area of bare white skin around eyes. Feet and legs grey black.
HEN Similar to cock in colouring. Eyes dark brown.

This is a popular bird in most countries, particularly in America where it is a most sought-after species. It is suitable both as a single household pet and as a garden aviary bird. When kept as pet birds care must be taken to ensure that they are securely caged or kept in a closed room under supervision. They have a large wing span and if they escape into the open can travel long distances in a short time.

Most Greater Sulphur-crested Cockatoos like personal attention and will dance and display to achieve it; if not appeased they call loudly and harshly. It is important that cockatoos, or any birds for that matter, are not teased or they will develop an aggressive nature – parrot-like birds can inflict quite severe wounds with their large powerful beaks. Fortunately, the vast majority are gentle and affectionate – it is we who make them otherwise. This species usually repeats words very clearly though it has a limited vocabulary.

The Greater Sulphur-crested Cockatoo has been widely bred in Britain, Europe and America during the last hundred years. Breeding pairs need large, strongly constructed aviaries with plenty of bark-covered branches to gnaw. They will use wooden barrels, large sections of rotting logs, or specially made boxes as nesting sites. These receptacles should be filled to a depth of at least 12 in (30 cm) with moist rotting wood, peat, wood chippings, or a mixture of all three for the birds to scoop out their nest hollows. The clutches are of three or four eggs and incubation lasts about twenty-eight days – the parents share this duty. The young birds leave their nests when they are between seven and nine weeks old and are under the care of their parents for another three or four weeks. During the rearing period the birds need large quantities of their usual seeds, soft foods, green vegetables and fruit. The adult birds must be left quietly while incubating and rearing if the young are to be raised successfully. Breeding pairs can become dangerous not only to other birds but also to their owners.

There are three subspecies.

Great White Cockatoo *(K. alba)* Plate 67
Syn: White Crested Cockatoo, Umbrella Cockatoo
COCK Overall length about 20 in (51 cm). Beak black. Eyes black. White overall except for slight tinting of yellow at base of inner wing and tail feathers. Feet and legs black.
HEN Coloured as cock except eyes are reddish brown.

The broad and rounded crest of this species gives it an appearance that is quite different from the more commonly seen species. Its slow and deliberate movements make it an interesting bird to observe either as a pet or in an aviary. Young birds are affectionate and make particularly good household pets. Birds are not often available, but they have been bred successfully in both Britain and America.

Leadbeater's Cockatoo *(K. leadbeateri)*
Syn: Major Mitchell's Cockatoo, Pink Cockatoo
COCK Overall length about 17 in (43 cm). Eyes black. Beak light yellow. General colour white with a soft rose-pink suffusion, darker on neck, breast, underparts and under wing coverts. Eye skin whitish grey. Crest very large and full, beautifully patterned with white, yellow and rose-red bands. Feet and legs light grey.
HEN Similar to cock in colour, eyes reddish brown.

The colouring of this species indicates why it is sometimes called the Pink Cockatoo. When its fine large crest is fully erect it looks extremely handsome. Leadbeater's Cockatoos are generally of a placid nature and more examples would be kept as pets if they were more plentiful and less costly. In America the supply of these birds is always exceeded by the demand.

Their breeding requirements are similar to those of the Greater Sulphur-crested Cockatoos, but their nesting boxes can be slightly smaller. A few pairs nest and rear young each year and they are considered good and careful parents.

Leadbeater's are definitely seen to their greatest advantage when housed in outdoor flighted aviaries. There are three subspecies *(K. l. molles, K. l. mungi* and *K. l. superflua)* that vary slightly only in their size and colouring.

Lesser Sulphur-crested Cockatoo *(K. s. sulphura)*
Plate 68
COCK Overall length about 13 in (33 cm). Eyes black. General colour white with yellow suffusion on ear patches, breast and under tail coverts. Long recurving crest sulphur yellow. Feet and legs dark grey.
HEN Similar to cock in colouring. Eyes brownish red. Slightly smaller.

This is a smaller version of the Greater Sulphur-crested which it resembles in many respects. Although quite widely kept it does not have the same appeal as the larger species. By nature it is very friendly and consequently makes a good safe family pet. Birds are easily trained to perform simple tricks and to repeat a considerable number of words. Being smallish they can be comfortably housed in the standard all-wire parrot cage. They are very active in aviaries where their acrobatic performances are always a source of amusement to their owners. They will breed more readily than the larger species and each year reports of successful breeding operations come from many countries. Considering their size, Lesser Sulphur-crested Cockatoos have very large and powerful beaks, which they use with great effect on any woodwork that is within reach. This should be remembered, particularly when they are allowed out of their cages.

There are six subspecies.

Roseate Cockatoo *(K. r. roseicapilla)* Plate 69
Syn: Galah, Rose-breasted Cockatoo
COCK Overall length about 14 in (36 cm). Eyes very dark brown. Beak light horn. General colour silvery grey above, paler towards rump. Neck, chest, stomach and underwing coverts deep rosy red. Scoop-shaped crest rose red and white. Flanks and under tail coverts pale grey. Tail grey. Bare eye skin dull pink. Feet and legs grey.
HEN Similar in colouring to cock. Eyes lighter.

When taken into a household as young birds Roseate Cockatoos can be quickly trained to become endearing, playful and gentle pets. Fully adult specimens are more difficult to train and are more suitable for the aviary. Their talent for talking is not great and varies considerably with individual birds, much depending on the age of the bird and the patience of its instructor. They can be kept singly or in pairs and will become very attached to each other and to their owners. It is thought that there are more Roseate Cockatoos kept as pets and in aviaries than any other single species of cockatoo. Their smallish size, reasonable cost, and kindly nature, all contribute to making them the most popular member of the cockatoo family. They are very much at home in flighted garden aviaries and are delightful to watch whether bathing or playing on their perches. Of all cockatoos they are the easiest to breed in captivity and many fine young are reared each year. At the present time, however, there is some difficulty in obtaining breeding pairs.

LORIES AND LORIKEETS

This group consists of many species and subspecies, most of which have spectacular vivid plumage colour. Many are confined to very limited areas of territory and are extremely rare, only appearing very occasionally in aviaries. They have brush-like tongues, which are used to lap nectar and soft fruits. The nature of their diet makes this group rather difficult for the ordinary bird keeper to manage and, apart from the two species described, are better left to the experienced aviculturist. The majority of species settle down well in captivity when given warm housing and some species have raised young in aviaries and even large cages. The group as a whole consists of birds that are of a friendly disposition to their own species and to their owners.

Chattering Lory (*Domicella g. garrula*) Plate 70
COCK Overall length about 12 in (30 cm). Beak reddish horn. Eyes red brown. General colour is rich crimson red; wings green, yellow at butts and under wing coverts. There is a band of yellow across the shoulders and the tail is reddish purple, suffused with green. Feet and legs reddish brown.
HEN Coloured like cock; difficult to sex.

This is a contented species with both sexes continually playing and chattering to each other. Were it not for the hygiene needed in their housing they would make ideal household pets. They nest quite readily in aviaries and in most instances young are successfully reared. Chattering Lories can be kept in aviaries in temperate climates but will always need a box in which to roost (the majority of lories and lorikeets prefer to roost in a box and it is essential that one should always be provided). They need similar fruits and nectar as prescribed for the next species and, like other members in the group, must have facilities for bathing.

Swainson's Lorikeet (*Trichoglossus haematodus moluccanus*) Plate 71
Syn: Blue Mountain Lorikeet, Rainbow Lorikeet
COCK Overall length about 12 in (30 cm). Beak orange red, tipped with yellow. Eyes brown. Head and throat purplish blue. Back, wings and tail bright green. Breast and under wing coverts rich vermilion red, the underparts blue, and the tail coverts yellow and green.
HEN Coloured like the cock but has slightly smaller beak and head.

Although it lives mainly on soft fruits and nectar, in captivity it will at times eat a little parakeet seed mixture; this, however, must be given in limited quantities only. A suitable nectar can be made up of equal parts of water, honey and baby food or condensed milk. Because of their diet, their aviaries must be kept perfectly clean to prevent an unpleasant odour. They settle down well in captivity and pairs have been known to breed both in flights and aviaries. Swainson's are susceptible to cold and need to be well housed during cold weather.

MACAWS

This group of large, long-tailed, brilliantly coloured birds with big, extremely powerful beaks, comes from tropical America. There are about twenty-four species and subspecies, ranging in size from the rare Dwarf Macaw of about 14 in (36 cm) to the large Hyacinth Macaw measuring 36 in (91 cm) or even more. Despite their size and fierce looking hooked beaks they are among the gentlest of the parrot-like species if trained and handled properly as young birds. Most pet macaws seem to delight in being handled and enjoy climbing or sitting on their owners. Most species, other than those reared in captivity, are taken from nests as partly fledged young and then reared by hand. This treatment makes them trusting and dependent on humans and dispels the fear normally associated with captivity. When taken as fully adult birds they are extremely difficult to train and not really suitable as household pets. Wherever they are seen, be it in private homes, aviaries or zoological gardens, they always command attention. A number of large establishments have trained macaws to fly at liberty in the gardens, returning home to sleep and feed. It is certainly a magnificent sight to see several of these large, brightly coloured birds flying in the open or playing around an old log. The four species described below have all nested and reared young in large garden aviaries.

Blue and Gold Macaw (*Ara ararauna*) Plate 72
Syn: Blue and Yellow Macaw
COCK Overall length about 30 in (76 cm). Eyes pale yellow. Beak black. Upper parts bright blue with the forehead, crown and rump having a greenish tint. Underparts deep rich yellow. Under tail coverts greenish blue. Undersides of wings and tail yellow. Flights and

outer tail purplish blue. Facial skin patches whitish grey veined with small black feathers and a black band around the throat. Feet and legs very dark grey.

HEN Similar in colouring to cock. Beak smaller.

This is the most popular macaw kept in captivity because of its attractive colouring, intelligence, playfulness, enquiring behaviour, and its mimic speech. Although not the largest macaw, it is a well-made bird with more than half its length consisting of the fine tapering tail. As household pets they are mostly kept on 'T' stands so that their tails do not get damaged and, of course, they have ample room to spread their large wings. In spite of having a very powerful beak they are gentle with humans. They have been bred on a number of occasions in Britain, Europe and America in accommodation varying from large cages to aviaries with very big wired flights.

Hyacinthine Macaw (*Anodorhynchus hyacinthinus*) Plate 73

Syn: Hyacinth Macaw

COCK Overall length about 36 in (91 cm). Eyes medium gold. Beak black. General colour deep rich cobalt blue with the wings showing the darkest shadings. Eye rings and skin around the base of beak orange yellow. Feet and legs black.

HEN Similar in colouring to cock. A little smaller overall.

This bird, about 6 in (10 cm) larger than the Blue and Gold Macaw, is scarce, expensive and much sought after. High prices are paid for single birds or possible breeding pairs. It is the most beautiful of all macaws; the large black beak and yellow facial skin contrast to advantage with its shining plumage of deep cobalt blue. On stands or in aviaries they command attention at all times. They are docile and affectionate and make good pets. Though they are hardy they do not reproduce in captivity quite as freely as the Blue and Gold; nevertheless, young have been successfully reared on many occasions and if more breeding pairs were available the numbers would rise considerably.

Red and Blue Macaw (*Ara chloroptera*) Plates 72, 74

Syn: Green-winged Macaw, Maroon Macaw, Red and Green Macaw

COCK Overall length about 34 in (86 cm). Eyes light yellow. Beak upper part light, base darker, lower part black. General colour dark crimson red. Tail coverts light blue. Wing coverts crimson red, green and blue. Flights blue. Tail blue with some red, except the two central feathers which are red tipped with blue. Facial skin area

Blue and Gold Macaw with good facial markings, on a circular hanging metal perch

pinkish, veined with small red feathers. Feet and legs greyish-black.

HEN Similar in colouring to cock. Beak thicker and shorter.

This delightful species has several names, all of which describe its rich colouring. It is similar to the Hyacinth Macaw in size and general temperament. It can be bought quite readily and at prices generally within reach of most bird lovers. They get along well with children and household animals as well as with their owners. These birds have been bred successfully in captivity in many countries, and have also been crossed with closely allied species. They make good and attentive parents and, like all macaws, the nesting and rearing periods are spread over several months. With care and attention all specimens will live to a great age (up to 60 years) whether kept as pets or as free-flying aviary birds.

Scarlet Macaw (*A. macao*)
Syn: Red and Yellow Macaw
COCK Overall length about 36 in (91 cm). Eyes light yellow. Beak, upper parts light, lower black. General colour brilliant scarlet deeper shade on head area. Wings red, yellow and blue. Rump light blue. Facial skin area pale pinkish and veined with small black feathers. Tail mainly deep blue with some red. Feet and legs black.
HEN Similar in colouring to cock. Slightly more slender in build. Beak smaller.

This brilliantly coloured bird is usually easy to obtain and to train. Although its general colouring is rich scarlet, it has some yellow and blue areas – hence the name Red and Yellow Macaw. When young birds are kept as single household pets they soon become very attached to their owners and quickly learn to repeat a limited number of words. Although their vocabulary is not great, their brilliant colouring and confiding manner makes them a popular species. Examples are mostly to be found in bird gardens and zoological establishments, on stands or in large flighted aviaries, where they always attract the visitors. Like the Red and Blue Macaws they will breed in captivity.

LOVEBIRDS

These small, short-tailed true parrots form an interesting group of attractive birds quite distinct from Budgerigars, which at times are misnamed Lovebirds. The popularity of these little parrots is due to their bright colouring, the freedom with which they reproduce, and their friendly behaviour to each other. One of the practices most interesting to owners is their method of carrying nesting material under their wings. This unusual method of transporting twigs and straws into the nest boxes captures the imagination of many owners and makes the raising of lovebirds additionally rewarding. Contrary to popular belief, lovebirds will live quite contentedly on their own as pets or in aviaries. There are numerous records of single pet birds of some species learning to repeat a few simple words.

Originally lovebirds were exported from their native Africa until it was found that they would breed in captivity and now the vast majority of aviary birds are bred from domesticated strains.

These have been developed in the same way as Budgerigar strains. Several of the more frequently bred lovebird species have produced colour mutations which have been established as free-breeding races by breeders using the Mendelian rules of inheritance. Closely related species can be crossed and the resultant fertile hybrids show colour characters of both the parent species. Selective pairings of second generation hybrids have produced pure strains of the new colours.

An interesting feature of the lovebirds is that they build nests in their nest boxes using dried coarse grasses, straw, twigs and strips of bark. To obtain satisfactory breeding results it is imperative that the nesting pairs are supplied with ample quantities of these materials. It is also essential that the nests do not get too dry and the bottoms of the box should be covered with a thick layer of moist peat, sawdust, rotting wood, or wood chips or a mixture of all four materials. The best breeding results are usually obtained when the nesting boxes are hung so they are in direct contact with the open air. There are about fourteen species and subspecies of lovebirds excluding the colour mutations.

Abyssinian Lovebird (*Agapornis taranta*) Plate 75
Syn: Black-winged Lovebird
COCK Overall length about 6½ in (16·5 cm). Eyes medium brown. Beak deep red. General colour rich green with lighter underparts. Forehead band and eye surrounds bright red. Wing coverts and flights brownish black. Tail green with wide black bar near tips. Feet and legs greyish.
HEN Similar in colouring to cock but without red on head.

This is the largest lovebird species. They settle down well in cage or aviary but are rather shy breeders. Pairs do occasionally nest and rear young but they cannot be considered as a reliable breeding species. They make attractive show specimens and are reasonably easy to train as such and in aviaries they live quite well with most species of the more commonly kept parakeets. They like climbing about and gnawing pieces of old decaying wood.

Black-masked Lovebird (*A. personata*) Plate 76
Syn: Masked Lovebird
COCK Overall length about 5½ in (14 cm). Eyes medium brown. Beak red. Head blackish brown shading into gold on lower neck and upper back. Rings around eyes white. Breast deep yellow, darker towards the throat. Lower parts, wings and back, bright green. Rump greyish blue. Flights blackish. Tail green. Feet and legs greyish.
HEN Similar in colouring to cock. Beak stouter.

Because of its handsome colouring and the prolific way in which it reproduces, this is the most widely kept lovebird. In addition to its normal colouring as described above there are blue, white, cinnamon, pied and lutino forms, each with its own particular attraction. The lutino mutation first occurred in America in 1935. Many Black-masked Lovebirds have been bred, like Budgerigars, in large cages but results are more satisfactory when they are allowed to breed in small flighted single-pair garden aviaries. They are quarrelsome and it is not safe to keep more than one breeding pair in the same enclosure; even mated birds will have a periodic squabble. In spite of this they rear their young satisfactorily, but it is far safer to remove the young as soon as they can feed on their own. After the young hatch the parents need an increasing quantity of various fresh greenfoods, and some pairs will take a little soft food. A few specimens are kept as pets and they settle down very well as such, but most Black-masked Lovebirds are to be found as aviary birds.

Fischer's Lovebird (A. fischeri) Plate 77

COCK Overall length about 5½ in (14 cm). Eyes medium brown. Beak red. General colour various tones of bright green. Eye ring white. Forehead red orange. Cheeks and throat pale red orange shading to gold. Top of head golden brown. Neck yellowish. Rump dull blue. Tail green with blue shading. Feet and legs light.
HEN Similar to cock in colouring.

In most countries Fischer's Lovebirds compete strongly with the similar sized Black-masked Lovebirds for popularity. The only objection to Fischer's is that they are rather difficult to sex. In some cases hens are a little stouter than the cocks but this is not a sure guide as there is considerable variation in the size of individual birds. They are the best species for the beginner, being prolific and reliable breeders. Breeding pairs should be kept in single enclosures as they are inclined to be vicious when nesting. Like all the lovebirds they are quite hardy providing they have dry, draught-proof quarters during cold weather. Hot conditions to suit them (they come from tropical Africa) if they have somewhere to shelter from the direct rays of the sun.

Nyasa Lovebird (A. lilianae)

Syn: Lilian's Lovebird, Nyasaland Lovebird
COCK Overall length about 5 in (13 cm). Eyes dark brown. Beak red. General colour green, paler on neck and shoulders, darker on back and wings. Forehead, cheeks and throat rich deep red orange. Back of head golden.

Upper tail coverts yellowish green. Lower rump deep blue. Tail green and yellow. Feet and legs grey.
HEN Similar in colouring to cock. Beak stouter and darker in colour.

This is the smallest species, with a very attractive colouring and an especially gentle nature. Nyasa Lovebirds are one of the few species that will live peaceably in colonies and this makes them a suitable variety for the breeder with limited space. Reports indicate that although they are free breeders in most countries they do not appear to do so well in America. Lovebird strains of all species vary considerably in their breeding potential, so it is possible that the strains of this species used by American breeders are not so prolific. A successful American breeder, David West, found that most strains of this species in the United States had been mixed with Peachfaces. Being quite small birds they can breed in cages and many fine broods are raised each year in such housing. This method is useful for those fanciers who have limited birdroom space provided they also have reasonably sized flights for housing the birds when they are not breeding and for the young birds as they develop. Nyasas are no exception to the general rule that lovebirds give the best breeding results when housed in outdoor flighted aviaries. Birds bred under such conditions are always stronger and more vigorous than those produced in more restricted accommodation.

Peach-faced Lovebird (A. roseicollis) Plate 78

Syn: Rosy-faced Lovebird
COCK Overall length about 6 in (15 cm). Eyes light gold. Beak light horn. Eye ring white. Back and lower breast soft pale green. Front of head soft rose red, deeper on crown and pale on cheeks. Throat rose red. Rump and upper tail coverts bright blue. Flights dark. Tail green with bands of red, blue and black. Feet and legs greyish.
HEN Similar in colouring to cock. Little paler in colour on head.

This is the second largest of the genus and has a fierce and pugnacious temperament. If housed in large outside flights they quieten down considerably since they are active birds and like plenty of flying space. Peach-faced Lovebirds are popular in most countries, particularly America. Because of their quarrelsome nature they must be housed in single pairs during the breeding period. They are prolific breeders and make good parents. If trained when young they will make excellent show birds and are highly regarded as such in Britain. A few specimens are kept as pets and have proved to be quite satisfactory even if a little noisy at times. Pied and Yellow mutations have occurred and strains of these are now being developed. The former mutation is quite common in the U.S.A.

Red-faced Lovebird (*A. p. pullaria*) Plate 79
COCK Overall length about 6 in (15 cm). Beak red. Eyes brown. General colour rich bright green with the underparts more yellowish. Face and top of head orange red, rump bright blue, shoulders, wing butts and under wing coverts black. Tail green banded with red and black. Feet and legs deep grey.
HEN Less bright throughout than cock, with under wing coverts green and wing butts yellowish.

Somewhat similar to the Abyssinian Lovebird, this species is a little smaller and has more red on head and face. It takes kindly to captivity although it is difficult to persuade it to breed. Providing they have a flighted aviary with plenty of flying space a small flock of Red-faced Lovebirds can be housed together without squabbling. Being handsome, they make good exhibition birds.

Parrotlets (*Forpus* species*)
This genus, of which there are some twenty species and subspecies, is the South American counterpart of the lovebird family. Occasionally examples of some species are offered for sale and they need the same general management as prescribed for the African lovebirds. They are mostly green in colour with the cocks having some blue or yellowish tinting on the head area; their beaks are smaller than those of lovebirds. It is possible to persuade most species to breed in captivity but they do not make particularly good parents and the hen can be very vicious. Most species are obtainable in America, and in Britain the Blue-winged Parrotlet (*Forpus passerinus vividus*), Plate 80, and the Celestial Parrotlet (*F. c. coelestis*) are those most frequently seen.

HOUSING
The accommodation required for parrots and their allies depends on the size of the birds and whether they are to be kept as single pets or in aviary collections for breeding. Round or square parrot cages (see illustration) are used extensively to house single parrots and the smaller cockatoos. These cages are specially made with the entrance, food and water doors fitted with fastenings that cannot be opened by the birds. They are made of heavy gauge galvanized or plated welded-metal bars that can withstand the onslaught of the most powerfully-beaked varieties. The hardwood perches fitted to such cages often have metal-capped ends to prevent the birds from destroying them too quickly. To enable the birds to exercise their beaks, bark covered branches should be fixed periodically inside the cages. The cages should be placed away from draughts, smoke, steam, or the direct rays of the sun.

Macaws, cockatoos and some parrots are best kept on 'T' stands (see Plate 73), to allow more freedom for tails and wings. The stands have sand trays as bases and the birds are usually tethered to the stands by light steel chains attached to one leg by a swivel. As most of the birds have been tethered from an early age the chains are not objected to and, once the birds become used to their owners and their surroundings, the chains can often be removed.

Aviaries for housing parrots can be of similar designs to those described for parakeets, though made of stronger materials. The uprights and cross pieces of the flights are

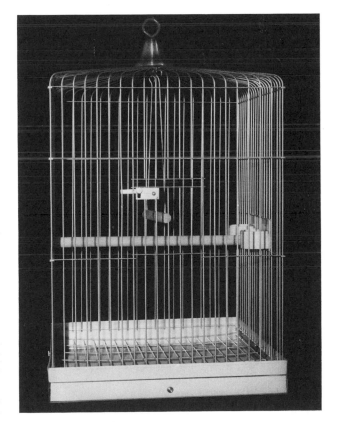

Square parrot cage (*Rymet Ltd*)

best made of angle iron or tubular metal and the wire should be heavy-gauge small-mesh chain link. Shelters can be made of very thick hardwood boards, brick, manufactured blocks or pre-stressed concrete slabs. All windows and any other wooden parts should be protected by stout wire-mesh screens. Perches for flights and shelters are best made from branches of apple, pear, plum, hawthorn, beech, alder, elm or pine trees, which can be renewed when they become damaged. The majority of parrots like wood to gnaw and doing so gives them natural exercise and helps to keep their beaks in good condition.

It is difficult to give exact size for parrot aviaries as these will depend on the species to be housed and the amount of space available to the owner. Large macaws and cockatoos need flights of not less than 30 ft (9 m) long, 15 ft (4·5 m) high and 12 ft (3·6 m) wide. For the smaller kinds about 20 ft (6 m) long, 9 ft (2·7 m) high and 6 ft (1·8 m) wide is sufficient. In comparison with flights suggested for parakeets these lengths may not seem adequate; however, it should be remembered that parrots do not fly nearly as much as parakeets, much preferring to climb. The floors can be covered with grass, sand, gravel, stone slabs or concrete and the shelter floors should be either stone slabs or concrete. To prevent escapes the flights and shelters should be examined regularly for weak spots, which must be repaired immediately – for it is surprising how very quickly birds will force a way out. The sleeping quarters must always be dry and draught-proof and the owners should, when the weather is bad, be able to shut in the birds.

Lovebirds and parrotlets can be housed in the same type of aviaries, pens and cages as Budgerigars (pp. 96–9).

FEEDING

The basic seeds used for feeding parrot-like birds are sunflower and safflower, to which are blended varying proportions of canary seed, cereals and various nuts. In addition different fruits, fresh garden vegetables, greenfoods, dates, figs, and other dried fruits are eaten in varying quantities by the different species. These ingredients can be bought separately and blended to the taste of the species or individual birds. The food must be stored carefully to keep it fresh and sweet. The owners of single pet birds will find that the specially blended packet seeds obtainable from pet stores are invariably the most economical.

Sunflower seeds can be white, black, striped or mixed,

and, as they all have the same food value, it is a matter of the individual bird's taste. Mixed sunflower seeds are, however, more readily obtainable than the separate sorts. Canary seeds should be the large Spanish type and it is essential to see that they are fresh, plump and hard. All seeds and cereals should be of the best quality, clean, and free from all extraneous matter.

There are a number of different blends of parrot seeds but they all seem to have a basic content of not less than 40 per cent sunflower. The balance of the mixture is made up of some or all of the following: safflower, maize (corn), wheat, dari, oats, hemp, canary seed and ground nuts. All kinds of fruits such as apples, pears, bananas, grapes, even peaches and nectarines will be eaten. Garden vegetables such as peas, beans, ripe tomatoes and melon seeds, carrots, celery, chicory and endives serve as excellent fresh foods. When fresh fruits are not readily available dried figs, sultanas, raisins, dates and various nuts can be offered. It should be realized, of course, that individual birds will not eat all the foods listed, but preferences will soon be discovered.

All parrot-like birds need grits, which can be obtained from bird stores in a grade suitable for the size of the bird. This material is essential for the birds to grind the food in their gizzards, and as the grits wear smooth by constant movement they are voided and must be replaced. In addition to grits, lime (calcium) is necessary and this can be offered in the form of cuttlefish bone and prepared mineral blocks. Although birds may go long periods without having these materials they certainly thrive when they have a constant supply. It has been noted that just before breeding times parrot-like birds, both cocks and hens, seem to have an increased desire to gnaw wood. This is probably because they need more cellulose at that time.

Although parrot-like birds do not drink a great deal, fresh clean water must always be there for their use. As well as drinking water, bathing water should be provided. Some parrot-like species will bathe in a shallow dish and others prefer to be sprayed. In outdoor flights the birds can bathe whenever it rains, when it is amusing to watch them enjoying themselves.

The large macaws need the same kind of seed mixture as parrots and cockatoos with extra nuts added. They are very partial to Brazil nuts, which they can crack easily with their powerful beaks, and they can be offered other kinds of nuts that are available. They like a reasonable quantity of fresh fruit and garden vegetables together with grit and lime. Although they are large birds they are slow moving and do not eat as much food in proportion to their size as the smaller, swifter moving parakeets.

The usual Budgerigar seed mixture (see p.99) can be given to lovebirds and parrotlets, with the addition of two parts sunflower seed and a small quantity of hemp seed. Different breeders of lovebirds have their own personal ideas on the use of sunflower because of its fattening nature; nevertheless, it is important to see that the birds have enough of this valuable food. Lovebirds need plenty of mixed grits, cuttlefish bone, old mortar rubble, mineral blocks, dried crushed domestic hens' egg shells, and they need the same kinds of greenfoods as Budgerigars. They are particularly fond of millet sprays which are useful additions to their diet especially when young are in the nest. When they have eaten the seeds from the sprays they will often use the stalks for nest building.

BREEDING

It is the general practice to house all breeding pairs of parrots in separate double-wired enclosures so that they can give their full attention to reproduction and not spend time and energy in unproductive squabbling or in serious fighting with other birds. Most parrots mature slowly, coming into their breeding cycle only when they are several years old – up to eight or ten years for the large kinds. The climatic conditions have a bearing on this fact; birds kept in warmer countries reach breeding condition earlier than those living in cooler, more extreme climates. This means that pairs are together in aviaries for several years before breeding is possible. Once pairs have mated they are likely to produce nests of young yearly for a very long period.

If pairs are ready to nest the kind of nesting receptacle is not of particular importance provided it is large enough and has a thick layer of material on the bottom. Hardwood barrels or half barrels, square, oblong or grandfather clock type boxes, large rotting logs, metal bins, can all be tried. If metal bins are used they should have some small holes in the sides and bottom for ventilation, wooden entrance perches, and wooden slats bolted on the insides to allow the birds easy entrance and exit. Metal has the advantage of being indestructible and does not need to be renewed. All nests, of whatever type, should be fixed high in the aviaries and perches arranged allowing the birds to climb into the boxes without difficulty. Nests for African Greys, Amazons and small cockatoos should be approximately 15 in (38 cm) square and 20 in (51 cm) high, and for the larger cockatoos and macaws some 18–20 in (46–51 cm) square and 24–36 in (61–91 cm) high (all internal measurements). Various types of nest boxes

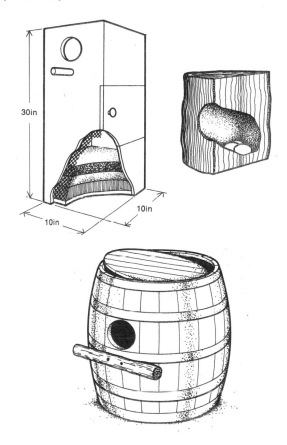

Grandfather clock, log and barrel nest boxes – note the cut away section in the first to show the wire against the inside front and the layered nesting material

30in

10in

10in

are shown above, the dimensions of which can be adjusted to suit the particular species concerned.

The period of incubation for most members of the parrot family is about twenty-eight days and it is five to eight weeks according to the species before the young are ready to leave the nest. When they emerge they are fully feathered and are fed by their parents for a further few weeks, gradually becoming less dependent as they learn to fend for themselves. During the time the young are in the nest the adult birds need their usual diet with an increased quantity of fruit and green vegetables. Most birds also like some soft food and there are various mixtures that can be given; for example, coarse insectivorous food mixed with cod-liver oil food or boiled mashed potatoes or both. Wholemeal bread and milk, raisins, boiled maize mixed crumbly moist with milk are liked by many birds. It will be seen that there are many nutritional foods that can be given to breeding pairs to assist them in rearing their young. A variation of diet helps considerably in the successful rearing of all species of young. Fortunately, breeders have a wide choice of foods to offer the birds, all of which have individual likes and dislikes; what is favoured by one species may be completely ignored by another and this can only be discovered by trial and error.

All the suggestions made in the section on breeding parakeets (pp.137–8) apply to parrots.

Lovebirds will happily use nest boxes of similar designs

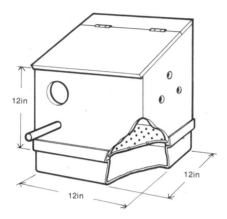

Special nest box for a lovebird – the box, with a perforated zinc bottom, is placed over a tray containing water. Water vapour can pass through the holes in the zinc and thus keep the eggs moist enough to ensure hatching.

to those described for Budgerigars (p.101) but they should be somewhat larger – a good size would be 10 in (25 cm) long, 8 in (20 cm) high and 6 in (15 cm) wide. Such a size gives the birds sufficient room to build their nests on 1 in (2·5 cm) or so of moist peat, etc. As moisture plays such an important part in the successful hatching of lovebirds' eggs, many breeders hang the nest boxes in open or partly open flights. Others use specially made nest boxes incorporating water trays at the bottom covered with perforated zinc: this prevents the eggs from becoming too dry which can lead to hatching failures.

The clutches of eggs laid by lovebirds vary from three to eight, the average being five or six. Eggs are laid on alternate days and the incubation period is twenty-one days so, like Budgerigars, there is a difference in the age of the hatching chicks. The young leave their nests when four or five weeks old and soon learn to feed themselves. When this stage is reached it is wise to remove the young from the breeding aviaries to prevent the young from being attacked by the adult birds.

The chicks can be ringed in the nest with closed metal rings or, later, with split metal rings and their numbers and particulars should be entered in a breeding register. The maintenance of accurate breeding records is of the utmost importance, particularly when colour mutations are being bred. Lutino (albino) forms are invariably sex-linked and pied, blue, yellow and white kinds recessive in their inheritance (see pp. 104–5). Colour-breeding lovebird varieties is increasing in most countries and is an added interest.

Aviary-bred British Birds

A number of species on the 'List of British Birds' have been bred successfully in captivity for many generations and are now considered to be adapted to domesticated conditions. The species are covered by the Protection of Birds Act of 1954 and its subsequent amendments. In Great Britain it is illegal to advertise or sell any British bird unless it is cage- or aviary-bred and ringed with a closed metal ring (band). It is also against the law to catch birds, to take their eggs, or to disturb their nests. Further information on the Protection of Birds Acts 1954–67 can be obtained from The Royal Society for the Protection of Birds, The Lodge, Sandy, Bedfordshire SG19 2DL, who publish a booklet *Wild Birds & the Law*.

Some British species have been naturalized in other parts of the world and now breed freely among the native bird populations. They, too, may not be sold in Great Britain unless they are cage- or aviary-bred ringed specimens. The same regulation applies to the related Continental subspecies

However, the law does allow a certain number of birds to be taken from the wild to strengthen breeding stocks and for educational purposes. Special licences are issued to approved persons to take a given number of a named species for these purposes. This protection helps to conserve diminishing species and at the same time allows domestication to proceed. In the future, it is possible that aviary-bred birds may be used to supplement any wild stocks that have become seriously depleted. Under the guidance of the British Bird Fancy Council the various specialist societies help and encourage their members to found domesticated strains of many native species. Whenever aviculturists and naturalists have the opportunity to compare notes both will benefit.

Species other than those described below are bred in captivity though on a smaller scale; Redpoll, Hawfinch, Chaffinch, and some of the softbilled species, for example, produce young in aviaries each year.

Blackbird *(Turdus m. merula)* Plate 81

COCK Overall length about 10 in (25 cm). Eyes black. Eyelids yellow. Beak deep yellow. General colour unbroken jet black. Feet and legs blackish brown.
HEN Dark blackish brown somewhat mottled on breast. Beak, feet and legs brown.

Blackbirds with normal plumage colour and the pied, white and albino mutations, have been bred in captivity for a number of years. Their friendly, fearless nature makes them ideal for domestication. In the wild they tolerate man's presence even when they are breeding. They like to live and nest near human habitation as they find a large proportion of their food in cultivated areas and gardens. Their beautiful mellow song is a feature of the British country and town environments.

Blackbirds rear young in captivity provided they have suitable sites in which to build their nest and only one pair is kept in an enclosure. They tolerate birds of the finch family but, as in the wild, will not share their territory with birds of their own species. Blackbirds, which are softbills, are easy to feed and they will thrive on an insectivorous mixture together with fruit and some live insects.

All the chicks reared, whether of the normal form or of colour mutations, should be ringed with the correct size of closed metal ring so they can be identified. Rare mutations may not be sold unless they too are closed ringed as they do occur occasionally in the wild. Blackbirds are a good species for the beginning breeder of softbills as they are hardy, easy to keep and breed, available in different colour forms and sing beautifully in cages and aviaries.

It has been calculated that in the wild two pairs of birds must each produce two nests of young to ensure that there will be one new pair of birds to breed the following season. The other young from these nests are killed either by predators, on the roads by motor vehicles, by severe weather conditions, or they die from other natural causes. In captivity the percentage of young that survive for the following season is extremely high as they do not face the same hazards. They always have plenty of good food, have no fear of predators, are kept warm and dry in all weathers, and consequently have a greater life expectancy.

Bullfinch *(Pyrrhula p. nesa)* Plate 82

COCK Overall length about 6¼ in (16 cm). Eyes black. Beak black. Head, wings and tail, purplish black. Band of buff and grey across wings. Upper back bluish grey, sides of neck, breast and stomach brick red. Lower rump and vent white. Feet and legs black.

HEN Similar to cock except the sides of neck, breast and stomach are vinous grey and the wing bands are duller.

These are a very handsome and distinctively-coloured members of the finch family, greatly admired by bird lovers. In their natural habitat they are rather shy and secretive yet in captivity they settle down quickly and become admirable aviary birds. Their song has no great musical value but they can be taught to whistle various tunes. Wild Bullfinches are disliked by gardeners and orchard owners as they destroy a great many fruit and flower buds in the spring while searching for insects.

Strains of this species have been bred in aviaries for many generations and by careful selection breeders have improved their quality and they have become domesticated. Bullfinches are ready breeders in aviaries and numbers have also been bred in unflighted pens and even in large cages. Undoubtedly they breed more freely in flighted aviaries and the resulting chicks are of better overall vigour and quality. Most pairs make reliable parents and seem to take a great pride in their young. In addition to their normal seed mixture they like greenfoods, soft fruits, berries and some soft food when rearing. They build very neat, compact nests starting with a small platform of twiglets on which they construct a cup of fine roots lined with wool, soft hair, and a few feathers. Sufficient of these materials should be supplied to the breeding pairs, otherwise nesting may be unsuccessful.

Colour mutations of Bullfinches appear from time to time – those showing an excess of black or completely black plumage are the most usual. A few examples of white birds occur; the cock birds have a rosy pink breast colour and are

Norwich Canary cock (right) and Bullfinch hen – a well-matched breeding pair for producing Canary × Bullfinch Mules

particularly beautiful. As far as I know neither of these mutations have been successfully produced in aviaries. I once had an all-black Bullfinch hen that had two nests of eggs with a normal cock, but both clutches were infertile. Similar reports have come from owners of melanistic Bullfinches so it is likely that the gene concerned affects their reproduction.

Bullfinches have been crossed successfully with other British finches to produce hybrids, and with Canaries to produce mules (the young from two finch-like species are usually known as hybrids, while those from a Canary and a species of finch are called mules). In these crosses hen Bullfinches are used – extremely few results have been reported when cock Bullfinches have been paired with a hen of other finch species.

Of all the hybrids the Goldfinch × Bullfinch are generally considered to be the most handsome, showing clearly the beautiful colours of both parents. The Canary × Bullfinch Mules are richly coloured and are much sought after by exhibitors particularly if the Canary parent is of the Norwich type.

Crossbill *(Loxia curvirostra scotica)* Plate 83

COCK Overall length about 7 in (18 cm). Beak blackish and crossed at tip. Eyes dark brown. General colour when in full breeding plumage pinkish crimson red with brown wings and tail. The non-breeding colouring is much duller, lacking the pinkish tone and between breeding periods the birds can be very mottled in their colouring. Feet and legs brown.

HEN Yellowish green, browner on back and greyish white on the underparts.

These are one of several species of birds with heavy powerful beaks, the ends crossed left over right or right over left. Although in the wild Crossbills are timid birds living high in the trees, they settle down extremely well to cage and aviary life. They do not mix much with other aviary birds and are better in separate aviaries, where a number of pairs can be housed together. Except for a few enthusiastic breeders they are not generally popular. They are bred quite regularly in aviaries as is their relation, the European Crossbill (*L. c. curvirostra*). Crossbill × Canary Mules have been bred at times and a very fine example of this cross gained the award as 'Best Bird in Show' at the National Exhibition of Cage and Aviary Birds, London, in 1964 and again in 1965.

Goldfinch (*Carduelis c. britannica*) Plates 84, 86
COCK Overall length about 5 in (13 cm). Eyes light brown. Beak whitish horn, dark at tip. Mask crimson red edged with white. Crown, sides of neck and wings black. Band of yellow on wings and white spots at ends of flights. Back brown. Upper tail coverts buff. Underparts white, washed with brown. Tail black with white tips. Feet and legs brown, lighter in aviary moulted birds.
HEN Similar to cock. Mask a little less in area and brightness.

These, like the Bullfinches, have distinct, brightly coloured markings; they also have a very sweet song. For centuries Goldfinches have been kept as pet singing birds in Great Britain and were especially favoured during the Victorian era. In cages, pens or aviaries they will nest and rear young with great freedom and there is an abundance of domesticated strains. To make their neat and compact little nests they need soft dried grasses, fine rootlets, short fine hair, natural wool, small feathers, and cobwebs for binding. Their clutches of eggs are usually four to six and the incubation time is thirteen days; incubation is carried out by the hen while both parents share the feeding.

In captivity and in the wild most pairs will have two nests each year. Cock Goldfinches mate readily with other British finches and Canaries (see p.57), giving rise to many beautifully coloured hybrids and mules (Plates 85, 86). A few specimens of pied and white Goldfinches have occurred in the wild but so far no domesticated strains of these mutations have been established.

Cage- or aviary-bred Goldfinches make good single household pets, becoming tame and friendly with their owners in a short time. Their song is soft and sweet and this often attracts people to Goldfinches in preference to other singing birds. In the house they are best kept in the all-wire or wire-and-plastic canary cages.

Greenfinch (*Chloris c. chloris*) Plate 87
Syn: Green Linnet
COCK Overall length about 6 in (15 cm). Eyes medium brown. Beak horn. General colour olive green, more yellowish on rump. Wings edged with bright clear yellow. Tail black, bright yellow at base. Feet and legs pinkish.
HEN Generally duller green having a brownish suffusion, yellow areas less bright.

Greenfinches are widely kept as aviary breeding birds because they reproduce freely. The shade of green varies in tone and brightness and there are 'yellow' and 'buff' forms in all shades; also, there are two established colour mutations – cinnamon and lutino – and both are sex-linked.

Their nests are larger and more loosely constructed than the Goldfinch's though the same materials are used for building. Clutches range from four to six in number and the hen incubates the eggs for thirteen days. Greenfinches eat seeds, berries, greenfood, fruit and some insects, the last particularly when they are feeding their young.

It is thought that blue, fawn, white and albino forms may be produced in time by using fertile mules paired with normal Greenfinches and lutino mutations. Experimental work is now going ahead to obtain these colours and the first steps look promising. In the initial cross-pairings Dominant White Canaries have been employed because normal Greenfinches are yellow-ground birds and to obtain required colours white ground is necessary.

Some Greenfinches are kept as household pets although not as frequently as Goldfinches. Their song is quite pleasing but their colouring is not particularly appealing to most pet owners. They are usually kept in mixed aviaries of British birds and for colour-breeding.

Linnet (*Carduelis c. cannabina*) Plate 88
Syn: Brown Linnet
COCK Overall length about 5¾ in (14·5 cm). Eyes dark brown. Beak dark horn. Forehead, centre of crown and breast crimson red. Nape and sides of neck mottled greyish brown. Wing and tail feathers blackish, edged with white. Chin and throat dull white, striped greyish brown. Stomach tinted white. Flanks brownish fawn. Feet and legs dark brown. In the winter time the crimson red areas are replaced by grey with dark mottling.
HEN Similar in colour to cock's winter plumage.

Linnets have been kept as singing birds for many generations and some people consider that few finches can surpass them for sweetness and variability of song. They breed well in captivity and were probably one of the first

British finch-like birds to be recognized as good aviary breeders. They are excellent parents and have frequently been employed to rear the young of other finches. Their nests are well made of grasses, moss, hair, wool and a few feathers. They are very adaptable and in aviaries will use almost any nesting materials that happen to be available. Clutches consist of four to six eggs, five being the usual number in captivity. Occasionally a pied specimen is seen although, as a species, they do not seem to mutate to any extent. Linnets are often used to cross with Canaries – their mules are highly regarded as singing birds because they have the fine song qualities of both parents.

Siskin (*C. spinus*) Plates 86, 90

COCK Overall length about 4½ in (12 cm). Eyes brown. Beak dark horn. General colour olive yellow. Throat and crown black. Rump yellowish. Wings barred with yellow and black. Underparts whitish. Flanks streaked with black. Tail black, yellow at base. Feet and legs brownish black.

HEN Upper parts greyish brown, streaked with blackish brown. Underparts whitish, streaked with dark brown. Yellow on rump, wing bands and base of tail. No black on head or throat.

These small, active, boldly made birds take easily to cage and aviary life, breeding quite freely in both small and large enclosures. There are a number of domesticated strains of the Siskin in several countries. They are much favoured by mule and hybrid breeders as they cross so readily with related species (see p.57). However, if kept in cages for long periods with access to unlimited quantities of oil-containing seeds they quickly become over-fat and unsuitable for breeding.

Siskins are thought to like some fruit-tree buds, but, in my opinion, it is the grubs in the buds and not the buds themselves they eat. Since their natural habitat is the mountainous and well-wooded areas, away from cultivated gardens, they are not troublesome to fruit growers to any degree. In the wild they feed mainly on the seeds of pine, birch, alder and spruce, and small insects.

Siskins nest somewhat later than most of the other common finches, probably waiting for their insect food to become plentiful. Their nests are beautifully made of mosses, down and other soft material and they need a good supply of these when breeding in aviaries. In captivity the average number of eggs per clutch is four and they usually hatch and rear them all if given plenty of insectivorous food and live insects.

Song Thrush (*Turdus philomelos*) Plate 89

COCK Overall length about 7 in (18 cm). Eyes golden brown. Beak horn. Upper parts olive brown. Throat light. Underparts yellowish, splashed with dark brown spots. Tail dark brown. Feet and legs brownish.

HEN Similar in colour to cock. Difficult to sex.

These are among the best loved of all the British song birds. Their song is sustained and melodious and, together with that of the Blackbird and Missel Thrush, forms an important part of the British spring bird song. In large and small gardens they are to be found busily engaged in searching for insects, worms, slugs and snails, which form the main items of their diet. The small losses of soft fruits to song birds are compensated for by the vast quantity of garden pests they annually consume.

Thrushes seem rather particular about where they build their nests and prefer good thick shrubs for building sites. It is not always possible for breeders to have such accommodation, so ingenuity must be used to find good substitutes. Bracken, heather, broom and pine branches can all be employed in making artificial sites that are acceptable to the birds. When rearing their young, the parents will eat a certain amount of insectivorous food but they must be given a reasonable quantity of live insects. captivity all their chicks are generally reared to full maturity since they are not subjected to natural hazards.

Two colour mutations of the Song Thrush are being bred in aviaries: cinnamon and dilute. The Cinnamon is a sex-linked form and follows the usual sex-linked inheritance, the Dilute may also be sex-linked although so far there is insufficient evidence to prove this. The mutants cross readily with the normal birds and domesticated strains of all three shades are being bred in captivity.

HOUSING

The majority of aviary-bred British birds are kept for breeding and exhibition purposes and therefore require a different type of housing from those kept solely for song and decoration. Exhibition birds should be housed for part of the year in aviaries or pens while the remainder can be kept in large stock cages. The cages used for housing Canaries (see pp.65–6) are quite suitable for most species of British birds, and aviaries and pens of the size used for Budgerigars will do for the birds when they are not breeding. When required for song and decorative purposes simply-designed flighted aviaries are ideal as they give the birds plenty of flying space and permit the owners to see them clearly. These aviaries should have sound, dry, draughtproof sleeping quarters, to which the all-wire flights are attached. Food, grit and water vessels should be kept in the sheltered part of the aviary with facilities for bathing in the flights. The flight perches should be tree branches varying in thickness, naturally arranged, and fixed so that the birds have plenty of flying space between them. The floors should be grassed, with some sandy areas, and thickly planted clumps of herbaceous garden flowers such as Michaelmas daisies, goldenrod, phlox and cosmos. A shallow pool for bathing can be made to look attractive with a surround of small rocks and rock plants.

Breeding-aviaries are best designed in ranges of small units, each to house a single breeding-pair of birds. They should consist of a sleeping and feeding section with planted all-wire flights as roomy as possible. Individual breeders have their own ideas for the internal arrangements of these breeding flights but the consensus of opinion is for heavy planting with shrubs and herbaceous plants. The floors of the sheltered portions should be either wooden or concrete and every precaution taken to keep out vermin. The perches in the shelters should be machined dowelling to facilitate quick and easy cleaning. Seed, water and grit vessels should be placed so they are clear of the perches so that filling and cleaning can be done with the minimum disturbance to the birds. Breeding birds are best left quietly on their own, visits to the aviary being limited to the daily feeding and watering routine and to ring the young.

FEEDING
Canary seed is the main ingredient of seed mixtures for British-seed eating birds, mules and hybrids; to this are added rape, hemp, sunflower, niger, teazel, and mixed wild seeds, in varying quantities according to species. Softbills need an insectivorous mixture together with soft fruits and live insects.

Most finches are extremely fond of niger which is a small black seed with a high oil content, but if given in too large quantities the birds will become over-fat. Hemp and sunflower seeds are also oil-bearing seeds and must only be given in controlled quantities. The smaller finch-like birds (Goldfinch, Siskin and Redpoll) prefer niger and some hemp. Bullfinch, Greenfinch and Hawfinch prefer the larger sunflower and hemp seeds. Birds in flighted aviaries naturally get much more exercise than those kept in cages and their allowance of oily seeds can be greater. Breeders have their own ideas as to how the seeds should

be given to the birds: some prefer a balanced mixture and others, including myself, give the seeds in separate dishes. The latter is less wasteful as the birds will eat the separate seeds in order of preference and not rummage about in a mixture to find the seeds of their choice.

In addition to seeds the birds need some form of soft food throughout the year, the amount being increased when they are breeding. They appear to prefer a fine insectivorous mixture with a small amount of cod-liver oil food added, made crumbly moist and given fresh daily. At breeding times some live food must be included in the diet. A constant supply of mixed grits, cuttlefish bone and mineral blocks, and fresh clean water for drinking and bathing are always necessary.

Greenfoods are essential and British birds will eat many varying kinds; they prefer them in their fresh green state but they also eat them when ripe and half ripe. The various wild weeds suggested for Canaries on p.68 are also eaten by the British finches, hybrids and mules, as well as the seeding heads of dock, hardheads (*Centaurea* species), plantain (*Plantago major*), thistles and oats. Most of these seeding heads can be dried and carefully stored for use during the winter months when ordinary greenfood is difficult to obtain. A further good greenfood liked by the majority of finches is sprouted seeds of canary, grass, rape, oats and wheat. When any of the cabbage family or lettuce go to seed whole plants can be put into the aviary and the birds will enjoy eating the seeds in their natural form.

There are several first-rate soft foods on the market especially blended to suit the requirements of the different kinds of soft-billed birds; the manufacturer's instructions should be followed. Although these are complete foods all the birds will benefit from a regular supply of live foods such as ants' eggs, gentles (maggots) and mealworms, which can be bought from bird stores. Various other insects can be collected from gardens and hedgerows to supplement and vary the standard diet. Snails are a useful extra for Thrushes and stone, brick or rock must be put on the flight floor for the birds to use as an 'anvil' to crack open the snail shells. Pieces of hard meat-fat and small amounts of raw shredded lean meat are beneficial and can be given periodically. The feeding habits of the different species vary somewhat and the owner will gradually find out the particular requirements of his or her stock of birds. Every effort must be made to keep the diet balanced.

BREEDING
All birds used for breeding must be fully mature

specimens of good quality and in perfect health. If the breeding pairs are not closed-ringed (banded) they should be marked with either split metal or plastic rings and the particulars carefully entered in a breeding register. This is the only safe method of keeping records of domesticated strains of any species and allows for controlled inbreeding to take place. I know of one strain of Greenfinches where the breeding records can be traced back over twenty-five years. These particular birds are of much better physique and colour than the vast majority of wild specimens and aviary-bred stock reared in uncontrolled conditions.

There seems to be a difference of opinion as to when the pairs should be put into the breeding quarters. Some think it best to leave the pair together all the time; others think they should be housed apart and allowed to mate just before breeding time. Both methods work quite successfully and it must be left to the individual breeders to follow the course they think best suited to their stock.

The correct nesting materials are essential for all aviary breeding birds. The materials should not be put in heaps on the flight floors but scattered around so the birds have to search for them. Manufactured wool, twine, horsehair, sewing cotton, nylon thread, fine wire, string and raffia must not be included; I have seen both adult and young birds badly damaged or even killed by becoming tangled up with one of these materials. Fields, hedgerows and gardens will provide plenty of soft dried grasses, fine twigs, rootlets, dried herbage stalks, mosses and vegetable down; these items can be collected throughout the year and stored in readiness for the breeding season.

It is most important that the birds are given ample supplies of grits and mineral-containing material throughout the year. It takes a long time for the birds to assimilate and accumulate in their systems the necessary quantities of minerals and vitamins needed to bring them into the right condition for producing families. Many birds fail to breed due to the shortage of such materials.

Breeding pairs should be left as undisturbed as possible; their owners should follow a strict routine of feeding and watering. This will help to keep the birds in a settled state and therefore add greatly to the chances of successful nesting and rearing of young. Just before the young are due to hatch a little soft food should be given to the adults and the amount gradually increased as the chicks arrive and begin to grow. Greenfoods, seeding heads and some live insects in increasing amounts must also be offered. In planted flights the birds will be able to find a small number of live insects themselves in addition to those supplied.

Only if breeders think that pairs will not object to their nests being inspected and the chicks closed-ringed should this be carried out. If there is any question of the chicks being deserted by nervous parents then the young should be split-ringed when they have flown. Closed-ringing should be carried out early in the day preferably when the birds have their morning food as the adults are less likely to be disturbed at that time. If closed rings are put on the young as late as possible there is little likelihood of their parents trying to remove them. When the young are safely feeding themselves they should be put into nursery aviaries to develop and moult and be given the same kinds of foods they have been having while with their parents.

I would like to put forward some suggestions on the possible breeding of white-ground Greenfinches by the use of hybrids. Red Factor Canaries were produced by using hybrids (mules) from crossing Red Hooded Siskins with Canaries (see p.59). There is every reason to believe that other crosses give a proportion of fertile hybrids (mules) and that the reverse process (back-crossing the Red Factor Canary hybrids with the Siskin) results in new coloured British birds. Linnets, Siskins and Greenfinches, and particularly the latter, would make good subjects for experiments.

Both cock and hen Greenfinches can be crossed with Canaries to produce mules and some of the fully mature cocks may be fertile. If these crossbred cocks are to prove fertile this does not happen until they are some three or four years old. Of Lutino and Cinnamon Greenfinches, the former are bred in the greatest numbers and are therefore more easily obtained. Dominant White Canary cocks mated with Lutino Greenfinch hens give Blue, and normal Green, Greenfinch Mules in cocks and hens. The young cocks will be Blue/Albino and Green/Lutino with the hens being just Blues and Greens. If cock Blue/Albino Greenfinch Mules are back-crossed to Lutino Greenfinch hens they give Blue, Green, Albino and Lutino Greenfinches, and mules of the same colours. Once this objective has been achieved strains of Albino and Blue Greenfinches could soon be established.

If fertile Blue/Albino and Green/Lutino Greenfinch Mule cocks are produced then, by back-crossing with Canaries instead of Greenfinches, Albino and Lutino Canaries should result. This Greenfinch cross-breeding experiment is being carried out in a number of places and it may not be too long before positive results are achieved. Similar crosses with Cinnamon Greenfinches, Siskins and Linnets have an equal chance of success. The future certainly holds much for the breeders of domesticated strains of British birds.

Exotic Birds

The term exotic means, of course, alien, or not indigenous, and thus implies different species to each reader according to where he or she lives. To the Australian reader, for example, the Gouldian Finch is not an exotic bird, but it is to a reader in the U.S.A. or Great Britain. In the context of this book the term should be construed as meaning birds not indigenous to Europe.

There is something fascinating in keeping and breeding birds from other countries and this is an increasingly popular section of the cage and aviary bird fancy. In different parts of the world there are a large number of species that vary greatly in size, shape and colouring, but only a limited number are suitable for general cage and aviary life. It is, perhaps, surprising how some species become quickly adapted to captivity and become domesticated. Export regulations wisely adopted by many countries to protect their bird life have resulted in concerted efforts to breed more species in captivity.

Because of the ease and the small cost at which many of the commonly imported kinds were obtainable, breeders have not, in the past, taken great pains to induce them to reproduce. It is realized today that this was not the correct approach to bird keeping and now there is a strong emphasis on getting all true pairs to breed and rear their youngsters in captivity. The majority of species discussed in this section of the book are those that are now reasonably common and have proved to be suitable subjects for domestication. There are, of course, numerous other species that periodically become available, but these should only be kept by experienced aviculturists as it is unforgivably wasteful for such birds to be in the hands of the inexperienced fancier. I would urge exotic-bird enthusiasts to make every possible effort to cooperate in building up stocks of species originating from countries that are now prohibiting the general export of birds. If this is done with reasonable success it is possible that limited export of these species may be allowed to approved breeders to strengthen, maintain, and develop the domesticated strains. Keepers of exotic birds should become members of one of their national or specialist foreign bird societies or one of the area societies. Membership of these societies introduces the enthusiast to other foreign-bird fanciers and facilitates the exchange of stock, and ideas on breeding methods. In Britain most of the societies are associated with and support the Foreign Bird Council – a body that deals with all matters that are of importance to exotic-bird keepers. The Avicultural Society of America is of great help in the U.S.A.

AUSTRALIAN FINCHES

These birds are not kept for their singing voices, which are practically non-existent, but for their colouring, and for the ease with which they will breed in many kinds of accommodation. Since the ban on the export of Australian birds over forty years ago practically all the stocks now available have been bred in captivity. The best known species is the Zebra Finch which, because of its world-wide popularity, is treated separately in rather more detail on pp.106 to 117. It is possible that some of the other freely breeding species have a similar development potential.

Bicheno's Finch (*Stizoptera bichenovii*)
Syn: Banded Finch, Owl Finch
COCK Overall length about 3½ in (9 cm). Beak whitish. Eyes brown. Upper parts brownish grey with dark bar-

ring. Forehead very dark, almost black. Cheeks, throat and underparts white. A narrow band of black runs across the middle of the chest from wing to wing and another, from the top of the eyes, completely circles the facial area. Wings dark brownish straw, spotted with tiny white dots. Rump white. Tail black. Feet and legs whitish pink.

HEN Similar to cock, but the black bars less clearly defined. Usually slightly smaller.

This is the smallest of the group known as Grass Finches. Although not as colourful as some Australian Finches, it has attractive ways and is quaint to look at. Whenever possible, and pairs can be obtained, it should be included in mixed aviaries of small finch-like birds. Until they are thoroughly acclimatized to their aviaries they are rather nervous and easily disturbed, but once they have settled down, most pairs will start to build nests and raise families. Most pairs prefer to build their own nests rather than make use of the conventional wooden nest boxes that are supplied for small exotic birds. When their chicks arrive they must be supplied with ample quantities of seeding grasses and chickweed, millet sprays, some small live insects such as greenfly, and live ants' eggs. Most are good attentive parents and will rear several nests in a season. Should any pairs seem to be a little temperamental with their eggs, they can be fostered out to Zebra Finches most of which will rear the young without any trouble. A subspecies – the Black-ringed (Black-rumped or Double-banded) Bicheno's Finch (*S. b. annulosa*) – has similar colouring except that the rump feathers are black instead of white. Not surprisingly this subspecies has been crossed a number of times with Bicheno's Finch and produced fertile offspring.

Cherry Finch (*Aidemosyne modesta*)

Syn: Modest Grass Finch, Plum-headed Finch
COCK Overall length about 4½ in (11·5 cm). Beak black. Eyes dark brown. Crown of head rich dark plum red. Upper parts dark brown, spotted with small white dots; the wing coverts and upper tail coverts are also well spotted with white. Tail blackish with a few white spots. Neck, underparts and sides of face white, barred with deep brown. Chin spot black. Feet and legs black.
HEN Similar to cock but without the plum head colour and black throat spot.

For some reason these birds seem rather more difficult to keep and breed than most of their relations and, consequently, are only popular with more experienced breeders. They can be successfully bred in large cages and pens, as well as flighted aviaries and are good parents.

They are similar to Bicheno's Finch in their feeding habits and can be given the same diet. There are a few records of Cherry Finches producing young when crossed with related Grass Finches and other small finch-like birds.

Diamond Sparrow (*Steganopleura guttata*) Plate 91

COCK Overall length about 5 in (13 cm). Beak plum red. Eyes brown. Head soft pale grey. Back and wings brownish. Throat grey. Underparts white with wide band of black over chest and along the flanks, where it is well spotted with large white dots. Feet and legs light red.
HEN Coloured like cock. Difficult to sex.

These are chubby thick-set finches with a striking colour pattern – it is this shape that has earned them the name of Sparrow. The courtship dance of the cock bird is very unusual and enables the sexes to be sorted out with a degree of certainty. Because of their bold shape, good colour, and friendliness in cages, they make fine exhibition birds. Diamond Sparrows always seem to thrive much better when they have plenty of space in which to fly; if kept in close confinement they tend to become too fat. Excess fat is a danger to the health of all species and such birds are of little use in the breeding quarters. Those species that are very prone to becoming overweight should not be kept in cages for long periods at a time.

When breeding they are somewhat quarrelsome and are likely to bully the more timid species; it is safer and they will probably nest more successfully if housed on their own. They are not particularly fussy where they construct their large, untidy nests; in planted aviaries they build their nests in shrubs, or if such sites are not available in wooden nest boxes and even in old nests of other birds. If the pairs are good healthy specimens they will rear broods of three to five chicks for a number of years. While the young are in the nests they will need extra greenfoods, some soft food, and a few live insects. Hybrids from crossing Diamond Sparrows with Zebra Finches, Long-tailed Grass Finches and Parson Finches, are the results of some of the pairings that have been recorded.

Gouldian Finch (*Erythrura gouldiae*)

Syn: Gouldian, Lady Gould's Finch, Purple-breasted Finch
COCK Overall length about 5 in (13 cm). Beak whitish pink with crimson-red tip. Eyes pale brown. Face blood red, with narrow border of black, bordered with brilliant blue gradually merging into the grass green of the upper parts. Chin and throat black. Wings grass green. Upper breast purple. Lower breast and underparts yellow with

some orange tinting. Tail black with the two central tail feathers long and finely pointed. Under tail coverts and vent white. Feet and legs pale pinkish.

HEN Somewhat similar in colour to cock only of a much duller tone.

In addition to the Red-headed Gouldian Finch described above there also exist, both in the wild and in captivity, two other forms – the Black-headed and the Yellow-headed, both of which are coloured the same apart from their heads. Only a small number of Yellow-headed birds are found in the wild flocks of Gouldian Finches, which consist mainly of the Red- or Black-headed varieties. The genes controlling red- and black-headedness are both sex-linked, the red being dominant over black; the gene controlling yellow-headedness is recessive.

These beautifully coloured finches can be considered as fully domesticated as all three forms have been consistently bred in captivity for a large number of generations. Under captive conditions mutations have appeared and have been established. From South Africa comes the White-breasted Gouldian finch, coloured like the species but the purple breast patch is replaced by a pure white area; it can be bred in all three head colours. This mutation appears to have been bred during the late 1950s and early 1960s and was exhibited for the first time in 1965. A Blue-breasted form has recently been reported and is now in the process of being established. A few years ago I was sent a colour transparency of a white variety that was being bred in the United States of America. These birds, although mainly white, did have the red or yellow areas but in a much reduced depth of colour. It will naturally be possible to breed all Gouldian mutations in the three different head colours as soon as they occur.

The general opinion among owners of Gouldian Finches is that as a species they are good breeders and parents although a trifle erratic in their nesting habits. Some pairs nest during the winter and others in the spring or autumn. This may well depend on the time of year they themselves were hatched as they come into breeding condition at about nine or ten months old. They make their rather rough nests of soft grasses in wooden nest boxes, of which they should have a plentiful choice. Some fanciers use half-open-fronted boxes, while others have found that their pairs prefer the Budgerigar nest boxes with circular entrance holes and perches. Both should be provided enabling the birds to choose for themselves, which helps them settle down to nesting more quickly. Plenty of soft dried grasses, moss, and a few feathers should be provided for nesting materials.

A family of Gouldian Finches – the cock (left) shows the colour delineation of the breast and the three young (centre) show the feeding guide-spots. The hen is on the right.

Clutches vary from three to seven in number and hatch after about fifteen days of incubation. The young birds have small phosphorescent spots at the base of the beak, which enable the parents to feed them in the dark.

Their general food requirements are simple, consisting of mixed millets, canary seed, millet sprays and plenty of seeding grasses and chickweed. When pairs are breeding they require the same kinds with extra seeding grasses and millet sprays. Some breeding pairs will eat a little soft food or wholemeal bread moistened with milk, although these items do not seem to be a necessity. At all times they must have plenty of grits, cuttlefish bone, mineral blocks, and some crushed charcoal. The Gouldian Finch is a delightful species to keep, breed and exhibit. The colouring is so vivid that it might almost be unnatural. A specialist society for Australian Finches was formed in Great Britain in 1972 and, undoubtedly, under its guidance Gouldian Finches and their mutations will be developed and will flourish to an even greater extent.

Long-tailed Grass Finch (*Poephila acuticauda*)

COCK Overall length about 7 in (18 cm). Beak yellow. Eyes dark brown. Crown and sides of head silver grey. Throat bib pear-shaped and jet black in colour. Eyes surrounded by elongated black ovals. Back rich fawn, deeper brown on wings. Breast pinkish fawn. Rump white with black band. Tail coverts and under wing coverts, vent and thighs white. Tail black, very long and tapering (about one third of the bird's total length). About the last inch (2·5 cm) of the two central feathers is very fine and hair-like. Feet and legs pale pinkish.

HEN Similar in colour to cock. Possibly a little smaller. Difficult to distinguish.

These are the best and most consistent breeders of all the Australian Finches except, of course, the Zebra Finches and are therefore an ideal species for fanciers embarking on the breeding of this group of birds. At nesting times they are apt to become quite spiteful to smaller and similar sized birds and are best kept on their own during this period. They like to build their nests in wooden boxes or small wicker baskets and need plenty of soft grasses for this purpose. The young should be removed from their parents as soon as they can properly fend for themselves.

Although not as colourful as some other species, their reproductive capacity makes them ideal birds for any breeding establishment, but unlike the Gouldian Finches they do not seem to produce mutations. There is, however, a subspecies that inhabits a different area of Australia known as Heck's Long-tailed Grass Finch (*P. a. hecki*), Plate 92; this is coloured just like *P. acuticauda*, except the beak, which is red instead of yellow. Both kinds will cross freely with each other and breeding records show the red-beaked variety is dominant over the yellow. The beak colours do not blend and by back-crossing the hybrids the two kinds reappear according to the Mendelian principles of heredity. When exhibited, the pairs must have the same coloured beaks. They are extremely difficult to sex by colour or size but it can be done quite accurately by watching for the clumsy courtship display of the cock birds.

Parson Finch (*P. cincta*)

COCK Overall length about 4½ in (11·5 cm). Beak grey black. Eyes dark brown. Top, back and sides of head silver grey with black stripes running from the eyes to the beak. Throat ornamented with large pear-shaped black bib. Back deep fawn. Wings brownish. Breast soft light fawn separated from the vent by an area of black. Rump black merging into white on upper tail coverts. Tail black and pointed. Feet and legs pinkish.

HEN Similar in colouring to cock but with head somewhat darker in shade. Generally a little smaller in build.

These are not so aggressive as the Long-tailed Grass Finches; nevertheless, they are best housed as single breeding pairs. Parson Finches are great nest builders and are not the least bit particular from what other nests they gather their material. Most fanciers have found them to be good breeders and they will rear their young without trouble. Their general habits are much like those of the Long-tailed Grass Finches with which they will

cross readily, producing hybrids that are said to be fertile. They make good exhibition birds but do not appeal to exhibitors in the same way as do the Long-tailed.

Ruficauda Finch (*Bathilda ruficauda*)

Syn: Rufous-tailed Finch, Star Finch

COCK Overall length about 4½ in (11·5 cm). Beak red. Eyes brown. Forehead, cheeks and throat bright vermilion with the cheeks heavily spotted with tiny white spots. Upper parts yellowish green. Breast and flanks yellowish olive green spotted with small white spots. Tail reddish brown. Feet and legs light pinkish.

HEN Similar in colouring to cock with less red on facial area.

These birds are much more slender and daintier in shape than the Grass Finches and are attractively coloured. They are good breeders in cages, and in aviaries

Ruficauda Finch

when they are not disturbed by more aggressive species. Generally speaking Ruficaudas do best when housed as single pairs either in large cages or in small aviaries. They need the same breeding management as other Australian Finches and, in the right conditions, will often rear two broods per year. While the growing young are in the nest they should be given reasonable quantities of small live insects in addition to their usual seed and greenfood.

Ruficaudas are useful birds for mixed aviary collections as they add colour in a different pattern of shades.

Other species in this admirable group, that are procurable from time to time, equally colourful and as free breeding, include the Pectorella Finch (*Lonchura pectoralis*), Chestnut-breasted Finch (*L. castaneothorax*). Masked Grass Finch (*Poephila personata*), Crimson Finch (*Neochmia phaëton*) and Painted Finch (*Emblema picta*).

MANNIKINS

Mannikins (not to be confused with Manakins) are a group of small birds with large, quite powerful beaks, mainly inhabiting Asia (*Lonchura* species), but some come from Africa (*Spermestes* species). They have much to recommend them, being hardy, inexpensive, and easy to house and feed. Previously, because they were freely imported to most countries, not enough thought was given to their breeding potential, which is quite high. However, fanciers now realize that it is better to breed the various species if the supply of birds is to be maintained. The chief colours of the mannikins are combinations of black, white, brown and grey, which can be most attractive although not as colourful as, for example, the Australian Finches. Taken as a whole they do not seem to produce colour varieties. Most mannikins exist quite well with other species provided, of course, that the aviary is not overcrowded. Given good peaceful conditions the majority of species will breed very well indeed. Even in mixed aviaries it is not unusual for a pair of mannikins to nest and produce young against great odds. It is rather difficult to be sure that the pairs are in fact true pairs as there is no colour difference between the sexes. This has led to a number of mixed pairings between different species which has resulted in hybrids. Bengalese (Society Finches) are the result of such crossings and, it is possible that other crossing would establish further hybrids.

Black-headed Mannikin (*Lonchura malacca atricapilla*)
Syn: Black-headed Munia, Black-headed Nun
COCK Overall length about 4½ in (11·5 cm). Beak silvery grey. Eyes dark brown. Head, throat and nape shiny black. Remainder of plumage deep rich chestnut brown with a black patch on the underparts. Feet and legs dark grey.
HEN Similar in colour to cock. It is difficult to distinguish between the sexes.

This is one of the most commonly kept species and will be seen in the majority of collections of small exotic birds. They are of a peaceful nature agreeing well with other small species, such as the waxbills. When housed with other birds they do not seem to breed readily although, in heavily planted flighted aviaries, true pairs will quickly nest. Under such conditions they may build their own nests or make use of wooden nest boxes. Plenty of dried grasses and mosses should be given so that those who wish to may construct the kind of nest they prefer. The toenails of all species of mannikins tend to grow rather long and it is important to ensure that they are clipped (see p.190) before the start of each breeding season. Many clutches of eggs are spoiled each year because owners fail to clip their birds' overgrown toenails. Black-headed Mannikins require the usual kinds of seeds, greenfoods and some soft food when breeding. A few birds will readily pair with related species – a fairly frequent occurrence in mixed collections.

Bronze-winged Mannikin (*Spermestes cucullatus*)
COCK Overall length about 4 in (10 cm). Beak grey. Eyes dark brown. Head and throat black with a metallic green sheen. Breast and stomach white. Back and wings chocolate with glossy black spots on shoulders. Flanks brownish grey marked with white. Rump beige marked with stripes of dark brown. Feet and legs black.
HEN Similar in colour to cock, and therefore difficult to distinguish.

These are one of the smallest and most handsomely coloured of the mannikins coming from Africa and fortunately they are successful breeders in captivity. They show their attractive colouring to the greatest advantage when housed in planted aviaries and they breed better under these more natural conditions. Pairs will, however, nest and rear young in large box-type breeding-cages or small unflighted pens. Like most members of the mannikin group they are hardy and will live quite happily in unheated aviaries throughout the year, provided they have access to dry draught-proof sleeping quarters. Their food requirements at all times are few and simple: they need only millet and canary seeds, millet sprays and greenfood. When rearing young they like a few small live insects and a little insectivorous soft food. As show birds

Pair of Black-headed Mannikins

they are excellent – they soon become tame and friendly and settle down well in show cages.

Java Sparrow *(Padda oryzivora)* Plate 93
Syn: Paddy Bird, Rice Bird, Temple Bird
COCK Overall length about 5 in (13 cm). Beak coral pink and very large. Eyes dark brown. General colour soft dove grey. Head and tail black. Cheek patches large and white. Stomach and under tail coverts white. Lower breast grey with a lilac tint. Feet and legs coral pink.
HEN Similar in colour to cock; difficult to distinguish between the sexes.

These are probably the most widely known of all exotic birds for they are imported into many countries in large numbers. It should be noted that they are a prohibited species in America. Present owners can continue to keep their stock but it is illegal to sell or give them away. The reason for this ban is economic: the Java Sparrows have established themselves in some southern states and farmers fear their eventual destructiveness to grain crops.

Their contrasting colours and silky plumage are outstanding. Their feathers are soft, smooth and bright, making the birds look as though they have been painted. It is often said when describing good show birds of other varieties, that 'their feathers are like those of Java Sparrows' which illustrates the impact the plumage of Java Sparrows has on the bird fancy. Wild Javas do not breed very freely in captivity, but the domesticated strains do, particularly the White (Plate 94) and Pied mutants that have been developed. Both of the latter are handsome birds and will cross readily with the wild type Greys to which the two mutations are recessive. A fawn mutation has been reported but information is sketchy and incomplete. Fawn in white-ground and Cinnamon in yellow-ground birds are always possible in the wild and the chances are greatly increased by the controlled breeding possible under domestic conditions.

Javas make ideal aviary birds and can be kept singly, in couples, or in true pairs, along with many other mannikins and finch-like birds. In spite of their large beaks, which give them a dangerous look, they are generally reasonably peaceful. At breeding times they do become a little more aggressive and will drive all other birds away from the vicinity of their nests. I have always found that Budgerigar-type nesting boxes are admirably suited and freely accepted by breeding pairs of Javas. Several boxes should be allocated for each of the breeding pairs and the boxes should be hung at varying heights in the aviary. When crossing Whites or Pieds with normal Greys for maintaining and strengthening the stocks, they should be bred under the strict control practised for all colour-breeding crosses.

On the whole Javas make first-rate parents and will rear strong healthy young on canary and millet seeds, millet sprays, greenfood and some soft food. They like paddy rice and the whole, unshelled grains of rice, which is their natural food, but they will live perfectly well in captivity for many years without this grain.

All varieties of Javas are somewhat difficult to sex; however, this can be done by watching for the cock bird's curious display. The cocks stretch out their necks and make a strange, little bubbly noise, while the hens sit quite still. It is advisable, once the sex of any bird has been definitely ascertained, to ring it with a coloured split ring and record it in the stock register.

Magpie Mannikin *(Spermestes fringilloides)*
COCK Overall length about 4½ in (11·5 cm). Beak top

Pair of Magpie Mannikins

dark, bottom light greyish. Eyes dark brown. Head black. Upper parts and wings deep rich brown. Chest and underparts white. Flanks black. Sides of underparts speckled black with brownish patch. Feet and legs dark brownish.

HEN Similar in colour to cock, sometimes a little smaller; difficult to sex.

This species is closely related to the Bronze-winged Mannikin but larger and more powerfully built, and can be considerably more aggressive to other species. It adapts itself very well to cage life and consequently makes a good exhibition bird. This feature and the pleasing colour, make it a popular mannikin with fanciers. At times, pairs will nest and rear chicks, but this is the exception rather than the rule as most pairs will not reproduce in captivity. Magpie Mannikins are more likely to breed, however, if housed on their own than they will in mixed flocks in a large aviary.

Silverbill *(Euodice cantans)* Plate 95
Syn: African Silverbill
COCK Overall length about 4½ in (11·5 cm). Beak silvery grey. Eyes brown. Upper parts pale brown. Underparts creamy buff. Wings dark brown. Rump and tail blackish. Feet and legs pinkish.
HEN Similar in colour to cock and therefore difficult to distinguish.

This is a very pleasing species that is imported in large numbers into many countries. The Silverbill's colouring is a little sombre, their nature peaceful and the cocks have a soft musical song. They are hardy, cheap, and breed well in many kinds of accommodation. Silverbills were the first exotic birds I ever bred in a small mixed flighted aviary – the parents produced four healthy chicks. This success was the start of my interest in the breeding of exotic birds, and since that time I have bred Silverbills under many varied conditions in cages and aviaries. I have always found Silverbills simple to breed as they require only ordinary seeds, greenfood, and some insectivorous soft food during that period. They usually like to construct their dainty nests in wooden nest boxes and require plenty of soft grasses, mosses and a few feathers. Several breeding pairs can be kept together in the same aviary quite amicably and, at times, will even feed each other's chicks when they are on the perches.

There is another species, the Indian Silverbill *(E. malabarica)*, Plate 96, which comes from India. In colouring they are much like the African species but are slightly larger and have distinctive white rumps. The Indian birds do not seem quite as hardy as the African, nor do they breed so readily. The two species are frequently crossed and the young they produce are fertile.

Spice Mannikin *(Lonchura p. punctulata)* Plates 97, 104
Syn: Nutmeg Finch, Spice Bird, Spotted Munia
COCK Overall length about 4½ in (11·5 cm). Beak dark silver grey. Eyes brown. Head, neck, back and wings a warm nutmeg brown shade, darker on head and throat. Breast and underparts nicely spangled with buff and brown. Tail dark. Feet and legs pale brown.
HEN Similar in colour to cock; difficult to distinguish between sexes.

This is another widely-kept mannikin that is hardy, easy to feed, and looks well with birds of similar size both in cages and aviaries. Their particular pattern of colouring acts as an effective foil to the more brightly coloured birds in a mixed aviary collection. They are equally at home in cages, settling down contentedly and living happily for many years. There are several other sub-species, periodically obtainable, that differ a little in size and colour pattern to the more common race. Numbers of hybrids are bred annually from the subspecies and other related mannikins and, like the pure kinds, make excellent show birds. Some years ago I saw a cock bird that was heavily marked with white but unfortunately it would not pair with any hen.

Tri-coloured Mannikin *(L. malacca)* Plate 98

Syn: Three-coloured Mannikin, Tri-coloured Nun
cock Overall length about 4½ in (11·5 cm). Beak light greyish. Eyes deep brown. Head, throat and underparts black. Upper chest and flank white. Back, wings and other parts warm chestnut brown. Feet and legs brown.
hen Similar in colour to cock and hence difficult to distinguish.

These birds are typical mannikins in their shape, size and general behaviour towards other birds. Most owners find this species attractive for exhibiting, decorative as aviary birds, but indifferent as breeding stock. Some pairs have been known to nest and rear young, mainly in well-planted aviaries, and when they do breed they invariably make good and attentive parents.

White-headed Mannikin *(L. maja)* Plate 99

Syn: Maja Finch, White-headed Nun
cock Overall length about 4½ in (11·5 cm). Beak light greyish. Eyes brown. Head, throat and cheeks white, changing to buff at nape and breast. Back and wings bright chocolate brown. Underparts, under tail coverts and middle of stomach very dark brown almost black. Tail rich brown. Feet and legs greyish brown.
hen Similar to cock but head colour usually not so clear.

White-headed Mannikins are even more commonly found in mixed outdoor aviary collections than Tri-coloured Mannikins which they resemble in many ways. Their food consists of mixed millets, canary seed, millet sprays, greenfood and a periodic dish of soft food. They are of a very friendly nature and tame quickly whether housed in cages or aviaries. Imported birds do not nest very easily which is rather disappointing, but with some patience and perseverance I feel that much freer breeding strains could be satisfactorily developed. They are hardy, easy to feed, and a likeable species, and deserve to have more time given to their culture. There is a sub-species, the Javan White-headed Mannikin *(L. m. fer-ruginosa),* which is black on throat and upper breast and larger in size. These birds are sometimes imported with their smaller relations.

Other species of mannikin such as the Bib-Finch *(Spermestes nana),* the Rufous-backed Mannikin *(S. bicolor nigriceps)* and the Sharp-tailed Finch *(Lonchura striata acuticauda)* are sometimes available and are all pleasing additions to a collection.

PARROT FINCHES

This group of brightly coloured birds comes from the Malayan Peninsula and some of the nearby islands. They are much in demand by keen breeders of exotic birds for their colour, their exhibition potential, and the free way in which they breed in captivity. Like many birds they are a little difficult to keep in confinement until they become fully accustomed to their new climatic conditions. Some strains have been bred in aviaries in Great Britain, Europe, America and Australia for so many generations that they can now be claimed to be thoroughly domesticated. Over the years most of the species have been crossed together and produced fertile offspring. These hybrids when back-crossed to their parent species will give young of the original species and hybrids in equal numbers in accordance with the Mendelian principles of heredity. This fact is very useful to breeders and prevents too close inbreeding when there is a shortage of a particular species. From all points of view, parrot finches are highly desirable birds in any collection of exotics.

Blue-faced Parrot Finch *(Erythrura trichroa cyaneifrons)*

cock Overall length about 4½ in (11·5 cm). Beak blackish. Eyes black. General colour bright grass green, darker on the upper parts. Facial area deep bright blue. Tail, rump and upper tail coverts red. Feet and legs dark brown.
hen Similar in colouring to cock but not so bright on face.

Since the idea that parrot finches were delicate and difficult to keep or breed was dispelled, considerable numbers of this vividly coloured species are bred each year in many countries. By nature they are of a peaceful disposition and several pairs can be housed together in an aviary for breeding. They make their nests of dried grass, moss, and feathers, in the usual box-type nests. The clutches of eggs vary from three to six and incubation takes twelve to fourteen days, with both parents sharing the feeding of the young. Most fully matured pairs raise two nests of chicks in a season. They prefer to breed in planted outdoor flighted aviaries although some pairs have been known to nest in indoor pens and even in large box-type breeding-cages. Several breeding pairs in planted aviaries invariably give the most satisfactory results as to the number of young produced. Their diet is canary and mixed millet seeds, millet sprays, some fine insectivorous food, plenty of seeding grasses and other greenfoods, and a few live insects. They cross readily with other members of the parrot finch family to produce fertile young.

Pin-tailed Parrot Finch (*E. prasina*) Plate 100
Syn: Pin-tailed Nonpareil
COCK Overall length about 5½ in (14 cm). Beak blackish. Eyes black. Head, throat and upper chest blue. Middle chest scarlet, fading and turning to golden brown on lower parts. Upper parts, wing coverts and secondaries bright grass green. Upper tail coverts vermilion red. Flights blackish edged with green. Tail greenish with the two long central feathers crimson red. Feet and legs pale brown.
HEN Similar in colour to cock but duller and without the blue and red areas.

Although imported a little more freely than other members of the group, wild birds are, unfortunately, rather difficult to acclimatize. Aviary-bred specimens, which are now becoming more plentiful, soon settle down to new quarters and feeding. Their gorgeous array of bright colours makes them very desirable birds for outdoor planted aviaries. It is unwise to keep Pin-tails in cages for too long a time as they quickly put on weight and this leads to ill-health. If housed in aviaries with plenty of flying space they will live and breed quite happily for many years. They have an even temperament and can safely be housed with other birds that are not quarrelsome. The usual finch-type nesting boxes are generally used by breeding Pin-tails but occasionally pairs prefer to build their own nests in the thick cover of a planted aviary. Attractive hybrids occur when Pin-tailed Parrot Finches are crossed with related species.

Red-headed Parrot Finch (*E. psittacea*)
COCK Overall length about 5 in (13 cm). Beak blackish. Eyes blackish brown. General colour bright grass green. Head, throat, upper chest, rump and tail deep rich red. Feet and legs dark brown.
HEN Similar in colour to cock but red areas not quite so deep in shade.

This and the Blue-faced Parrot Finch are probably more commonly seen than other members of the group. Though relatively expensive to purchase, the willingness with which most pairs reproduce makes their acquisition well worth while. They make excellent aviary birds mixing well with their own and other species and not quarrelsome even when breeding. Like all parrot finches they nest in covered wooden boxes similar to those used by most exotic finches. They need the same management and food as described for the Pin-tailed. A constant supply of grit, cuttlefish bone, mineral blocks and crushed dried domestic hens' egg-shells (the last ingredient is very valuable for all parrot finches) should not be forgotten.

Royal Parrot Finch (*E. cyaneifrons regis*)
Syn: Blue-bellied Parrot Finch
COCK Overall length about 5½ in (14 cm). Beak blackish. Eyes dark brown. Head, face and tail vivid red. General colour peacock blue, lighter on chest area and becoming suffused with green towards vent. Wings green. Feet and legs brown.
HEN Similar in colour to cock with smaller facial area and duller in general tone. Flanks more greenish.

This most brilliantly coloured species was unknown in European aviaries until 1934 – the year of its first importation. It rivals the Gouldian Finch with its gorgeous intense colouring, and certainly earns its common name. It is more heavily built than the other parrot finches, but rather nervous and easily startled when first introduced into new quarters. Because of their timid nature the birds are not very satisfactory breeders in captivity, although a few young have been raised in various countries. With suitably planted aviaries, and care and patience on the part of owners, it should be possible to establish much freer breeding strains. The general management and its food requirements are same as that of the other species, although to the diet should be added sweet apple, for which the bird has a great liking. In their wild state, their food mainly consists of various soft fruits and their seeds. Royal Parrot Finches are lovely birds but rather difficult to keep and so only practicable for very experienced aviculturists.

Other species that are occasionally obtainable are: the Blue-collared (*E. serena*), the Tri-coloured (*E. t. trichroa*) and the Peale's (*E. pealei*) Parrot Finches; all need the same management as those species already described.

OTHER FINCH-LIKE SPECIES
This section embraces various species that do not belong to large groups but which are regularly imported. The laws governing the movement of South American birds have recently been tightened considerably and their export has

been prohibited. Prior to these regulations some species of American birds had been imported into different countries and exist in various numbers in collections. The present owners of such birds should make every effort to encourage the birds to reproduce and thus form aviary breeding strains. If this is not done American species will have to be omitted from most ordinary collections of birds.

Pope Cardinal *(Paroaria dominicana)*
Syn: Dominican Cardinal
COCK Overall length about 7 in (18 cm). Beak, top dark grey, bottom whitish. Eyes brown. Head and throat crimson red. Upper parts grey with some black and large black shoulder patches. Some grey on flanks. Tail dark grey. Feet and legs greyish.
HEN Similar in colour to cock, but red areas usually not quite so bright. Difficult to distinguish from the cock bird.

This species is very similar in colour to the Red-crested Cardinal except that it does not have the distinctive crest. In their native Brazil they are one of the most popular singing birds and their song is sweeter and more varied than their near relation – the Red-crested Cardinal. They require the same kind of food and general management as that species but are generally more difficult to breed. A few pairs have been reported as breeding quite freely but others housed under the same conditions have made no attempt to nest. Of course, this can happen in any species because all pairs are individual in their acceptance of captive conditions.

Red-crested Cardinal *(P. cucullata)* Plate 101
COCK Overall length about 7½ in (19 cm). Beak whitish, dark at tip. Eyes golden brown. Head, throat and chest bright red. Upper parts soft grey, darker on wings and tail. Underparts white with some grey on flanks. Feet and legs blackish.
HEN Similar in colour to cock. Red areas usually not quite so bright. Difficult to distinguish sexes.

These South American birds have many enthusiastic owners both in their own country, where they are widely kept as singing birds, and in many others, particularly in Europe. Their erect red crests set off by their grey and white plumage together with their fearless behaviour make them fine birds for planted outdoor aviaries. Their song is quite pleasing, although the number of notes used is limited when compared with those of well-known singing species such as the Thrush or Blackbird. It is best to house this species with strong birds like weavers, whydahs and the larger mannikins for, even if they are not particu-larly aggressive, a peck from their strong beaks could seriously damage small birds such as waxbills. They have been kept quite successfully with Budgerigars and Cockatiels. In planted aviaries they often build their own fairly large nests of grasses and dried herbage in thick bushes. Sometimes pairs ignore natural sites and use open-type boxes, baskets or even a food dish should it be conveniently placed for their purpose. When the young are in the nests they require quite large amounts of live insects in addition to their usual canary, millet and sunflower seeds, fruit and greenfood. They cross quite freely with closely related species such as the Pope and the Yellow-billed Cardinal and produce fertile young. Some years ago, in a mixed aviary of weavers, I had a Pope cock and a Red-crested hen, which reared two broods of four young in a nest built in a large flat grit pot on an open shelf. The young were reared mainly on insectivorous food, apples, maggots and mealworms. This example proves that some pairs will nest in the open quite unconcerned of what is happening around them.

Virginian Cardinal *(Richmondena cardinalis)* Plate 102
Syn: Red Cardinal, Scarlet Cardinal, Virginian Nightingale
COCK Overall length about 8½ in (22 cm). Beak bright red. Eyes golden brown. Upper parts and tail brick red. Head, crest, cheeks and underparts bright red. Base of beak surrounded by narrow black band which widens at throat to form a bib. Feet and legs brownish red.
HEN Upper parts brownish olive. Crest, thighs and tail dull brick red. Underparts dark fawn. Band around beak and bib dusty black.

The largest and generally considered to be the most strikingly coloured of all the cardinals, this species is one of the earliest exotic birds from the New World to be kept in European aviaries. The North American race is a little larger than the Mexican, which is even more brilliant in its colouring and consequently in greater demand. Observations have shown that when they have moulted in captivity Virginian Cardinals rarely regain the vividness of colour they had in the wild. There are some points of resemblance between its song and that of the Nightingale *(Luscinia megarhynchos)* but there can be no real comparison with the sweetness and variation of the Nightingale's voice. Once acclimatized, Virginian Cardinals are tough and can be housed in outdoor aviaries throughout the year. They thrive on the diet described for other members of the cardinal family and, in addition, some birds will eat certain berries, such as those of the hawthorn, rowan and bramble (blackberries). Breeding has been restricted by the small number of hens exported, cock birds being preferred because of their colour and song. When true pairs are obtained they nest reasonably well and rear their young to full maturity. During this period they need more fruit and live insects, and some coarse insectivorous food. With perseverance it should not be difficult to establish domesticated strains of these very delightful birds.

From time to time the Yellow-billed Cardinal (*Paroaria capitata*) and the Green Cardinal (*Gubernatrix cristata*) are also imported and can be managed in the same way as the Virginian Cardinal. In addition there are some sub-species and related species that are sometimes exported in mixed consignments, all of which are attractive additions to a collection.

Cuban Finch *(Tiaris canora)* Plate 103
Syn: Melodious Finch
COCK Overall length about 3½ in (9 cm). Beak greyish. Eyes brown. Crown, back, wings and tail yellowish olive green. Forehead and mask black surrounded by wide bright yellow-orange area. Upper breast blackish merging into pink-tinted grey on the underparts. Feet and legs very dark brown.
HEN Similar in colour to cock but without black on upper breast. Forehead and mask dark brown. Yellow areas paler.

These delightful little finches come from the island of Cuba. Unfortunately, they are not very common in aviaries but there are stocks in breeding establishments in Great Britain, Europe and America. Cuban Finches are easy to manage, feed and breed. They are extremely active birds, well suited for housing in large aviaries, where they look their best if kept in small flocks. They are peaceful birds among themselves, but somewhat aggressive to other species at breeding times. Single pairs do well in flights containing weavers, whydahs, or similar sized birds. In such conditions they often use weavers' old nests in which to construct their own dainty ones. Some nest boxes should also be supplied for the use of any pairs who will not build their own or cannot find one to take over. Plenty of soft grasses and a few feathers are sufficient for nesting material. In addition to panicum, small canary seed, white millet and greenfoods they will need fine insectivorous food and small live insects when the young are hatched. Most pairs will hatch and rear two nests of young per year, but to prevent the parents harassing the earlier chicks it is advisable to remove them before the second clutches hatch. They are such good parents that

some breeders allow them out of the aviaries to search for food. Obviously, this cannot be continued once the young are ready to fly.

A related species, the Olive Finch *(T. olivacea)*, also from Cuba, is not as attractive in its colouring as the Cuban and is seldom found in aviaries.

Green Singing Finch *(Serinus mozambicus)* Plate 105
COCK Overall length about 5 in (13 cm). Beak light brown. Eyes pale brown, surrounded by black oval patches with streaks of yellow above and below. Head, mantle and back dark green, with the feathers having a dark grey central streak. Wings and tail very dark almost black with some pale yellow edging. Rump, underparts and throat lemon yellow, paler on the underparts. Feet and legs yellowish.
HEN Similar to cock in colour but duller, the green having a brownish tint and the yellow area paler. The throat has some brownish spots.

These little African Finches, related to the Canary, are always welcome inhabitants of any aviary collection of small birds. They are active, quite pleasing in colour, and have a nice song. They settle well in captivity and have a quite extraordinary life span. Individual birds have been reported as living from twelve to twenty years and one pair, seen by the author, was reputed to have lived for some twenty-four years, the only visible sign of age being heavy scaling on their legs. Most pairs will nest and rear young both in cages and aviaries, and need only some soft food to supplement their normal diet of seed and green-food. They use open-fronted nest boxes in cages and pens, while in planted aviaries they generally prefer to build their own nests with grasses, etc. Green Singing Finches will pair readily with the smaller types of Canaries. Any cocks produced from these crosses have very fine singing voices.

One closely related species, the Grey Singing Finch *(S. leucopygius)*, is much duller in colouring but this is compensated for by a very fine song (Plate 104). They breed equally well in captivity and cross readily with the Green Singing Finch. There are several other related species and subspecies, examples of which are sometimes to be seen in mixed collections, all needing similar management.

Green Twinspot *(Mandingoa nitidula)* Plate 106
COCK Overall length about 4½ in (11·5 cm). Beak dark grey. Eyes brown. General colour olive green with deep

orange above and below the eye and around the beak. The throat is yellowish green, rump orange, and the breast and underparts are black, spotted with small white dots. Feet and legs brownish grey.

HEN Similar to cock but paler, the face area being dull yellow.

This species belongs to a small group of African birds that live mainly in forest areas. It is comparatively rare in aviaries. Twinspots are somewhat delicate when first imported, but after settling down they are reasonably hardy although they cannot be wintered without heat. Their diet is mixed millet seeds, millet sprays, some small canary seed, a little soft food and greenfood, particularly seeding grasses and chickweed. Young have been reared from the Green Twinspot both by the parent birds and also by Bengalese foster parents.

Melba Finch *(Pytilia melba)* Plate 107
Syn: Crimson-faced Waxbill
COCK Overall length about 5 in (13 cm). Beak red. Eyes dark brown. Forehead, throat, cheeks and tail crimson red. Head and neck grey. Beak and wings olive green.

Pair of Aurora Finches, cock on left

Yellow bar on lower breast. Stomach whitish, broken with black barring and spots. Feet and legs brownish yellow.
HEN Paler in colour and without red on the head.

An attractive bird which, when fully acclimatized, is reasonably hardy. When not nesting it mixes well with other species of similar size. At breeding times only single pairs should be housed with other birds because when defending their nesting areas they can become quite dangerous. Most pairs prefer to build their own dome-shaped nests but some nesting boxes should be available for those that prefer a ready-made site. Although it is usual for eggs to be laid and hatched few young reach maturity. This is probably because their owners do not supply the correct food for them to rear their young successfully. Melbas should have plenty of millet sprays, seeding grasses, seeding chickweed and other seeding greenfoods, small live insects, a fine insectivorous soft food, panicum millet, white millet and canary seeds. Better breeding results would probably be achieved if the breeding pairs were each kept on their own in small planted aviaries.

Other species of *Pytilia* periodically seen in aviaries, are the Aurora Finch *(P. phoenicoptera)* and Red-faced Finch *(P. afra)*. They require the same general management and food.

Red Hooded Siskin *(Spinus cucullatus)*
Syn: Hooded Siskin and Venezuelan Red Siskin
COCK Overall length about 4 in (10 cm). Beak blackish brown. Eyes brown. General colour bright vermilion red. Head and wings black. Tail dark with black markings. Feet and legs blackish.
HEN Upper parts grey with some vermilion suffusion on back and chest. Rump light vermilion. Underparts orange red with some white.

This species is frequently misnamed the Hooded Siskin by bird breeders in many countries – a name which belongs to *S. magellanicus* or *S. ictericus* (Plate 108). *S. cucullatus* should be correctly called Red Hooded Siskin, which perfectly describes their unusual colouring. It is a somewhat delicate species until fully acclimatized and even then it requires a certain amount of heat during cold weather. Most of the imported birds are cocks, which mate readily with small Canary hens to produce hybrids containing the Red Factor in the genetic make-up (see p.59). Hens are not so common and do not settle down to nesting in captivity. Red Hooded Siskins must have reasonable quantities of niger seed if they are to thrive and most will eat some canary seed and perhaps a little sweet red rape. Greenfoods such as seeding grasses, chickweed, shepherd's purse and seeding dandelion heads also form an essential part of their diet. When the young hatch, the parents require some soft food, either a Canary-rearing food, or a mixture of that and a fine insectivorous food. Aviary life seems to suit them and they spend much time in the bushes and herbage looking for small insects. For cross-breeding experiments cock birds can be kept in cages – an environment in which they are equally at home.

Ribbon Finch *(Amadina fasciata)* Plate 98
Syn: Cut-throat

COCK Overall length about 5 in (13 cm). Beak light horn. Eyes medium brown. General colour soft dark biscuit with the upper feathers edged with black. Underparts have a slight pinkish suffusion and the black edging of the feathers is much finer. Throat, and below the eyes, whitish and below this is a wide crimson band. Tail dark brown. Feet and legs light brown.

HEN Similar in colour to cock but without the crimson throat band.

This is one of the best-known and most universally kept of the small hardy African seed-eating species. It is cheap to purchase and easy to obtain. Birds can be kept in large cages, pens or aviaries, in any of which they thrive extremely well. Breeding will start more quickly if they are kept in outdoor aviaries. When breeding they are pugnacious and should only be mixed with other species that are able to defend themselves; at other times they can be housed with most smaller species. They are somewhat sparrow-like in their nesting habits, building large untidy nests in boxes with almost any kind of material that is available. The average clutch is five and both parents share the incubation and chick rearing. Although Ribbon Finches are of a seemingly trusting nature, they will desert their eggs and young if their nests are inspected or disturbed. During the breeding period they need their normal seed diet supplemented with plenty of fresh greenfood, live insects and soft food; some pairs will take wholemeal bread and milk. The young birds should be removed from their parents when it is seen that they are able to fend for themselves. Recent enquiries indicate that quite large numbers of this species are now being bred annually and some fanciers have several generations of aviary-bred birds.

There are some subspecies, distinguished by variations in colouring, which are occasionally found in consignments of the normal kind. Another member of the genus is the Red-headed Finch *(A. erythrocephala)*, which is a little larger and the cock's head is completely red (Plate 104). Given the same treatment they can be bred as easily as the Ribbon Finches and the two species will cross-breed. Both species make fine exhibition birds as they quickly adapt themselves to cage life.

Saffron Finch *(Sicalis flaveola)* Plate 109
COCK Overall length about 5½ in (14 cm). Beak light brown. Eyes dark brown. Forehead and crown rich bright orange becoming more yellow at the sides of the head. Upper parts greenish yellow streaked with dark brown. Underparts clear yellow. Flights and tail yellowish with dark brownish-grey markings. Feet and legs light brown.

HEN Similar in colour to cock but much duller. Orange areas less rich in shade.

This species is very popular and freely imported from South America, where it is a common bird. In captivity they are hardy, easy to feed and breed, and the cocks have a pleasant song. They eat canary seed, mixed millets, a small quantity of hemp with greenfood, and some soft food; when the young are in the nests the quantities of the latter two items should be increased. They make good cage birds and most pairs so housed will nest if not disturbed too much by their owners. As aviary breeding birds they are excellent and will nest and rear young freely using ordinary finch nesting boxes. It is this fact as well as their hardiness, song and colouring that makes them such popular birds with the beginning breeders of exotic birds. They usually have two clutches of four or five eggs per year and will rear a high proportion of their young. It should not be difficult to develop good free-breeding domestic strains of this species and several related kinds which become available from time to time. Cock birds will pair with hen Canaries to produce richly coloured young, the cocks of which have a melodious song.

Among the related species that are sometimes seen in aviaries are Pelzelni's Saffron Finch *(S. pelzelni)*, Plate 110, and the Yellow Finch *(S. arvensis)*. Both are smaller and have less rich colouring.

DOVES
The smaller members of the pigeon family are generally known as doves and some of them can be successfully kept as aviary birds in mixed collections. There are a large number of species in the world, many of which have been domesticated and developed beyond all recognition by many years of cross-breeding. Most of the commonly

imported species are simple to feed and house, hardy, and some are regular breeders. Soberly coloured and tolerant to other bird species, they make a suitable contrast in collections of more brightly coloured birds. Although non-aggressive to birds of other groups, they can be vicious towards other members of their family. Moreover, their repeated cooing notes can be monotonous in a limited area and some fanciers may consider this to be a drawback. The four species described below are all easy to obtain and keep and are mostly seen in general aviaries.

Barbary Dove (*Streptopelia roseogrisea*) Plate 111
Syn: Ring-necked Dove
COCK Overall length about 9 in (23 cm). Beak orange. Eyes golden. General colour light fawn with a pinkish suffusion on breast. Black ring around back of neck. Undersides of tail black and white. Feet and legs pinkish.
HEN Similar in colour to cock; difficult to distinguish sexes.

The best known member of the dove family, this is the domesticated form of the African Collared Dove. There is also a white form generally called the Java Dove. Many Barbary Doves carry the white character in their genetic make-up and it is not unusual for pairs to produce young of both colours. An apricot-coloured form and a frilled form, which has rough feathers like a Frill Canary, exist in America and both are recessives like the White.

Barbary Doves can be kept in aviaries containing even the smallest waxbills which they will not harm in any way. They are very free breeders and lay their two white eggs almost anywhere. They should be given suitable flat baskets, earthenware nest pans, or wire-mesh platforms, so they can build their flimsy nests of small twigs and pieces of straw in safety. Their food consists of millet, small wheat, dari, with fresh greenfoods and an occasional dish of soft food. If handled when very young they become extremely tame and are very suitable as first pet birds for young people.

Cape Dove (*Oena capensis*) Plate 112
Syn: Harlequin Dove, Masked Dove, Namaqua Dove
COCK Overall length about 8 in (20 cm). Beak purplish at base tipped with yellow. Eyes golden brown. Head, neck, mantle and wing coverts silvery grey. Front of head and throat black. Breast and stomach white. Upper parts brownish grey. Lower back buff with white band between two blackish ones. Wings chestnut brown with metallic blue patches on coverts. Tail blackish and long (about half of overall length). Feet and legs purple brown.

HEN Similar in colour to cock, but duller and without black on head and throat. Beak dark horn.

This South African species is known by a number of widely differing names which may confuse beginners into thinking that they are separate species. They are imported into Great Britain and Europe in considerable quantities and find favour amongst aviculturists who like peaceful birds to populate large mixed aviaries. Aviary-bred and fully acclimatized pairs will, under good conditions, breed quite regularly. Breeding birds should be given a number of small-wire mesh platforms fixed high in the aviary on which to build their nests. Their own choice of sites is often very poor, the nest consisting of only a few twigs and pieces of straw placed on a ledge or in a bush. Each year many eggs and young are lost through falling out of these flimsy nest structures – the wire mesh helps to prevent this. The pairs are inclined to be nervous when breeding and are always more successful when not unnecessarily disturbed. Their food requirements are simple, consisting of white, yellow and panicum millet with greenfoods and grits; some birds will also eat a little canary and maw seed. No extra foods are needed at breeding time for, like all the dove family, the young are fed with food prepared in their parents' crops (crop milk).

Diamond Dove (*Geopelia cuneata*) Plate 113
COCK Overall length about 7½ in (19 cm). Beak horn grey. Eyes red, surrounded by an area of red skin. Head, neck and tail warm lavender grey. Upper parts pure light grey. Vent area light grey. Wings rosy grey covered with tiny white dots. Feet and legs red.
HEN Similar in colour to cock. Back and wings somewhat more brownish in shade. Somewhat difficult to distinguish from the cock.

This is one of the smallest doves suitable for the aviary. The original stock came from Australia so long ago that the species can be said to be truly domesticated. They breed well but need help in nest construction. Eggs are often laid in most precarious positions with little to prevent them from falling and smashing on the aviary floor. Canary nest pans or little platforms of small-mesh wire with a few twigs and some straw should be placed in high positions and most pairs will make use of this material to build safer nests. Good, healthy breeding pairs will often hatch and rear six to ten chicks in a single season. To add further interest to their breeding there are mutant dilute silver and cream forms. Diamond Doves can be kept in mixed collections of exotic birds as they do not disturb other inhabitants with the exception, of course, of other doves. Diamond Doves need the same food and treatment as Cape Doves.

Necklace Dove (*Streptopelia chinensis*) Plate 114
Syn: Chinese Necklace Dove, Spotted Chinese Turtle Dove
COCK Overall length about 13½ in (34 cm). Beak black. Eyes orange brown. Head grey, paler in front and nape light reddish with a wide black necklace spotted with white. Upper parts brown and underparts tinted with red. Wings dark grey and brown, lighter at edges. Feet and legs red.
HEN Smaller and paler in colour than cock and has yellow eyes.

This handsome little dove is found over a wide area of Asia; in Africa there are some subspecies which vary slightly in their colour pattern. It takes extremely well to captivity, but requires a large secluded aviary for it is a timid bird when nesting and if disturbed deserts its eggs. When the hen is sitting her mate will drive away all other birds from the nesting area. They are hardy, long lived, and once settled produce chicks with great regularity. Hybrids with related species have been bred.

Necklace Doves have escaped from captivity in Southern California, where flocks of them are now part of the local fauna.

Other doves, rarer in captivity, require much the same general management as the foregoing species, but special attention should be paid to their acclimatization.

SOFTBILLS
This term is used to describe those birds that feed upon insects, fruit and nectar; it distinguishes them from those that eat seeds (the 'hardbills'). Among the birds included in this category are bulbuls, tanagers (p.175), toucans (p.175), sunbirds and humming birds. Some of them need so much special care that they are best kept in zoological or bird gardens, where the necessary time and money is available. Perhaps one of the greatest difficulties lies in their refusal to accept a diet that replaces their natural one. There are, however, some species that are comparatively hardy, not too expensive and make good subjects for those aviculturists who have already successfully managed the hard-billed groups and wish to gain further experience. Because of the nature of the food eaten by these species they require special housing and cleaning so that their aviaries, birdrooms and cages, are always clean and have no unpleasant odour. When kept in temperate countries many of the soft-billed species will require heat and extra light during certain periods of the year. It will be seen from these few notes that soft-billed birds as a whole are not for the inexperienced bird keeper.

Golden-fronted Fruit-sucker (*Chloropsis aurifrons*) Plate 115
Syn: Golden-fronted Bulbul
COCK Overall length about 8 in (20 cm). Beak black. Eyes brown. General colour bright green, darker on wings and tail, paler and more yellowish on underparts. The cheeks and throat are deep blue bordered with black which widens to form a bib broadly edged with yellow. The forehead rich golden orange extending to the centre of the crown. Feet and legs yellowish.
HEN Coloured like the cock but slightly less bright overall.

This species is related to the bulbuls and like them the cocks have a fine song. If kept as a songster cocks should be caged on their own. It is not a good species for a mixed aviary since it is pugnacious towards others and greedy. Its main diet is sweet soft fruits, nectar, a few live mealworms, and a little insectivorous food. Golden-fronted Fruit-suckers like to bathe quite frequently and whether kept in cage or aviary should have the necessary facilities for a daily bath.

Greater Hill Mynah (*Gracula religiosa javanensis*) Plate 116
COCK Overall length about 13 in (33 cm). Beak orange, lighter at tip. Eyes darkish. General colour black with metallic green sheen on back. Flights black, marked with white. Back of eyes and ear coverts covered by folds of bare, vivid yellow skin. Feet and legs dark.
HEN Similar in colour to cock and therefore difficult to distinguish.

These birds are generally kept as single household pets because of their great talent in mimicking the human voice and many other sounds. Words repeated by the mynahs are often claimed to be clearer than those of talking parrots but this is usually a reflection of the talent of the individual bird. Talking mynahs are in great demand in most countries for, like parrots, the sound of one language is just as easily mimicked as another. If the mynahs are kept in aviaries and are not trained to mimic humans they mostly repeat the calls of the other birds, mammals, and sounds around them. One of the reasons why mynahs are so tame and friendly is that most birds imported are young, hand-reared individuals and consequently have no fear of human beings and rely on them for their food. The popularity of mynahs as talking birds is emphasized by the fact that special cages are made to house them, and a food mixture specially blended to suit their requirements. In addition to their standard insectivorous mixture they need a daily supply of live insects and ripe soft fruits. Dried fruits, such as currants, raisins, sultanas and dates, are a useful variation of diet and are best mixed with their insectivorous food. Mynahs like to bathe daily and they should always be given the opportunity to do so as it helps to keep their plumage clean. At exhibitions mynahs always attract the visitors both for their unusual head colouring and their endless chatter.

The Greater Hill Mynah has been bred in Europe, Great Britain and America, particularly in California. The Lesser Hill Mynah *(G. r. indica)*, a subspecies, is also a good imitator and often kept for that purpose. Other members of the genus can be obtained and all need a similar diet and general management.

Green Glossy Starling *(Lamprotornis chalybeus)* Plate 117
Syn: Green-winged Glossy Starling
COCK Overall length about 8 in (20 cm). Beak black. Eyes golden yellow. Upper parts metallic glossy green. Ears, rump and upper tail coverts bluish. Stomach dark blue. Tail metallic glossy green blue. Feet and legs black.
HEN Similar in colour to cock, slighter in build.

These are strong, restless birds and like other members of the genus need a little heat during cold weather. They are best housed on their own in single pairs in large cages or in flighted aviaries as they are inclined to be quarrelsome with most other and their own species. In both types of accommodation they are equally active. To keep them in good feather, Green Glossy Starlings must be provided with good bathing facilities and they will often bathe several times during a day. Each year a few pairs produce young in Budgerigar-type nesting boxes in which they build their rough nests of straw, hay and moss. They are good attentive parents and rear their young without any particular trouble. Their diet is coarse insectivorous food, ripe fruits, mealworms, gentles (maggots) and some finely chopped raw meat. When the young are in the nest the live food and meat allowance must be increased by the addition of worms, snails, and ants' eggs. They usually make good show birds, either singly or in pairs, but they do need extra attention to get them show steady.

Other members of this genus such as the Purple Glossy Starling *(L. purpureus)*, Plate 118, and the Purple-headed Glossy Starling *(L. purpureiceps)* are two other good species for the beginner in softbills, needing a similar diet and general treatment. The Spreo Starling *(Spreo superbus)*, Plate 119, considered to be the most beautiful of the glossy starlings, is not often imported, but it has been bred in aviaries a number of times in Great Britain, Europe and America.

Pekin Robin *(Leiothrix lutea)* Plate 120
Syn: Japanese Nightingale, Pekin Nightingale, Red-billed Robin
COCK Overall length about 6 in (15 cm). Beak wax red. Eyes golden. Forehead dark yellow. Upper parts olive green. Underparts pearl grey. Throat bright yellow shading into reddish orange on the upper breast. Wings dark olive green marked with bright yellow, orange and red. Tail black, forked at end. Feet and legs yellowish.
HEN Similar in colour to cock, a little duller overall.

This hardy little bird is the most widely kept of the softbilled species. Although similar in size and shape to the English Robin it is not related to it. They are lively birds and the cocks have a pleasing song which has undoubtedly earned them their Nightingale names. Their colours are most attractive and are seen at their best advantage when the birds are housed in large cages or unplanted aviaries. In planted aviaries Pekins spend most of the time hopping about in the thickest parts of the natural cover and therefore will be seldom seen. For breeding purposes they need well-planted aviaries and should be housed on their own as they are notorious for eating other birds' eggs. Fully acclimatized specimens can be wintered in unheated birdrooms and aviaries in most countries, hence their popularity with bird keepers. Their food is varied: insectivorous food, live insects, fruit and some seed, such as canary and mixed millets. Unless they are allowed to bathe whenever they wish their plumage can soon get stained and ragged. Even under ideal conditions, as a breeding species they are not particularly reliable for although numerous pairs build nests and lay eggs, few young reach maturity.

There is a subspecies *(L. l. calipyga)*, which comes from the mountainous regions of India and specimens are sometimes imported. It requires the same treatment.

Red-eared Bulbul *(Otocompsa jocosa)* Plate 121
Syn: Red-whiskered Bulbul
COCK Overall length about 8 in (20 cm). Beak brownish. Eyes brown. General colour brown, head and crest black. Cheeks white with red ear mark. Breast white. Under tail coverts red. Feet and legs pale brownish.
HEN Smaller, with red areas duller and the brown colour warmer in tone.

This species and the Red-vented Bulbul *(O. emeria)*, which has no white and is more blackish (Plate 122), are the two more commonly seen bulbuls in captivity. They are pleasing birds with fine singing voices and will quickly become very tame, taking titbits from the owner's fingers. They thrive well on a diet of insectivorous food, live insects and soft fruits. In well-planted aviaries pairs do periodically produce nests of young but they cannot be described as free breeders.

Shama (Copsychus malabaricus indicus) Plate 123
Syn: Indian Nightingale
COCK Overall length about 10 in (25 cm). Beak black. Eyes blackish brown. General colour shining blue black with white on rump and sides of tail, the underparts are bright chestnut brown. Feet and legs dark yellow.
HEN The black areas of the cock are replaced by greyish brown and the chestnut by reddish fawn.

This is a delightful species that takes kindly to aviary life, preferably as single specimens for true pairs constantly squabble. They have sometimes been bred in captivity in large planted enclosures. The song of the cock, which may be kept as a single singing bird, is beautifully sweet and clear and not overpowering. Their tails account for about half of their total length and both sexes use it freely for display, giving them the appearance of miniature Magpies. They need a similar diet to that of the Pekin Robin, but they do not eat any seed.

Zosterops (Zosterops palpebrosa) Plate 124
Syn: Indian White-eye
COCK Overall length about 4 in (10 cm). Beak dark horn. Eyes brownish. General colour clear olive green, paler on underparts and brighter on throat with flanks pale grey. Eyes are surrounded by a narrow ring of white which is characteristic of all the group. Feet and legs brown.
HEN Coloured like the cock and thus difficult to sex.

This is the most popular species of a large and wide-ranging genus of small active gentle-natured birds behaving similarly to Tits.

In an aviary Zosterops are amusing to watch because of their constant acrobatic search for insects. Numbers of pairs housed in aviaries rear young each year in Great Britain, Europe and America. As show birds they are favoured by beginners in the softbill field.

Two other species seen fairly frequently are the Chinese Zosterops (Z. simplex) and the Cape Zosterops (Z. capensis). Zosterops feed on small insects, nectar, soft ripe fruits and fine insectivorous food.

TANAGERS Plates 125–128
The tanagers are a large group of South American species that live mainly on soft fruits and most of them are very brilliantly coloured. After keeping Pekin Robins or Glossy Starlings, tanagers are, for many fanciers, the next step. They range in size from 4 in (10 cm) to 7 in (18 cm). The desire to add tanagers to a collection of softbills is understandable as there are so many beautifully coloured species from which the bird keeper can make a choice. One of the most striking and freely imported species is the Scarlet Tanager (Ramphocelus brasilius or Piranga olivacea), the cocks of which have a striking vivid blood red colour set off by velvety black wings and tail, and the hens a reddish brown shade. Other beautiful species are the Superb Tanager (Calospiza fastuosa), whose colours are shining emerald green, black, orange and yellow; the Black-eared Golden Tanager (Tangara arthus palmitae) with rich gold and black-marked plumage; the Blue-winged Tanager (Tanagrella cyanomelana) with its blue colouring and the Purple (Violet) Tanager (Tanagra violacea) with a combination of purplish violet and deep yellows. These, and other less spectacularly coloured ones, all have iridescent plumage and make fine birds for experienced aviculturists.

TOUCANS Plate 129
These and the related toucanets and aracaris, are perhaps more suitable for zoological or bird gardens and specialist aviculturists. Their large beaks and quaint shapes make them attractive to the general public when seen in large specially designed garden aviaries. A few examples, such as the Toco Toucan (Ramphastos toco) and the Sulphur-breasted Toucan (R. sulfuratus), are kept by private collectors in birdrooms and aviaries, and occasionally they are seen at cage bird exhibitions. Their diet consists of fresh and dried fruits with some coarse insectivorous food.

WAXBILLS
A large group of small, nicely coloured birds, among them being the smallest seed-eating species kept and bred in captivity. A number of species are freely imported and are quite often chosen by new bird keepers as a first venture into exotic birds. There are many valid reasons for this – the more common species can be purchased at a reasonable price, their requirements are simple, they are easy to manage in both cage and aviary, also there is a good range of colours, and most species can be bred in captivity. The majority of waxbills come from Africa and

the surrounding islands. They are all cleanly built, slim birds of a few inches in overall length, active, bright, quick moving, but with little singing voice. They can be kept anywhere in town or country and are equally at home in cages, pens or aviaries, at all times of the year and in most countries. If given suitable facilities most species will nest and rear young. There are few collections of exotic birds that do not contain some members of the waxbill family.

Avadavat *(Amandava amandava)*
Syn: Red Avadavat, Strawberry Finch, Tiger Finch

Pair of Red Avadavats, cock on right

COCK Overall length about 4 in (10 cm). Beak red. Eyes red brown. Head, neck, breast and rump vivid fiery red. Back, flights and tail rich dark brown. Upper tail coverts, flanks and wings covered with minute round white dots. Feet and legs pinkish. Out of the breeding season the cock is coloured much like the hen.
HEN Various shades of brown, paler on breast with a small number of white dots on wings.

Vast numbers of Avadavats are exported from the Indian subcontinent each year and specimens are found in aviaries all over the world. Once they have settled down in the aviaries they will be found to be one of the hardiest members of the group. Throughout the year the cock birds sing their pleasing little songs which, in a mixed

collection, compensates for their out of season loss of colour. In well-planted aviaries most pairs will build their own domed nests in thick bushes and breed. If natural sites are not available some pairs will use small wooden nest boxes. Their diet is panicum millet, millet sprays, soft food, greenfood and a few live insects, most of which they will find for themselves in planted aviaries. If breeding is to be successful (and this applies to all waxbills) the number of breeding pairs housed in each aviary should be restricted to a minimum.

The Green Avadavat (*A. formosa*), which as the name suggests is mainly green in colour (Plate 130), has white bands on the side of its body and is more expensive to purchase. This species is more difficult to manage, but given careful treatment when first imported it will settle down and quite often pairs do nest.

Cordon Bleu *(Uraeginthus bengalus)* Plate 131
COCK Overall length about 4½ in (11·5 cm). Beak red. Eyes dark brown. Curved ear patches crimson red. Upper parts soft warm greyish brown. Chest and underparts clear bright sky blue. Tail dark, long and tapering. Feet and legs pinkish.
HEN Similar in colour but without red ear patches.

When first seen these charming little birds appear to be delicate, but this is not so once they have become acclimatized. They quickly settle down in cages, pens or aviaries, and in the latter will often nest and rear young. When breeding, the cock birds can become very aggressive and will drive all, even larger, birds away from their nesting area. The nests are generally constructed of soft grasses and feathers in wooden nest boxes, and both parents share in incubating and feeding their young. They need the same kind of feeding as Avadavats, with extra greenfood and live food when the young arrive. As they settle down so quickly in cages they make good show birds for new exhibitors.

Two related species, less frequently seen, are the Blue-breasted Waxbill (*U. angolensis*) which is similar in colour but without the crimson ear patches (Plate 132), and the Blue-headed Waxbill (*U. cyanocephalus*), which has a completely blue head (Plate 133).

Firefinch *(Lagonosticta senegala)* Plate 134
COCK Overall length about 4 in (10 cm). Beak red. Eyes brown. General colour crimson with tiny white dots all over sides and back; tail and flights reddish brown. Feet and legs reddish brown.

HEN Greyish brown dotted with white, red on rump and upper tail coverts.

These are somewhat delicate when first imported, especially the hens, but once they are acclimatized they are generally hardy and long lived. In a planted aviary, or an unplanted one with plenty of nesting boxes, they will generally nest and rear young, and are good attentive parents. They do well in a mixed aviary of waxbills and small finches as they do not interfere with other nesting pairs. Like all waxbills they periodically need a small amount of soft food, and, when rearing young, some maggots, chopped mealworms or aphids (plant-lice) should be added to their diet. As exhibition birds they are very popular and good pairs frequently win in mixed common waxbill classes.

Golden-breasted Waxbill *(Estrilda subflava subflava)*
Plates 134, 135
Syn: Zebra Waxbill
COCK Overall length about 2½ in (6·5 cm). Beak red. Eyes reddish brown. Upper parts brown, tinted olive green. Throat greyish. Bright red stripes over the eyes. Flanks barred with fine dark grey stripes. Breast and stomach rich orange deepening to red orange in centre. Tail blackish brown. Feet and legs pinkish.
HEN Similar in colour to cock. Underparts dull light yellow. Red eye stripes absent.

In spite of their minute size and fragile appearance these tiny waxbills are quite hardy when acclimatized and can be wintered in most countries without artificial heat. They will live and thrive in cages, pens or aviaries, the wire mesh for which should be ⅜ in mesh (9·5 mm). Many pairs nest each year but in captivity have proved themselves to be rather poor parents as few chicks are reared to maturity. This may be due to the fact that the breeding pairs do not get sufficient small live insects when the chicks arrive. They will make their nests in wooden boxes or nest baskets but prefer weavers' old nests. Their usual food is panicum millet, millet sprays, plenty of seeding grasses and other greenfoods, and a little insectivorous food.

A related species, the Large or Giant Golden-breasted Waxbill *(E. s. clarkei),* is larger but not so brightly coloured and needs the same general treatment.

Lavender Finch *(E. caerulescens)* Plate 136
Syn: Grey Waxbill
COCK Overall length about 4 in (10 cm). Beak red. Eyes deep brown. General colour soft lavender grey, lighter on cheeks and throat, darker on flanks, where it is heavily spotted with tiny white spots. Black streaks run from base of beak to the eye. Rump and central tail feathers rich crimson. Feet and legs blackish.
HEN Similar in colour to cock, difficult to distinguish between the sexes.

The delightful two-tone colour scheme of this species blends well in a mixed collection of waxbills. They are more difficult to acclimatize than most waxbills but once this has been achieved they settle down well to cage and aviary life. They will usually nest with reasonable freedom in planted aviaries, where they build their own nests of soft grasses in thick cover, or they make use of nesting boxes. Lavender Finches need the usual waxbill diet and must have some live insects throughout the year with a greatly increased quantity when they are rearing young. They are most highly thought of as exhibition birds and pairs in good condition usually do well in waxbill classes.

A related species, the Black-tailed Lavender Finch *(Estrilda perreini),* with its black beak, legs and tail, is sometimes imported and needs similar treatment.

Orange-cheeked Waxbill *(E. melpoda)* Plate 137
COCK Overall length about 4 in (10 cm). Beak red. Eyes reddish. Upper parts soft reddish brown. Underparts warm grey. Cheek patches bright orange. Rump and tail coverts bright red. Tail red brown. Feet and legs pinkish.
HEN Similar in colour to cock and therefore difficult to distinguish.

This is a commonly imported species, cheap to buy, hardy in most climates, and with a good life expectancy, all of which make it suitable for the beginner. It is not a free breeder although true pairs will sometimes nest and rear a few young. Unless a number of birds are purchased at the same time and observed carefully it is most difficult to select true pairs. Cock birds will display before the hens with a lot of tail flicking and bobbing up and down. Hens are usually much shyer than their mates and when identified should be ringed with split plastic rings. In addition to the usual waxbill food they are exceedingly fond of seeding grasses which should be given whenever supplies are available.

Red-eared Waxbill *(E. troglodytes)* Plates 134, 137
Syn: Common Waxbill, Grey Waxbill, Red-cheeked Waxbill, Senegal Waxbill
COCK Overall length about 4 in (10 cm). Beak red. Eyes reddish brown. Upper parts dark warm grey. Underparts lighter grey with a pink wash which becomes deeper in

shade towards the centre of the lower chest. Narrow red stripe above the ears on each cheek. Tail red brown. Feet and legs pinkish.

HEN Similar in colour to cock and therefore difficult to distinguish.

This species is also freely imported, cheap and hardy. Being difficult to sex it is not unusual to find that 'pairs' are in fact the same sex. Because of the ease with which they can always be obtained few efforts are made to get them to reproduce. However, although it is said they are not particularly good in that respect, if given the use of planted aviaries, where the inhabitants are not overcrowded, there is no reason why true pairs should not nest and rear families. They are attractive little birds in mixed aviaries and seem to stand cold weather conditions quite well without extra heat being provided. Red-eared Waxbills need the same general treatment and food as suggested for the Orange-cheeked species and also make good birds for the beginner in exotics.

There are numerous other species and subspecies of waxbills that become available from time to time, all of which are useful for collections of small seed-eating birds. Among those most frequently seen are the St Helena's Waxbill (*E. estrilda*), Dufresne's Waxbill (*E. melanotis*), Plate 138, and the Yellow-bellied Waxbill (*E. melanotis quartines*). Very beautiful rare species are the Violet-eared Waxbill (*Granatina granatina*) and the Grenadier Waxbill (*G. ianthinogaster*), Plate 139, which are rather delicate and are birds for the experienced owner.

WEAVERS

An extensive group of African birds that are generally considered to be very hardy, little trouble to keep, have unusual colour patterns and are fairly inexpensive and easy to obtain. Most of the more common species are excellent birds for starting mixed collections of hardy exotic species. Very few members of the family have been bred in captivity although they spend a great deal of their time weaving their beautifully-shaped nests. However, they are frequently used for nesting in by other small birds. Much pleasure can be derived by owners from watching the birds at their work of nest building. A good display of weavers can be seen at the Smithsonian Institute Zoo, Washington, D.C. It is only during the breeding periods that the cock birds assume their beautiful colouring – for the remainder of the time they are coloured like the hens in various shades of brown. Another interesting feature of the weavers is the way in which the cock birds display to their mates.

They stretch out their necks and dance up and down on their perches, uttering a series of squeaky notes. Because of their colouring the majority of imported weavers are cock birds and thus hens are often difficult to obtain. For exhibition purposes it is always preferable to have a pair of the same species. Many weavers are similarly coloured although with different patterns, therefore only a few will be described.

Napoleon Weaver (*Euplectes a. afra*) Plate 140
Syn: Yellow Bishop
COCK Overall length about 4½ in (11·5 cm). Beak horn coloured. Eyes blackish. General colour bright yellow. Sides of head, throat, lower breast and stomach black. Wings and tail dark brown. Feet and legs yellowish. Out of the breeding season coloured like the hen.
HEN Shades of brown with some dark markings. Little smaller than cock.

This hardy, attractively-coloured species is a great nest builder in captivity and occasionally hens will lay eggs and rear young. In this event, the birds will need extra quantities of live insects in addition to their insectivorous food, greenfood, millet and canary seeds. They are rather lethargic birds in cages and are undoubtedly best seen in aviaries, where they are extremely active. Pairs make excellent show specimens when they are in colour and being hardy they are good birds for the beginner.

Orange Weaver (*E. orix franciscana*) Plates 141a, 141b
Syn: Orange Bishop
COCK Overall length about 4 in (10 cm). Beak horn. Eyes blackish. General colour shades of orange red. Head and breast black. Tail and wings dark brown. Feet and legs yellowish. Cock when out of the breeding season coloured like the hen.
HEN Shades of brown with some dark markings. Little smaller than cock.

When first imported the cocks, if in full colour, are not orange red but a wonderful rosy red of extraordinary brightness. After moulting in captivity they rarely, if ever, regain that rich red shade. These beautiful birds are the most freely imported of the group and can always be obtained at reasonable prices, which makes them popular. Their general habits and feeding are similar to the Napoleon Weaver, and the two species, when seen together in an aviary, make a picture with their vividly contrasting colours.

Red-billed Weaver (*Quelea quelea*) Plate 142
Syn: Quelea
COCK Overall length about 5 in (13 cm). Beak deep red. Eyes golden. Head, throat, back of neck and chest buff, heavily suffused with deep rosy red. Face mask black. Wings and tail dark brown mottled with light brown. Feet and legs yellowish.
HEN Shades of brown. Beak yellow.

One of the more sedately coloured weavers, it is quite pretty in a quiet way. It is imported in great numbers to many countries. It is very hardy and one of the most industrious nest builders – placing its nests in every conceivable spot in all types of aviaries. It requires the same treatment and feeding as the two previously mentioned species.

There is another form commonly known as Russ's Weaver, which has a brown instead of a black face, and a few examples are sometimes found in batches of Red-billed Weavers. Both are tough little birds and mix in well with all other types of weaver and the larger finches.

Some further species of weavers seen at various times and which add variety to collections are the Grenadier Weaver (*E. o. orix*), the Crimson-crowned Weaver (*E. bordeacea*), the Taha Weaver (*E. afra taha*), Plate 143, and the Rufous-necked Weaver (*E. cucullatus*).

WHYDAHS

Allied to the weavers, the whydahs are notable because of the beautiful plumage of the cock bird of most species during the breeding season, and for their parasitic breeding habits. The former feature is one of the attractions of these hardy, easy to keep, African birds. Their parasitism takes the form of the hens laying their eggs in the nests of smaller birds leaving the hosts to hatch and rear the chicks. Each species of whydah generally chooses a particular species of waxbill or mannikin to act as host. Because of this feature it is only on extremely few occasions that whydahs have actually been bred in captivity – they are therefore kept mainly for decorative and exhibition purposes. They need the same general management as the weavers with which they can be safely housed. It is not a good idea to include whydahs in the same enclosures as small finch-like birds, especially if the latter are required for breeding purposes, for the whydahs not only interfere, but their rather clumsy flight will disturb the smaller birds. Aviaries consisting of collections of whydahs and weavers in full colour make an unusually attractive and colourful sight.

Giant Whydah (*Coliuspasser progne*)
Syn: Long-tailed Widow bird
COCK Overall length including tail about 25 in (63·5 cm). Beak black. Eyes red brown. General colour including massive long tail black. Shoulders marked with cream and orange patches. Feet and legs brownish. Cock, when out of colour is like the hen.
HEN Mainly lightish brown with some darker streaks. A little smaller than cock.

These are the largest and considered to be the most spectacular of all the whydahs, but unfortunately they are not very frequently imported into Great Britain and Europe and when specimens do arrive they are in great demand. Their food consists of mixed millets, canary seed, millet sprays, greenfood, a little soft food and a few live insects. They are good birds for mixed collections as, unlike many whydahs, they are in no way aggressive to their smaller companions. When flying in an aviary with their long 18 in (46 cm) tails flowing behind they make an impressive sight. They are fortunately long lived, hardy, and do not require any heat in cold weather in most countries.

Paradise Whydah (*Steganura paradisaea*) Plate 144
Syn: Widow bird
COCK Overall length including tail about 18 in (46 cm). Beak dark horn. Eyes blackish. Head black. Upper chest and collar chestnut brown. Stomach buff. Vent white. Remainder of plumage black. Feet and legs brown. Cock, when out of colour, is like the hen.
HEN Shades of brown and buff with some dark streaks.

This is the most widely known of the whydah family and is freely imported into all countries. The bright colouring and fine long tails of the cock, the friendly nature and hardiness are all features which make it an attractive bird to keep. They will live quite happily in large cages in which they can be exhibited, but undoubtedly their quaint beauty is always seen at its best when the birds are flying in large flighted aviaries. All they need in the way of food is mixed millet and canary seed, greenfood, millet sprays, and a few live insects.

Pin-tailed Whydah (*Vidua macroura*) Plate 145
COCK Overall length about 12 in (30·5 cm). Beak light red. Eyes golden. Forehead, crown and nape of neck glossy bluish black. Cheeks, throat, neck band, rump and upper tail coverts white. Upper parts black. Underparts white with black crescent on breast. Feet and legs greyish.
HEN Buff and browns with dark stripes. Beak light pinkish brown. Feet and legs pale brown.

One of the smaller species and probably the most widely kept of the whole group. They are pleasing in their colouring but unfortunately the cocks can be most aggressive towards other smaller birds and should not be housed with them in confined quarters. In mixed aviaries of larger species, including weavers and other whydahs, the Pin-tails make useful additions. Like all their family they are easy to feed, and can be wintered outside in most countries which makes them popular among amateur bird keepers. Food and management are as described for the two previous species.

Other whydahs seen quite frequently are the Yellow-shouldered (-winged) Whydah (*Coliuspasser macrocercus*), Plate 146; the Yellow-backed Whydah (*C. macrourus*); the Red-shouldered Whydah (*C. axillaris*); and the White-shouldered (-winged) Whydah (*C. albonotatus*), Plate 147, which only has tail plumes of medium length. The cocks of these species when in breeding plumage are all black except for the coloured markings indicated by their names. Two very attractive and rare species are the Queen Whydah (*Vidua regia*) and Fischer's Whydah (*V. fischeri*), Plates 148a, 148b, both of which have long wire-like tail shafts, the ends of which are wider.

Related to the whydahs and often classified with them is the:

Combassou (*Hypochera c. chalybeata*) Plate 149
Syn: Steel Finch
COCK Overall length about 4½ in (11·5 cm). Beak whitish. Eyes brown. At breeding time the whole plumage is a shining steel blue black and at other periods it is a mixture of drab buffs and browns. Feet and legs red brown.
HEN Similar to cock's out of colour plumage.

Like the whydahs this species is polygamous and parasitic in its breeding behaviour, but the cock does not grow a long tail. They make excellent hardy birds for a mixed aviary with their gleaming black plumage setting off the colours of the other occupants. Combassous take extremely well to cage life and make fine exhibition birds for the beginner.

QUAILS

Quails belong to the pheasant family and some of the smaller species make fine additions to large planted garden aviaries. They are easy to feed, living on the seeds mainly used for the other birds in their aviaries. Most species require a little wheat and soft food and live insects, particularly when rearing young.

Button Quail (*Turnix lepurana*)
Syn: African Button Quail, Bustard Quail
COCK Overall length about 5 in (13 cm). Beak blackish grey. Eyes yellow. Head barred with light yellow and deep brown. Upper parts brownish yellow with lighter edge to mantle feathers. Back and sides brownish, spotted with black. Feet and legs flesh coloured.
HEN Overall length about 6 in (15 cm). Head brown with a stripe of reddish yellow over the crown and above the eyes. Sides of head brownish. Mantle cross-banded with black edged with yellow. Throat and chin white with rust-coloured stripe across breast. Sides yellowish brown with black drop-like markings and underparts white.

In this species the larger and more colourful hens play the dominant role in the family, but the cocks choose the nesting site and scratch a hollow, which they line with soft, fine grasses. The clutches of eggs, 6–10 in number, are laid in these nests and the cocks carry out most of the thirteen days of incubation and take charge of the brood. When the young hatch the parents should be given soft food, extra live insects and plenty of chopped greenfood. The chicks grow rapidly and at six to eight weeks are the same size as their parents.

The Australian Button Quail (*T. pyrrhothorax*), which is slightly larger, is sometimes obtainable, and requires the same management.

Chinese Painted Quail (*Excalfactoria chinensis*) Plate 150
Syn: Blue-breasted Quail
COCK Overall length about 4½ in (11·5 cm). Beak black. Eyes hazel. Cheeks white, outlined in black. Throat black; broad white band across upper breast and sides of neck. Chest and flanks blue grey. Lower chest and underparts deep chocolate brown. Feet and legs yellow, with black claws.
HEN Lacks black and white markings and the blue grey on chest and flanks. General colour dull browns, mottled on upper parts.

These are the smallest of the quails and make excellent inmates for planted aviaries. Like all quails they are ground birds and thus add life and colour to aviary floors. Unlike the Button Quail the hens do the incubating and rear the young while the cocks defend their families fiercely against any intrusion onto their territories. The young develop quickly and are independent of their parents at about five weeks old. They breed quite freely and require the same kind of treatment as described for the previous species. There is a dilute mutation known as Silver that is now being bred in Great Britain, Europe and

America, and White and Pied forms have also been evolved. These mutations are recessive.

Other species of quail that are sometimes included in aviary collections are the Common Quail (*Coturnix coturnix*), the Harlequin Quail (*C. delagorguei*) and the Rain Quail (*C. coromandelica*). The first–mentioned species is the only European quail.

HOUSING

Exotic birds are generally kept to add decoration to gardens and thus they are generally housed in aviaries. The cages, pens and aviaries described on pp. 65-7, 96-9, 113-4 can easily be adapted for use. Except for the small waxbills the wire cage-fronts and wire-mesh flights will need no alteration. For these very small species the wire mesh should not be more than ⅜ in (9·5 mm), a ¼ in (6·5 mm) being ideal. If it is painted with a flat black, non-poisonous paint, it will be almost invisible, giving a better view of the birds. During periods of cold weather a few species may need to be housed in heated quarters and the ranges of pens used for Budgerigar and Canary birdrooms are very suitable. Electricity is undoubtedly the best method of heating and lighting as it is easier to control and certainly safer than naked flame or gas heaters, where there is always the possibility of fumes being given off which can quickly upset the birds. The majority of species described in this section do not require artificial heat in cold weather once they have been acclimatized, but they should have dry, draught proof sleeping quarters. When new flighted aviaries are built they should be sited so that the prevailing winds do not blow directly into the openings of the shelters. The flights themselves can be of any shape as long as they give the birds the maximum amount of flying space and at the same time plenty of natural cover. Evergreens are undoubtedly the best bushes to grow in such flights as they will give shelter all through the year. Cotoneasters and *Lonicera nitida* are useful quick growing shrubs, while the deciduous Russian vine (*Polygonum baldschuanicum*) is ideal for growing up the sides of the flights as it covers a great amount of space in a very short time. Lavender, broom, gorse and some conifers are other quick growing shrubs. It is often useful to have some shrubs growing in large pots or barrels so they can be moved about to give the birds a change of nesting sites. For ground cover, there are several excellent ornamental grasses as well as the ordinary varieties which will all help to improve the aviary. Herbaceous plants such as Michaelmas daisies, goldenrod and phlox will encourage insects and also make building sites for certain species. Some of the more vigorous heathers planted on mounds will add colour and again provide nesting places and also a certain amount of nesting material. All these plants and shrubs can be obtained at local nurseries or garden centres.

Some fixed perching will be needed in the flights and natural bark-covered branches from such trees as apple, pear, plum, cherry or hazel, are all well suited for this purpose. The perching used should have branches of varying lengths and thicknesses. This exercises the birds' feet and prevents stiffness. It is important to site the perches so that the birds' droppings do not foul growing plants and shrubs. The ground beneath the main perching areas should be covered with sand or fine gravel so that cleaning is easy and will not cause disturbance.

If the sleeping quarters are not made of brick or similar materials, they should be lined with hardboard or strawboard to prevent draughts and conserve heat. The inside walls of the sleeping quarters should be decorated with white distemper or emulsion paint to give the maximum amount of reflected light. All windows should be completely covered with small-mesh wire-netting frames and it should be possible to open the windows from the outside to prevent unnecessary disturbance when the birds are nesting. The perching should be fixed clear of all food, water and grit vessels and in good positions for roosting in the most sheltered parts of the building. Some small species like to roost under cover and some open-fronted boxes should be fixed high on the aviary walls. It is advisable to have a small lip on these sleeping boxes on which a little sawdust or peat moss can be sprinkled to keep them fresh and clean. If this information is read in conjunction with the information given on housing other groups of birds aviculturists should, by using their own inventiveness, be able to produce some very fine and practical aviaries.

FEEDING

The staple seeds used for feeding most seed-eating exotic birds are panicum, yellow, brown, white and Japanese millets, and all canary seeds. Some species will also take small quantities of hemp and niger seeds as well as mixed wild flower seeds. Most good seed firms market blended mixtures to suit the different types of exotic seed-eating birds and these mixtures are probably the most useful for owners of small collections. Bird keepers with large mixed aviaries will find that it is cheaper to buy their seeds separately in bulk and blend their own mixtures or give them to the birds in individual kinds. In large aviaries the various seeds are best given in separate dishes so that the amount of each seed can be controlled by the owner. Birds only eat what they need of the different seeds and waste is thereby eliminated. Strict control is only needed with the fattening seeds such as hemp and niger. Only the best quality seeds should be bought and carefully stored in containers with well-fitting lids, as damp, mouldy or stale seeds are a potential source of many bird disorders.

Millet sprays are a valuable form of food for practically all species throughout the year. Newly imported birds will always eat plenty of millet sprays even if they are choosy about other foods and this will help in getting them established. Young birds in nests are usually better fed by their parents when millet sprays are provided. Sprays are also helpful in getting young stock weaned on to hard seeds prior to being removed from the care of their parents.

Although certain species are called 'seed-eating' birds they also need some form of soft foods and live insects to maintain them, even when not breeding, in perfect health. All types will benefit substantially if periodically given soft food and this can be cod-liver oil food, insectivorous food, a blend of these two, or wholemeal bread moistened with milk or honey and water. Each owner will discover by trial and error which form of soft food is most suitable for his own particular stock of birds. Any uneaten soft food must be removed at the end of each day as it can quickly go sour. Live food, such as mealworms or gentles (maggots), can be given in limited quantities to satisfy the needs of each species. When the young are in the nests the amount of soft food given to all species should be increased. The special food required by softbills can be bought already made-up from pet stores.

The provision of greenfood is often the controlling factor between successes and disappointments in rearing to full maturity many species of exotic birds. The favourite greenfoods of many kinds are seeding grasses and seeding chickweed and the other greenfoods suggested in the section on Zebra Finches and Bengalese (p.114). Only fresh greenfood obtained from uncontaminated sources should be given to the birds and when wilted should be removed daily. If birds are housed in aviaries that have planted flights they will be able to find a certain amount of insects and greenfood for themselves. This search for food will give the birds exercise and a very beneficial change of diet.

To keep all groups of exotic birds in good strong feather and robust health they must have as much grit and other mineral elements as they require. The correct grits, bird sand, cuttlefish bone, and mineral blocks can be obtained from all good bird-seed stores. These items can be supplemented with clean sea or river sand, crushed raw chalk, old mortar rubble, and dried crushed domestic hen's egg-shells. It is often useful to grate a little cuttlefish bone so that the smaller birds can eat it more easily, but they should also be given a few whole pieces to keep their beaks a reasonable length. Exotic birds often like a little granulated charcoal which is best given mixed with their grit.

Most species like to bathe frequently and facilities for this should be supplied whether they are housed in cages, pens or aviaries. The vessels used for baths must be shallow and when the chicks are being reared should not contain more than ½ in (13 mm) of water. The feathers of young birds are soft and if they happen to fall into several inches of water they quickly become sodden and the birds will drown. Water for drinking purposes should be supplied in addition to bath water although the birds will probably drink both. During warm weather and in hot countries the water in all vessels should be renewed daily and if necessary both morning and evening.

BREEDING

Throughout this section the importance of encouraging as many species as possible to reproduce their kind has been stressed and the following notes should be helpful to intending breeders. The breeding periods of the different species in a mixed collection of exotic birds can, when added together, be quite long, thus providing their owners with months of anticipation. After about two or three breeding seasons bird keepers will discover the times (April to September) when their species are likely to nest and can prepare accordingly. To achieve successful results there are certain points which should be observed at all times: only fit, vigorous birds should be considered as breeding stock – the pairing of closely related birds should be avoided; unmated birds of either sex must not be allowed in with breeding pairs; overcrowding should be avoided; only compatible species should be housed together. If these points are observed and the birds are suitably housed and correctly fed there is every possibility that many pairs will build nests, lay eggs, and rear young.

The principal materials used by the majority of species for constructing their nests are soft dried grasses, dried mosses, pieces of dried herbage, small feathers and cow hair. Plenty of these materials should be available whether the breeding pairs make their own nests completely or make use of nest boxes, baskets, or hollow logs in which to build. To allow the birds a choice of sites many more nesting receptacles should be provided than the actual number of pairs in the aviary. Doing this will help to prevent undue squabbling amongst the pairs over any particular nesting place.

Some breeding pairs do not seem to mind having their nests inspected whereas others will take a strong objection to the slightest interference. This being so it is far more practical to leave the nests strictly alone rather than risk the loss of eggs or young through inquisitiveness. This does, of course, prevent the chicks from being closed-ringed (banded) and therefore split metal or coloured plastic rings should be used soon after they have left their nests and can be positively identified. It is a good plan to have a few pairs of Zebra Finches or Bengalese breeding so that should any special exotic pairs desert their eggs or chicks they can be quickly fostered by these reliable parents. The use of foster parents can be of great value when breeding, for example, some of the Australian Finches, which may be temperamental – many nests of chicks are saved each year by this method of rearing.

Gouldian Finches (p.160) have been highly bred and colour forms other than those found in the wild have been evolved from mutations. The head colours of the normal Red and Black-headed Gouldians are sex-linked and follow the usual sex-linked rules (see p.105). The red head colour is also dominant over both black and yellow. The Yellow-heads and White-breasteds are recessive birds and breeding follows the rules given on p.104. The characters for yellow-headedness and white-breastedness can be carried in split form by both the Red- and Black-headed cocks and hens. Should the birds have a double set of chromosomes of these two characters the colours will then be visible in their plumage.

Mutant forms of exotic species all follow the general Mendelian laws of inheritance (see, for example, pp.103–5). If a colour break does occur, the first step in establishing it is to mate the mutant to a normal of the same species. By pairing the progeny of this first cross according to the prescribed rules of inheritance their genetic make-up can be discovered and in due course the new colour form can be stabilized.

Although numerous rare and common exotic species can be bred quite regularly in captivity there are others whose breeding patterns are somewhat erratic and, of course, there is no guarantee that any pair of birds will reproduce. It is this uncertainty that makes the breeding of birds so fascinating and the sight of young from a greatly prized pair of exotics flying strongly in the aviary is a thrill to all bird owners.

Genetics

In the sections on Canaries and Budgerigars the theoretical colour expectations of certain crosses are given and readers may wonder by what method they are calculated. The passing on from one generation to another of all features that go to make living things are governed by a set of rules, known as the Mendelian principles of heredity. Genetics, as this science is called, is a complex subject and needs special study. For the purpose of breeding birds it is only necessary to understand certain elementary rules.

All the colour and other characters of birds are controlled by extremely small bodies, called genes, which are situated in filament-like structures, known as chromosomes, located in the birds' cells. The chromosomes are always found in pairs of the same size and shape, each with their own complete sets of genes, except for the chromosome pair controlling sex which, in hen birds, differ in size. The sex chromosomes of cock birds, known by the symbols XX, are of equal size, whereas in hens there is one long (X) and one short chromosome (Y), forming

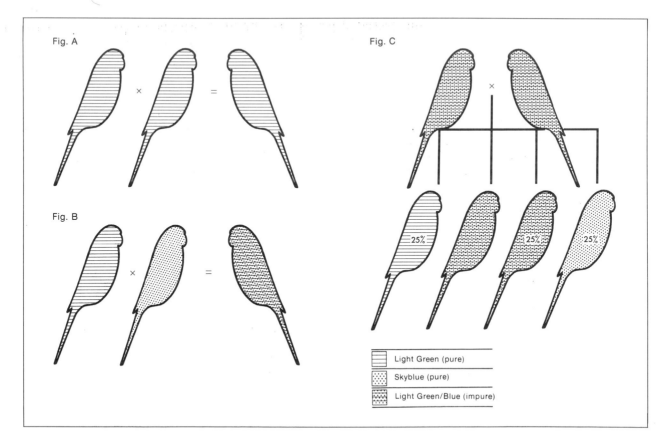

Fig. A

Fig. B

Fig. C

25% 25% 25%

Light Green (pure)

Skyblue (pure)

Light Green/Blue (impure)

an unequal pair (XY). It is the presence of the Y (short) chromosome half in the genetic make-up of an individual bird that causes it to be a hen. As far as is known, the Y chromosome half does not, in birds, carry any colour or other genes, its sole purpose is to determine the sex. The characters controlled by the genes in the X part of the sex chromosomes are known as sex-linked genes, the inheritance of which is explained later.

Hens produce small cells, known as ova which, during mating, are fertilized by even smaller bodies, the sperms, passed on by the cock birds. During the formation of these sex cells the number of chromosomes is halved so that each fertilized ovum (the egg) has a full set of chromosomes.

The genes in the chromosome pairs of each chick can be pure (identical) or impure (different) depending on the characters passed on by the parents. For example, a pure Light Green Budgerigar paired with a pure Light Green Budgerigar can only produce pure Light Green young (Fig. A), whereas a pure Light Green paired with a pure Skyblue can only give impure (Light Green/Blue) young (Fig. B). When two impure (Light Green/Blue) birds are paired together they will produce pure Light Greens, impure Light Green/Blues and pure Skyblues in the proportions 1: 2: 1 (25%, 50%, 25%) respectively (Fig. C). This proportion, when calculated over a considerable number of pairs, is always the same in those cases where only two characters are considered but if more than two characters are involved there are more, and smaller units.

Sex-linked characters, *all of which are recessive*, are inherited in a somewhat different manner because of the peculiarity of the pair of chromosomes that control sex. For example, a cock having sex-linked genes paired with a non-linked hen will produce cocks that carry the sex-linked gene and sex-linked hens. The opposite mating of a non-linked cock with a sex-linked hen will produce cocks carrying

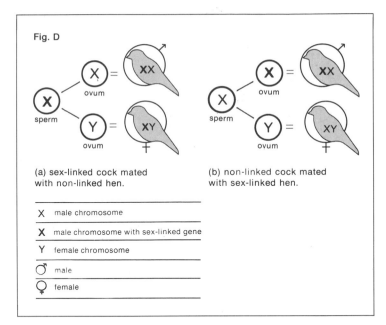

Fig. D

(a) sex-linked cock mated with non-linked hen.

(b) non-linked cock mated with sex-linked hen.

X	male chromosome
X	male chromosome with sex-linked gene
Y	female chromosome
♂	male
♀	female

the sex-linked gene and non-linked hens. These results are shown in Fig. D. In the first example (a), the cock produces sperm containing the male chromosome with the sex-linked gene (**X**) and the hen produces ova with the male chromosome without a sex-linked gene (X) and an equal number of ova with the female chromosome (Y); in the second example (b), the cock produces sperm containing male chromosomes without the sex-linked gene (X), while the hen produces ova with the male chromosome having the sex-linked gene (**X**) and an equal number of ova with the female chromosome (Y).

Dominant colour characters can be carried on one or both members of a chromosome pair and in both cases are *visible* in the birds' plumage. It should be noted that there is no visual difference in the colour of birds having a single or double quantity of any dominant colour character in their genetic make-up. It is impossible for any recessive, or sex-linked coloured bird, to be a carrier of dominant colour characters.

Ailments

DAVID J. COFFEY

B.VET.MED. MRCVS

The majority of cage and aviary birds are singularly free from ailments and, of course, because of protection from, or lack of, natural predators, their life expectancy is many times greater than birds in the wild. However, although the owner can do much to prevent the onset of illness by meticulous attention to such factors as cleanliness, proper diet, and allowing the birds plenty of room, some birds do become sick.

Successful diagnosis and treatment of animal disease requires a long training and considerable experience. By far the most difficult task is identifying the particular disease, and this is not a job for the unqualified. In nearly all cases of suspected illness a visit to the veterinary surgeon is the quickest, cheapest and most satisfactory solution for both the owner and the bird. A wide range of laboratory facilities to aid diagnosis and pharmaceutical drugs which cannot be obtained by the general public are available to veterinary surgeons. Home treatment of any sick bird is fraught with danger to the animal itself but thankfully, rarely to the owner.

Sick birds are usually all too easily identified. They generally show a marked change of behaviour which may be accompanied by such recognizable symptoms as discharges, diarrhoea, unusual lumps or bleeding.

When a sick bird has been identified it should be placed on its own in a small, clean hospital cage which is heated to a temperature of around 85–90 ° F (28–32°C). This cage should preferably be in a separate room which is well ventilated but free from draughts. Care should be taken to attend to sick birds after daily maintenance has been completed on healthy stock. When a sick bird has completely recovered it should be hardened off before being returned to its usual quarters. All utensils should be of a material which is easily sterilized either with a disinfectant or by boiling. Owners should wash their hands well immediately after handling sick birds or the utensils lest they transfer infection to healthy stock. All hospital cages and apparatus must be thoroughly cleaned and sterilized after use.

If a sick bird which has been placed in a hospital cage and given simple remedies does not respond within twenty-four hours, the advice of a veterinary surgeon should be sought with all haste.

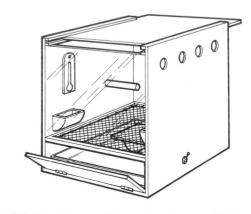

Hospital cage – the size will depend on the type of bird for which the cage is intended. The electric light bulb, which is placed under a sheet of asbestos, can be switched on from the exterior and switched off once the desired temperature has been reached.

ABSCESSES Occasionally, psittacine birds, particularly Budgerigars, develop abscesses. They are due to bacterial infection, possibly following an injury. They are most easily and successfully treated with antibiotics.

ASPERGILLOSIS This is an unpleasant condition caused by the inhalation of spores of the fungus *Aspergillus fumigatus*. It is relatively common in parrots but rarely seen in the smaller psittacines (including Budgerigars) and the seed-eating passerines. The symptoms are rather vague. Occasionally the bird has difficulty in breathing and may show a discharge from the nostrils. A positive diagnosis is usually only possible following a post mortem examination. Parrot owners are advised to add potassium iodide to the drinking water at the rate of 2½ grains to every 2 fluid ounces of water as a preventative measure. No treatment has been found as yet which is consistently successful. Good hygiene, as in all things, may help to prevent the onset of the condition.

ASTHMA This condition is rare but may occur in parrots and related birds, including Budgerigars. The cause is unknown. Indeed it probably has a number of quite unrelated causes including infection of the lungs and air sacs, aspergillosis, inhalation of poisonous fumes and dust or pollen laden air. Symptoms vary considerably but include difficulty in breathing, gaping beak, squeaking noise when breathing, and ruffled feathers. The unfortunate sufferer may have attacks frequently, or they may be several months apart. A cure is rare but alleviation of the symptoms is possible. Perfect ventilation is a good general adjunct treatment; airy runs are better than indoor situations in this respect. Veterinary attention is advisable.

BEAK TRIMMING see OVERGROWN BEAK AND CLAWS

BROKEN LIMBS These should be dealt with by a veterinary surgeon as unskilled attention can often cause permanent damage.

CAKED FEET see SORE FEET

CANCER Like all animals, birds are unfortunately susceptible to various types of cancer. Some types of cancer are visible to the owner while others are hidden from view, affecting the internal organs of the body. Symptoms are very variable and depend both on the type of cancer and on the organ which is afflicted. Birds with cancer may lose condition, sit with ruffled feathers, show swellings, be paralysed, show apparent sex changes, have diarrhoea or vomit. Some types of cancer in birds can be removed by surgery but the more malignant cases are impossible to treat and it is best to put the bird painlessly to sleep to avoid unnecessary suffering.

CERE COLOUR CHANGE A change of colour from blue in the cere of the male Budgerigar to brown is due usually to a cancer of the male reproductive organs – the testicles. No treatment is possible and the kindest thing is to put the bird painlessly to sleep when he shows signs of distress. The abdomen will often be seen to be greatly enlarged.

CHILLS see COLDS

CLAW TRIMMING see OVERGROWN BEAK AND CLAWS

COCCIDIOSIS This disease is rare but may be seen in a wide variety of caged birds. It is due to microscopic organisms known as Coccidia. On rare occasions a very acute form of the disease occurs causing convulsions and sudden death. More commonly, the affected bird appears dull, loses weight, refuses food and perches with ruffled feathers. It may show diarrhoea, vomiting and consume large quantities of grit. The disease can only be confirmed by laboratory examination of the droppings. Diagnosis is complicated by the fact that healthy birds can carry heavy infestations of coccidia without showing any symptoms of ill health. It would appear that an environmental stress factor like poor feeding, overcrowding or bad ventilation is necessary to trigger the coccidia into action. Treatment is successful if the bird is treated early enough and usually consists of adding one of the sulpha drugs to the drinking water.

COLDS Birds do not have a specific infection like the human common cold. Any discharge from the eyes or nostrils should be viewed with suspicion and veterinary advice sought.

CONJUNCTIVITIS This refers to a painful inflammation of the eyes. There are several causes including bacteria, viruses, fungi and physical irritants. Affected birds may rub their eyes on a perch, blink, and have a discharge which can be clear or pusy. Diagnosis may require laboratory tests but most cases will respond to daily applications of an antibiotic. Make sure that this is not just a symptom of a more serious condition. Do not neglect it.

CONSTIPATION This occurs when the bird is unable to pass its droppings. It is very rare in birds but can be recognized by excessive straining to pass droppings but with scant achievement. Any droppings passed will be small, dry and very hard. Treatment consists of ensuring that there is an adequate supply of greenfood, adding vitamins of the B group to food or water and in bad cases, which fail to respond to these milder administrations, dosing with liquid paraffin. If all else fails enemas can be given by a veterinary surgeon. A word of warning. Do not confuse a clogged cloaca, due to diarrhoea-encrusted feathers, with constipation or your treatment will make matters worse. A correct diagnosis should be obtained from a veterinary surgeon.

CROP IMPACTION This condition can occur in most species of bird. It is characterized by a swelling in the lower neck, and the bird trying to be sick. The cause is not clear. This needs the attention of a veterinary surgeon since surgery is sometimes needed to correct the condition. Recovery rate is not good.

CYSTS Yellow skin cysts are quite common in Budgerigars, where they are frequently seen in the wings. The treatment is surgical removal.

DEAD-IN-SHELL There is a variety of quite unrelated reasons for the failure of an egg to hatch. One or both parent birds may be infertile. Infertility itself is complex: it may be temporary because the bird has been ill and is being bred from before the period of convalescence is complete; it may be due to immaturity, the bird simply being physically too young to breed; or age – as birds become old the tissues become senile and in some cases the reproductive organs fail to function. There may be inherited factors, one or other parent carrying what is termed a lethal gene, which prevents the egg, although fertilized, from developing. This is particularly true in one form of embryonic mortality in the Canary. It is also

Two examples of dead-in-shell. Note that the shell and membrane are stuck to the body

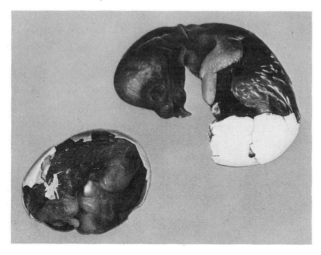

known that certain minerals and vitamins, notably Vitamins of the B Group and E, if absent from the diet of the parent birds can cause failure to hatch. A build-up of toxic substances, for example D.D.T., can also interfere with hatchability. While this has not been a problem in cage birds so far, it is something against which we must be on our guard. Several infections, notably Salmonellosis, are notorious for their ability to kill the embryonic chick.

Other possible reasons are: the shell is too thick, the chick being unable to break out; the chick may not be strong enough to break out; the chick may be stuck to the inner membrane; and, finally, even if the egg is fertile, alive, and contains adequate nutrition, the parent may, because of abnormal behaviour, fail to incubate properly, causing the egg to become chilled and the embryo chick to die.

Failure of eggs to hatch is, sadly, quite common in many species of cage birds. Careful post mortem examinations may be valuable in establishing the particular cause and owners are advised to seek professional help if the problem is causing concern.

DIARRHOEA This is a symptom not a disease. It simply means that the bird is passing watery droppings which do not have the usual form. It accompanies a great many diseases and should not be treated without first obtaining a correct diagnosis.

EGG BINDING This describes a condition where the female bird is unable to lay her egg. It is commonest in young birds and in all birds near the beginning of the breeding season. Sadly it is all too common in cage birds. The symptoms are sudden onset of straining, often with obvious swelling around the vent. The bird gets very distressed, feathers ruffle and she sits at the bottom of the cage. An egg can usually be palpated through the abdominal wall but where doubts exist an X-ray will often confirm the diagnosis. This is a very difficult condition to treat. The bird should be placed in a warm environment and a little liquid paraffin or glycerine smeared on the vent until the services of a veterinary surgeon can be secured. Even in professional hands treatment too often ends in tragedy.

ENTERITIS This word means an inflammation of the small intestine. It is usually accompanied by diarrhoea because the inflamed gut is unable to function correctly and the food, instead of being properly digested, passes through the intestine in a watery state. The inflammation may be caused by an infection, dirty food or poisonous chemicals. The droppings are very watery and without form. In other words diarrhoea is present. They are frequently greenish in colour. Many birds with enteritis drink more than usual and some have a craving for grit. The bird usually has a dirty vent (cloaca) and is seen straining. This condition may be affecting the intestine alone or may be part of another disease. For example, enteritis often accompanies Salmonellosis, Psittacosis and Coccidiosis. Diagnosis and treatment should be left to a veterinary surgeon as difficult cases may need laboratory tests and powerful antibiotics.

FEATHER PLUCKING There are a variety of reasons for feather plucking. Some, like nest lining in breeding birds, are normal; some are due to boredom, all too commonly seen in parrots kept in small cages with nothing to do and nowhere to do it, and others are due to incorrect feeding. Occasionally it is due to a skin disease, perhaps caused by skin parasites, or again, it may result from impacted preening glands. Sadly the condition is common. In some cases the plucking continues until the skin is broken and bleeding occurs. The bird will even continue to pluck and bite itself although it becomes painful to do so. The treatment obviously depends on the cause. The skin should be examined for parasites, the diet corrected where necessary but above all, when boredom is the reason, give the bird space to fly and more to do.

FRENCH MOULT At the present time largely confined to Budgerigars, the cause is unknown. It may be due in part to over-breeding, in part to incorrect feeding and in part to

Two Budgerigars suffering from French Moult, a severe case on the right

an inherited factor. Some young birds become affected while still fledglings. The condition is fairly common in breeding birds. Some nestlings show abnormal feather growth. In adult birds continuous moulting occurs, particularly of the wing and tail feathers. Affected birds are often permanently disfigured. No successful treatment has been discovered.

GOITRE This is a condition in Budgerigars, more common in the hen. It has been suggested that breeding precipitates the disease. Afflicted birds produce an audible squeak during each breath. It is slow in onset and the appetite remains normal. The bird often puts on weight and may have fits. The condition is due to incorrect functioning of the thyroid gland. Treatment consists in removing the bird from the breeding colony and supplying iodine either in mineral blocks, by using commercial seed which has iodine added or by placing two drops of colloidal iodine in half a fluid ounce of water, and use as drinking water.

GOUT An uncommon condition affecting Budgerigars and parrots which follows an attack of kidney infection. It results from a deposit of a hard white substance around the joints of the legs, wings and neck. An affected bird is clearly uncomfortable, continually raising its feet from the perch and stretching its wings. It can be improved by massaging and manipulating the affected parts under an anaesthetic.

HEART DISEASE Old birds of all types suffer sudden collapse and death due to heart disease. It may be preceded by fainting fits. Any bird which faints should be taken to a veterinary surgeon to establish the cause and receive heart drugs.

INTESTINAL TROUBLES see DIARRHOEA; ENTERITIS

LICE Lice are occasionally seen in birds. Afflicted birds show that their skin is irritating them by rubbing and scratching. They are often more active than usual, flying from perch to perch apparently unable to settle. Do note, however, that similar symptoms are seen in any skin condition and a definite diagnosis should be made before treatment is started. One of the most effective and safe treatments for lice is pyrethrum powder.

LISTLESSNESS The first symptom of many diseases.

LOOSE DROPPINGS see DIARRHOEA; ENTERITIS

NASAL DISCHARGE A symptom of many diseases.

NEPHRITIS This means inflammation of the kidney.

Nephritis is quite common in all types of birds and is recognized when the bird becomes lethargic and ruffled and drinks large amounts of water. The droppings are abnormally white. Nephritis may also accompany a number of other diseases so correct diagnosis is essential. Treatment should be left to a veterinary surgeon.

ORNITHOSIS see PSITTACOSIS

OVERGROWN BEAK AND CLAWS Most birds never need their beaks and claws cut, but there are individuals that do need such attention. If the claws are overlong there is always the danger of a bird getting caught up and damaging its leg, and the eggs of a nesting hen may be punctured and consequently spoiled. Overlong beaks represent a health hazard as they prevent the bird from eating correctly. Overgrowth is possibly due to inherited factors and birds so afflicted should not be used for breeding. Basically the job is as simple as cutting one's own finger and toe nails. A small pair of sharp nail clippers or scissors, confidence, and care not to cut the vein, see the task completed. The illustrations show how the bird should be held and by holding the bird's foot up to the light it is possible to see where the vein (quick) in each claw ends, the cut being made *beyond* of this. If the vein cannot be seen only the tip of the claw should be cut. The beak should be cut in the same way. Should the owner have insufficient confidence for this task, a veterinary surgeon will do it.

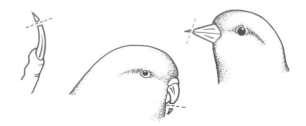

Claw and beak trimming – the photographs show two methods of holding small birds for claw trimming. The dotted lines in the diagrams indicate the cuts, which in all cases should be well clear of the veins (quicks) within the claws or the mandibles. Centre, a parrot-type bird with the upper mandible being trimmed; right, a finch-type bird having the beak trimmed.

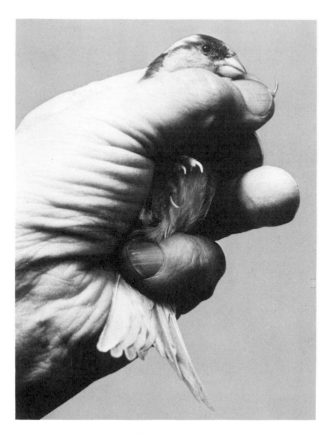

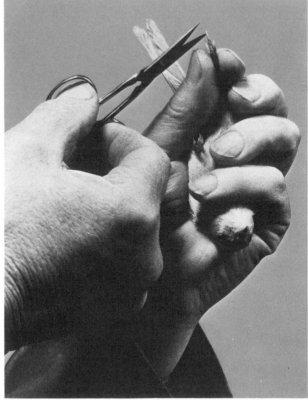

PSITTACOSIS (ORNITHOSIS) This disease is not only a danger to the health and life of many kinds of birds but causes a very unpleasant and sometimes fatal disease in man. It is caused by a virus. Psittacosis is commonest, and takes a most virulent form, in the psittacine birds. It is commonly imported with parrots and for this reason there is a strong argument for re-imposing import restrictions. Some individual birds act as carriers and show no symptoms. Others may be lethargic, have ruffled feathers, show green diarrhoea, difficulty in breathing accompanied by a discharge from the eyes and nostrils. There is commonly loss of weight. The disease may be progressive ending in convulsions and death or the bird may show a slow recovery, with a long period of convalescence needed. Suspected cases should be taken for veterinary advice since diagnosis can only be affirmed following laboratory tests. Treatment is possible if the condition is seen in the early stages.

RED MITE This little demon is scientifically known as *Dermanyssus gallinae*. It is sadly fairly common. Birds show skin irritation and restlessness (*see* Lice) but in addition untreated birds become anaemic and can die. The mites are most active at night, creeping from their lairs as darkness falls. Treatment consists in dusting with an insecticide, moving the afflicted creature to a clean cage during the day while the mites are resting and finally cleaning the cage thoroughly with gamma benzene hexachloride.

RHEUMATISM see GOUT

RICKETS Occasionally seen in all birds, particularly in young Budgerigars. The condition is due to an incorrect diet which is low in Vitamin D and contains incorrect proportions of the calcium/phosphorus ratio in the diet. Afflicted birds have short misshapen legs with enlarged joints. They are weak and unable to fly. The treatment, which is successful if the condition is diagnosed in the early stages, consists of feeding calcium and phosphorus in the form of bone meal and adding Vitamin D3 to the diet.

SALMONELLOSIS This is due to a variety of bacteria generally called *Salmonella*. It is serious because it is sometimes fatal to birds and because it can be transmitted to human beings. Sadly quite common. The symptoms include general lethargy, diarrhoea, dysentery and excessive thirst. Convulsions and sudden death can occur. Definite diagnosis depends on laboratory identification of the offending bacteria in the droppings. Veterinary treatment is definitely required since antibiotics and related substances are essential.

SCALY FACE AND SCALY LEG This condition is due to the small mite *Cnemidocoptes pilae*. It causes yellow-white encrustations on the beak, around the cere and eyes and, less commonly, on the legs and vent. Severe cases cause a deformity of the beak. Diagnosis is fairly easy and is based on the appearance of the beak, cere and eyes. It can be confirmed by examining a scraping of the crust under a microscope when the mites will be seen. Treatment is straightforward: the crust should be removed as far as possible burn the removed crust and a 10% solution of benzyl benzoate applied to the affected parts daily for a few days.

SORE EYES see CONJUNCTIVITIS

SORE FEET If droppings and seed husks get stuck to the feet they can cause irritation and sores will develop. If it is noticed that a bird is in this condition, the feet should be dipped in warm, disinfected water and the hard lumps gently washed away. When the feet are clean a bland ointment should be applied. The affected bird should not be returned to its original cage or aviary until the sores have completely healed. The perches must be kept perfectly clean to prevent reinfection.

TUMOURS see CANCER

WORMS All birds can be affected with parasitic worms but psittacines are particularly susceptible. Afflicted birds lose condition, may become thin and sometimes show diarrhoea. Diagnosis is confirmed by finding worm eggs in the droppings. Diagnosis and treatment should be undertaken by a veterinary surgeon.

Appendices

GLOSSARY

Addled Fertile eggs in which the developing embryos have died and disintegrated at an early stage.

Albino A mutation in which all dark pigments are absent from the plumage leaving only white; the mutant has red eyes and pink legs and feet.

Backcross Mating the young of a pair back to their parents.

Breed see *Type*.

Broken cap The clear area on the head of a Canary that is broken with dark feathers.

Buff and Yellow Types of feathers. The terms are principally used for describing Canaries. Buff (or mealy) feathers are edged with white giving them a frosted appearance that does not appear on yellow feathers.

Cap The whole of the top of a bird's head.

Cere The small patches devoid of feathers above the beak of some birds, e.g. Budgerigars.

Chromosomes Minute thread-shaped bodies, to which the genes are attached, that are contained in the reproductive cells.

Clear Birds without dark feathers in their plumage. Also indicates infertile eggs.

Clutch The eggs laid by a hen at a single setting.

Cobby Bird with a short thick body.

Colour break A sudden genetic change, partial or complete, of the normal colour; a mutation.

Colour-food A soft food containing a red colouring agent used to enrich the natural colour of certain birds, e.g. Canaries.

Consort The plain-headed mate of the crested (Corona) Gloster Fancy Canary.

Contour A bird's outline.

Coppy Another name for crest.

Corona see *Crested*.

Counterpart A similar mutation with a different ground-colour.

Coverts The feathers above the secondaries on the wings and those above the long tail feathers.

Crestbred Non-crested birds bred from one crested parent.

Crested A bird that has a crest (Corona) of feathers. The crest may be natural to the species or the result of a mutation.

Dilute A plumage colour that is paler than the normal shades.

Domesticated A species that has been consistently bred in captivity for many generations.

Dominant A colour or other feature that is produced by a gene, despite the presence of other genes (recessive); mostly used when describing colour characters of Budgerigars and Canaries (see also *Recessive*).

Double buffing The pairing of two buff-feathered birds.

Double character A double quantity of the same colour character in the bird's genetic make-up.

Double yellowing The pairing of two yellow-feathered birds.

Even-marked A clear bird having the same coloured areas on both sides of its body.

Fancy A name used to describe certain type breeds, particularly of Canaries.

Flighted The stage after the bird's nest feathers have moulted.

Flight feathers The long wing feathers.

Flue The soft downy feathers next to the bird's body.

Foul feathers Light-coloured feathers on an otherwise all dark-coloured bird.

Frosted see *Buff and Yellow*.

Genes Microscopic bodies situated on the chromosomes which control the inheritable characters.

Genetic make-up The inheritable characters possessed by the species or type concerned.

Gizzard The organ in which a bird's food is ground up with the aid of small sharp stones swallowed by the bird.

Grizzled A mixture of dark and light colour on the same feathers giving a pepper and salt effect.

Ground-colour The basic colours of white or yellow on which all other colours are superimposed.

Hybrid The result of crossing two different species (see also *Mule*), or of well-marked varieties within a species.

Inbreeding Pairing birds that are of close blood relationship.

Insectivorous food A soft food that is prepared from various kinds of dried insects.

Jonque An old name for yellow.

Lacing A darker colour pencilled on a light ground.

Lethal gene One that kills the chicks before they are hatched.

Line breeding The pairing of blood-related birds to form a strain or line.

Mantle The area between the neck and the back.

Mealy see *Buff and Yellow*.

Melanistic Having extra black pigment in the plumage.

Mendel's Law The rules of inheritance that set out the expected behaviour of all inherited characters in breeding experiments.

Mis-marked A dark bird having an odd light feather or a light bird with a dark feather.

Mule In Britain the hybrid result of crossing Canaries with certain British birds; in America the term can refer to any cross involving a Canary and another species.

Mutation The sudden chromosomal change of colour or character. Sometimes called a 'sport'.

Nest feathers The first feathers of a chick.

Normal Except in Budgerigars and Zebra Finches the wild type – not a mutation.

Orange ground see *Red Factor.*

Outcrossing The pairing together of unrelated individuals from different strains (see also *Inbreeding*).

Overall length The measurement from beak tip to tail end.

Pallid see *Dilute.*

Pied A bird whose colour is broken with light areas.

Pin feather A feather still encased.

Plainhead A bird without head crest.

Recessive A colour or other character that is carried by a gene that has no visual effect.

Red Factor The genetic factor introduced to Canaries by crossing a Canary with the Red Hooded Siskin; colours of the resultant hybrids range from orange to almost red.

Ring code numbers Personal numbers issued by specialist cage bird societies to their members for the closed metal rings used for identification purposes.

Saddle The upper back area.

Self All one colour.

Sex-linked Recessive characters that are carried on the chromosome that determines sex. In birds such characters are passed from mother to son (see p.185).

Sexual dimorphism Seen in birds where the markings and/or coloration differ in the two sexes, e.g. Orange Weaver.

Single character Bird having only a single quantity of a particular character in its genetic make-up.

Soft food Blended mixtures of biscuit (cracker) meal and other ingredients.

Split The oblique stroke (/) used in the genetic description of the colours of a bird in which one colour character is dominant and the other recessive. The former is placed before and the latter after the stroke; e.g. Light Green/Blue indicates that the bird carries in its genetic make-up a light green character that is dominant (and therefore seen) and a blue character that is recessive (and therefore not seen).

Stance The posture of a bird.

Strain Related birds bred systematically by a fancier to produce a line with consistently desirable heredity.

Suffusion The over-laying of one colour by another.

Theoretical expectations The results that, according to Mendel's Laws, should be obtained from a particular pairing.

Ticked A small dark mark on a light bird or a light one on a dark bird.

Tours Special arrangements of song notes as sung by Roller Canaries.

Type The visual form (colours, shape, markings, etc.) of a breed, variety or species as required by the specialist societies for exhibition purposes (see also *Wild type*).

Underflue Small, soft feathers close to a bird's body.

Unflighted A bird that still has nest feather flights.

Vent The area between the back of a bird's legs and the top of the tail.

Wild type The form of the species as found in the wild.

Wing butts The bend of the wings when lying close to the body.

FURTHER READING

A large number of books are available on all aspects of aviculture; those listed below are a selection which, it is hoped, the reader will find useful for continuing his studies. It is possible that some are out of print but the public library system should be able to help and, of course, second-hand bookstores are always worth a visit. Should there be any difficulty in purchasing new books from a local bookseller British readers should contact K. & R. Books Ltd., 1847 Melton Road, Queniborough, Leicestershire and American readers, Audubon Publishing Co., 3449 North Western Avenue, Chicago, Illinois 60618.

In general, books of a purely ornithological nature have not been listed, but it is suggested that the reader should acquire one or two, for they contain many facts that will help the aviculturist to understand better the birds in his care. The following are particularly recommended: *A New Dictionary of Birds* edited by Sir A. Landsborough Thomson published in Great Britain and the U.S.A. by Nelson, unfortunately now out of print, has a wealth of information on all aspects of ornithology, and *The Dictionary of Birds in Colour* by Bruce Campbell published in 1974 by Michael Joseph in Great Britain and Viking Press in the U.S.A. which has more than 1,000 illustrations in colour and an informative text.

Armour, M. D. S. *Exhibition Budgerigars*, K. & R. Books, Leicester

Armour, M. D. S. *Inbreeding Budgerigars*, K. & R. Books, Leicester

Bates, H. and Busenbark, R. *Finch and Softbilled Birds*, T. F. H. Publications, Neptune City, N.J. and Reigate

Bates, H. and Busenbark, R. *Guide to Mynahs*, T. F. H. Publications, Neptune City, N.J. and Reigate

Bates, H. and Busenbark, R. *Introduction to Finches and Softbills*, T. F. H. Publications, Neptune City, N.J. and Reigate

Bates, H. and Busenbark, R. *Parrots*, T. F. H. Publications, Neptune City, N.J. and Reigate

Bedford, the Duke of, *Homing Budgerigars*, K. & R. Books, Leicester

Bedford, the Duke of, *Parrots and Parrotlike Birds*, T. F. H. Publications, Neptune City, N.J. and Reigate

Brooks, W. E. *Guide to Canary Breeding and Exhibiting* (2 edn), K. & R. Books, Leicester, 1950

Carr, V. A. V. *Mule and Hybrid Birds*, K. & R. Books, Leicester, 1959

Clear, V. *Common Cagebirds in America*, Bobbs-Merrill, Indianapolis, 1966

Dean, W. *New Colour Canaries*, Colourmaster, St. Ives, 1974

Groen, H. D. *Australian Parakeets: their Maintenance and Breeding in Europe*, Litteria Scripta Manet, Gorssel (Holland)

Hart, E. H. *Budgerigar Handbook*, T. F. H. Publications, Neptune City, N.J. and Reigate

House, C. A. and Smith, A. W. *The Norwich Canary*, K. & R. Books, Leicester

Immelman, K. *Australian Finches* (2 edn), Angus & Robertson, Sydney and London, 1972

Low, R. *Parrots of South America*, John Gifford, London, 1972

Lynch, G. *Canaries in Colour*, Blandford, London and Hippocrene Books, New York, 1971

Petrak, M. L. et al. *Diseases of Cage and Aviary Birds*, Ballière-Tindall, London and Lea & Febiger, Philadelphia, 1969

Rogers, C. H. *Budgerigars* (revised edn), John Gifford, London, 1975

Rogers, C. H. *Zebra Finches* (new edn), K. & R. Books, Leicester, 1975

Roller Canary: Breeding and Training, American Cage-bird Magazine, Chicago

Roots, C. *Exotic Birds*, Cassell, London, 1975

Roots, C. *Soft-billed Birds*, John Gifford, London, 1970 and Arco, New York, 1971

Rutgers, A. (ed. Rogers, C. H.) *Budgerigars in Colour* (3 edn), Blandford, London and International Publication Service, New York, 1973

Rutgers, A. and Norris, K. A. (eds), *Encyclopedia of Aviculture* (Vols I & II; Vol III in preparation), Blandford, London

and British Book Centre, New York, 1970, 1972

Shackleton, W. H. *Yorkshire Canary: Breeding and Management* (4 edn), K. & R. Books, Leicester, 1969

Siskins: their Care and Breeding, American Cage-bird Magazine, Chicago

Soderberg, P. M. *Waxbills, Weavers and Whydahs*, T. F. H. Publications, Neptune City, N.J. and Reigate

Sparks, J. *Bird Behaviour*, Hamlyn, Feltham, 1969 and Bantam, New York, 1971

Stroud, R. *Digest on the Diseases of Birds*, T. F. H. Publications, Neptune City, N.J. and Reigate

The New Colour Canary, Canary Colour Breeders' Association, Broadstairs and Audubon Publishing Co., Chicago, 1974

Vane, E. N. T. *Guide to Lovebirds and Parrotlets*, K. & R. Books, Leicester, 1959

Most of the societies listed below publish magazines, bulletins or newsletters for their members and additionally there are the following national publications:

American Cage-bird Magazine (monthly), 3449 North Western Avenue, Chicago, Illinois 60618

Avicultural Bulletin, 4729 Norwich Avenue, Sherman Oaks, California 91403

Cage and Aviary Birds (weekly), Surrey House, Sutton, Surrey

LIST OF SOCIETIES

As has been suggested elsewhere in this book there is nothing better the interested reader can do than to join a cage bird society. Societies may be classified as: international, national, area (including state and county), and specialist. There are, literally, hundreds of societies in Great Britain and the U.S.A., as well as the rest of the world – far too many to list here. The vast majority are local but as they are, generally, affiliated to parent societies it is these that are listed below. Their secretaries will be happy to provide information not only on the parent body but also on the local affiliated societies. The request for information should always be accompanied by a stamped addressed envelope or an international reply coupon, as is appropriate. Other useful sources of information are the *American Cage-bird Magazine*, which includes a directory of American cage bird societies in each issue, and *Cage and Aviary Birds* in which many British societies advertise their shows week by week. Thanks are due to these magazines for help in compiling the following list.

AUSTRALIA

General
Avicultural Society of Australia, P.O. Box 48, Bentleigh East, Victoria
Canaries
Australian Canary Colour Breeders' Association, 24 Unwin Road, Sydney, N.S.W.

CANADA

General
Canadian Avicultural Society, Inc., E. Jones, 32 Dromore Crescent, Willowdale 450, Ontario, M2R 2H5
Canadian Institute of Bird Breeders, C. Snazel, 4422 Chauvin Street, Pierrefonds, Quebec
Budgerigars
The Budgerigar and Foreign Bird Society of Canada, Inc., Mrs B. Sanford, 17 Appian Drive, Willowdale M2J 2P7, Ontario
Canaries
Dominion Roller Canary Association, Inc., K. Swann, 9822 106 Street, Edmonton 14, Alberta, T5K 1B8

GREAT BRITAIN

General
The Avicultural Society, H. J. Horsewell, 20 Bourdon Street, London W1
The Junior Bird League, Miss Rosemary Low, c/o Cage and Aviary Birds, Surrey House, Sutton, Surrey
Bengalese
The National Bengalese Fanciers' Association, E. J. Hounslow, 2 Bridge Street, Griffithstown, Monmouthshire

British (aviary-bred) Birds
British Bird Breeders' Association, P. Howe, 3 Station Road,
Lower Stondon, Henlow, Bedfordshire
National British Bird and Mule Club, W. Lewis, Milnsbridge,
Bicton, nr Shrewsbury, Salop
Budgerigars
The Budgerigar Society, A. R. Secombes, 12 Abel Close,
Hemel Hempstead, Hertfordshire
Canaries
Border
Border Fancy Canary Club, G. A. L. Gordun,
9 Woodburn Terrace, St Andrews, Fife
British Border Fancy Canary Club, J. Fishwick,
11 Russell Avenue, High Lane, nr Stockport, Cheshire
International Border Breeders' Association, J. Houston,
'Radbourne', 10 Knockbuckle Road, Kilmacolm,
Renfrewshire
Gloster
Gloster Breeders' Association, C. Harris, 32 Beanwood Road,
Headington, Oxford OX3 9LF
Gloster Fancy Canary Club, A. J. Phillips,
8 Shurdington Road, Cheltenham, Gloucestershire
International Gloster Breeders' Association,
Mr & Mrs A. Watkinson, 9 Queensway, Worksop,
Nottinghamshire
Norwich
Norwich Plainhead Club, A. Taylor, 11 Robina Road,
Sutton, St. Helens, Lancashire
Yorkshire
Yorkshire Canary Club, J. K. Cooper, 3 Como Grove,
Girlington, Bradford, Yorkshire, BD8 9QA
Other Varieties
British Roller Canary Association, Mrs B. McBride,
5 Ewart Road, Bowring Park, Liverpool 16
British Roller Canary Club (1901), R. Barron,
7 Chasemore House, Dawes Road, Fulham, London SW6
Canary Colour Breeders' Association, Mr & Mrs J. Pitcher,
16 Detling Avenue, Broadstairs, Kent
Fife Fancy Canary Club, W. Lumsden, 10 Roomlin Gardens,
Kirkcaldy, Fife, Scotland
Lizard Canary Association of Great Britain, L. G. Wood,
31 Gipping Way, Sproughton, nr Ipswich, Suffolk, IP8 3BE
Old Varieties Canary Association, G. Fagence,
13 Broadwater Gardens, Harefield, Uxbridge, Middlesex
Foreign (Exotic) Birds
Australian Finch Society, A. C. Crook,
22 Finches Gardens, Lindfield, Sussex
Foreign Bird League, Mr & Mrs C. W. Stevens, Spen Cottage,
Greenmore, Woodcote, Reading, Berkshire, RG8 0RB
Parrots
The Parrot Society, N. D. Cooper, 17 De Parys Avenue,
Bedford
Zebra Finches
Zebra Finch Society, J. A. W. Prior, 103 Horncastle Road,
Lee, London SE12

NEW ZEALAND

General
The New Zealand Federation of Cage Bird Societies,
M. D. Neale, 31 Harker Street, Christchurch 2

UNITED STATES OF AMERICA

General
American Federation of Aviculture P.O. Box 1125,
Garden Grove, California 92642
National Cagebird Exposition, 1805 48th Street, Des Moines,
Iowa 50310
Budgerigars
American Budgerigar Society, Inc., Elizabeth M. Tefft,
2 Farnum Road, Warwick, Rhode Island 02888
Canaries
Cooperative Canary Breeders' Association, Miss Jane Scott,
3659 Edenhurst Avenue, Los Angeles, California 90039
Border
American Border Fancy Canary Club,
Mrs Madeline Mysliwiec, 1413 Britton Street, Wantagh,
L.I., N.Y. 11794
International Border Fancy Canary Club, John F. Ross,
10091 Dixie Avenue, Detroit, Michigan 48239
Gloster
International Gloster Breeders' Association (U.S. Chapter),
Mark E. Whiteaker, P.O. Box 471, 216 E.7th Street,
Trenton, Missouri 64683
National Gloster Club, Mrs Elsie Bradbury,
7 Washburn Terrace, Brookline, Massachusetts 02146
Norwich
American Norwich Society, Frank Martin, 805 N. Kaley,
Orlando, Florida 32806
Yorkshire
Yorkshire Canary Club of America, Mrs Madeline Mysliwiec,
1413 Britton Street, Wantagh, L.I., N.Y. 11794
Other Varieties
American Association of Roller Canary Breeders,
John Dziekan, 3529 W. National Avenue, Milwaukee,
Wisconsin 53215
American Singers Club, Inc., Mrs Janet Commons,
410 31 Barrington Road, Wauconda, Illinois 60084
Greater North American Color-bred Judge Association,
Gino Abbate, 136 Murray Street, Elizabeth, N.J. 07202
National Institute of Red Orange Canaries, Inc.,
Mrs Fran Ritchie, 5844 Sunrise, Clarendon Hills,
Illinois 60514
United States Association Roller Canary Culturists,
Francis J. Kelly, 3729 Bronx Boulevard, Bronx, N.Y. 10467
Zebra Finches
The Zebra Finch Society of America,
(Affiliated with Zebra Finch Society, England),
David W. Seabury, 8204 Woodland Avenue, Annandale,
Virginia 22003

Index

SCIENTIFIC AND COMMON NAMES